I would like to express my gratitiude to those who offered their ideas and their time to this effort. I sincerely appreciate their contributions.

Nancy Geddie, Jim Hanna, Al Egan, Lynn Adams, Hedda Wierstra, Ron Morrish, Joanne and the good people at Citizen Press

A special thank you to award-winning artist Mary Prittie for allowing me to use her painting of the Port Colborne Train Station on the cover of this book.

OUR ITINERARY

PREFACE

Life is a journey . . . not a destination. How many times have we heard people repeat this statement. Yet I never stopped to consider its full meaning until recently. Life is not about getting somewhere. Life is not about being judged by others for what we have. It is about the experiences we have and the personal learning, growth and understanding that comes from those times. Life is about using our strengths for our spiritual betterment. Life is about enjoying the time we have as fully as we can.

Many of us struggle to understand why our lives have twisted and turned as they have. We ask "why me?" Why not the other guy? Why can't my life be like theirs? Many of us decided very early in our lives how we would cope with adversity. Many of us formulated attitudes, perspectives and strategies that, in fact, work to keep us from enjoying the kind of lives we pursue. Some of us embarked on great ambitious quests for the illusive answers to "why has my life turned out like this?" and "why do I do the things I do?" only to be stymied time and again. The truth is those answers, if found at all, won't matter much. What would we do with that information anyway? How would those answers serve to make our lives any better or more enjoyable right now? It is learning how to live a more peaceful and fulfilling life in this day and the next that is important.

The spirit of this work is couched in this belief: "We will not experience any new learning opportunities, personal growth, inner peace or serenity unless we consider four very important points: it is necessary for us to seek out and understand our spiritual selves; it is important for us to connect our spiritual selves, our inner world, with our outer world; we not only have the **right** to determine our futures, we have the **power** to determine them; and we can learn great lessons from our pasts but we don't have to live in them or re-live them." This is the spiritual "journey" we all must take if we are to grow and become all we can be. The word "journey" speaks of the time, effort, and risk we are willing to spend to "travel"--to look inside ourselves--and to do what we need to do so that we can live the life we deserve.

Use this book as a road map to help you discover the hidden treasures that exist within you. When we are able to learn of our strengths and to face our fears we will be guided toward other spiritual journeys. It is part of our natural evolution to journey again and again.

INTRODUCTION

I am constantly awed by the resiliency and raw will to live that I see every day in the clients I serve. Many come to me in crisis. Most come, their lives in disarray, not understanding that they possess, within themselves, the resolve and resources necessary to work through most of the problems that stand between them and better times. I help them search for and recognize their inner strengths so they can use them to have more of what they want from life. I see myself as someone, just as I myself had someone, who is willing to listen and help them understand that life is to be embraced and explored, not feared or considered hopeless. There are always new roads to travel--new things to learn about ourselves and about our fellow travellers and there is more than one way to get to where we want to be.

Our focus should not be to avoid controversy or adversity. We need to accept them as an unavoidable part of life and learn to deal with them in ways that limit the effect they have on the quality of our lives. We have enormous potential to be all we can be if we could harness and utilize the spiritual strength and natural inner resources we possess. Most of us aren't aware that we have them. Many of us seek our strength, our drive, and our ambition from external sources. By doing so we set ourselves up for disappointment and failure time and again. The answers we seek are within us not outside of us.

This book is about the inner journey we must embark upon if we are to recognize and take advantage of the talents, strengths, and resources we already have. The keys and secrets to our happiness and success aren't related to money or power. Happiness and success are related to our ability to handle the issues and challenges that come our way every day. The more successful we are doing that the happier we will be. There are those who would disagree. There are those who would say, "Give me some of that cash and I'll show you happiness." There is no doubt life would be easier but that doesn't mean better. Look around and you will see many sad and lonely affluent people struggling to find the same answers to the same situations that face us: "I hate my job and I don't know what to do about it." "My relationship is falling apart and I don't know how to fix it. What can I do about that?" "I don't know how to be a parent to my kids. I've been away for so long they don't know me and I don't know them." "How do I get people to trust me again?"

I have come to understand the importance of learning how to successfully manage each of eight challenges I am likely to face in my lifetime. They need my constant attention if I am to have all that I want from this life:

1. Any personal or spiritual growth or progress will be difficult unless I continue to pay attention to how I feel about myself and how I take care of myself. This is where my journey began. I understood that I have resources I can use to become more competent and with competence comes a growing belief in myself. My self-esteem increases when I feel good about my abilities and my capabilities. My inner satisfaction and my desire to continue to grow are fuelled by the increasing value I place on myself. Self-value means self-esteem.

2. Learning how to problem solve--to break down and simplify the issues that face me so that I will not become overwhelmed by them is necessary for my inner peace. When I can manage myself in a way that allows me to focus on the main issue to be dealt with I am more successful. One thing at a time is enough for me.

3. Being aware of the stress I cause myself helps me to stay more healthy both physically and mentally. With this awareness comes a need to develop some skills to reduce or manage the impact the stress I experience can have on me. I realize that I can't eliminate all the stress from my life. I also know that some stress is actually good for me. It keeps me alert and can provide opportunities for me to learn more about myself. My life is less stressful if I keep it simple.

4. When I am able to tell others what I need from them, why that is important to me, or why their behaviour is unacceptable, and if I can do it in a way that does not hurt them or myself, I feel better. It means that I am putting myself first without putting someone else second.

5. I need to be aware of the times when I feel like doing what I want to do and not what I need to do. These are the times when I can get myself into a great deal of difficulty very quickly. If I am to work toward what is in my own best interests it will be important for me to stay focused on my goals, what I want to accomplish.

I keep my mission statement close by to help me and remind me of what is important when I get wilful. It is also important for me to build some "goof-off" time into my days or weeks so that I will not have to be responsible all of the time. **Balance** is extremely important to me.

6. Being vigilant in my day-to-day life both to recognize what angers me and to deal with it as soon as I feel ready to do so are important. Unchecked anger eats at me like a cancer, and others usually suffer because I haven't done what I needed to do at the time I needed to it. This comes from doing #4.

7. Most of us are either in a relationship of some kind or would like to be. As human beings we need to feel as though we belong somewhere and that there are others who value us in some way. I know that awareness of my wants and needs and understanding the wants and needs of my partner are vital if I want my relationship to have a chance. I understand that it will be difficult to have the kind of relationship I want until I can acknowledge the importance of, and begin to work on, the above six challenges in my life. If I can manage this aspect of my life I know that I will be happier and more successful.

8. Taking the time to stop and assess what I have learned, to recognize some new strength or skill that I have developed, and to feel good about what I have accomplished are extremely important to my sense of self. It's enlivening to say, "I like the way things are working out" or "I like the way I managed that situation." It helps me maintain and appreciate the gains I have earned and my hard work. It also brings me full circle. When I feel good about what I have done, what I have earned, and how I did it, my self-esteem and the image I have of myself are strengthened. When I feel stronger and more self-assured I'm likely to accept new challenges with a renewed attitude about my chances of success. The journeys into my heart and mind continue and I grow.

Many of life's failures are people who did not realize how close they were to success when they gave up.--Thomas Edison

The keys to living the kind of life we want are within us all. We need to recognize them and to manage them to the best of our ability. The responsibility is ours and ours alone. As it should be.

MANAGING ME . . . IT'S AN INSIDE JOB

1.

LEAVING THE TERMINAL

EVERYTHING I DO EITHER ADDS TO OR DIMINISHES ME AS A PERSON.

Self-esteem has more to do with how we choose to define ourselves than it does with any long-term therapy or a prescribed medication. We are not the sum total of our spiritual or psychological injuries. We are not defined by our wounds. We build a positive self-image of ourselves as we would build anything else, with hard work and by following a plan. There is no magic here. We all have the capacity to develop a positive sense of who we are. We can determine who we will be and how we might feel by the choices we make for ourselves each day. We can be the authors of our own stories. It is and always will be up to us.

Developing a positive sense of self, a positive self-image, is all about **DOING**. This is the key to building self-esteem. Our sense of self is enhanced when we do something positive for ourselves--something that makes us feel good, and helps us see ourselves as capable and competent. It can also be enhanced when others speak highly of us for how we conduct ourselves or for what we do.

However, when we are not feeling positive we can depend on other people to help us and support us to a degree that is not healthy. We even allow others to influence us and, in some cases, make our decisions for us because we don't have any confidence in our own abilities. For us to build our self-esteem **we** have to take the responsibility to pursue what **we** consider to be important to us, not what is important to someone else. This will depend upon our recognizing what resources and assets we possess. We need to develop the skills that will move us closer to our goals. With skill building and development comes confidence. We all have a reasonably clear idea of what we want but often become confused as to how to get it. Again, we can utilize the strengths that we already have.

Our sense of self has little to do with other people. Other people don't see the world through our eyes. They don't know what it feels like to be us. They don't know what is right for us. They only know what is right for them. This is as it should be. This is not to say that we don't enlist the help of others. This does not mean that we disregard others' suggestions. It does mean that **WE** make the final decisions about how we live our lives based on what we feel is in our own best interests and not the interests of others. The more we can do this the more competent and capable we become. We will make some mistakes but we can learn from those. We will make some good decisions as well. We'll grow from those too. This is how we continue to build our esteem.

We all need to get some positive feedback from people who love us and care for us. We all need the strokes that come from our mates, bosses, friends and family. This enhances our sense of self and our self-esteem. But we need to hear only the people we trust--those who are willing to support us, not control us.

I don't believe people have to be in analysis or have some cathartic experience before they can move on to feeling better about who they are and where they are going. There are many people who feel an emptiness deep in their souls. Their spirits have been damaged by events that in many cases were beyond their control. They feel that they are defective and undeserving of a life filled with happiness.

There are professionals who promote the belief that we cannot move into the future until we have healed our past. I disagree. It is possible to discover and develop our inner strengths, to feel increasingly more positive about ourselves and then go back, if we feel the need, and do any healing work that needs to be done. For a great number of us there is nothing but sadness and hurt back there. Why would we want to spend any more time ruminating over it? When we do that it feels as if we are being victimized all over again. The way for us to become more positive and to feel stronger is to be in the present. When we focus on the past we focus on what is wrong with us and we get into the "fix it" mode: "I'm broken somehow and I have to fix myself or have someone else fix me." I see more benefits by focusing on the strengths we used to survive our pasts and then build on them. The first perspective suggests prevention and the latter suggests promotion. It's similar to the choice of working to prevent war or focusing on promoting peace.

Living in the present keeps us focused on what we need to do **today.** When we are today-focused we begin to move ahead instead of being stuck. We begin to accomplish things that are important to our growth. Our futures begin with our todays. I am not, for one moment, suggesting that we negate the past. I am not suggesting that we should forget the awful experiences that many have suffered. I am saying that we continue to give our negative experiences more power than they deserve the longer we stay mired in horrible memories that we cannot change anyway. If there are things that need to be said to others, we should do it when we feel good about the skills, strengths and supports that we have developed so that we can deal, successfully, with any negative outcomes.

*** It is important to know that sometimes medical intervention may be necessary. A few people have chemical imbalances that require some form of medication. Some need medical assistance to manage anxiety or panic attacks. Still others may have a psychiatric illness that requires medication. It may be difficult for a person to feel positive if an untreated state of depression exists. However, I don't believe that medication should last a life-time unless there is a substantiated medical diagnosis. Many of the clients I have worked with have been able to cease taking their medication once they developed alternate methods of dealing with the underlying issues--stress or anger management skills, for example.

If you decide to stop taking your medication you should do so only after consulting a physician whom you trust and who is oriented to a wellness approach to healing.

What is it?

What is "esteem"? There are as many definitions as there are people. It is a very personal thing. Given the choice many people, if they were truly honest with themselves, would likely choose to be praised and recognized for who they are and to be seen as being good at doing something in particular than to have sex or possess money. Don Lowry, Founder of True

Colors, publisher and educator, explains esteem this way: "The purpose of all behaviour is to have esteem. All human endeavours are about having an identity or esteem. That means that all actions are concerned with one's self-image. That means that behaviour, what we do, is defined as an individual's attempt to feel good about him or herself." Nathaniel Branden, Ph.D., theorist and author, sums up self-esteem this way: "How we feel about ourselves affects virtually every aspect of our experience from the way we function at work, in love, in sex, to the way we operate as parents, to how high in life we are likely to rise. Our responses to the happenings in our everyday life are shaped by who and what we think we are. Self-esteem is the key to success or failure. Self-esteem has another value. It also holds the key to understanding ourselves and other people. I cannot think of a single psychological problem that is not traceable to a poor self concept. Positive self-esteem is a cardinal requirement of a fulfilling life."

Self-esteem is the essence of a satisfying life experience. It means that I have confidence in my ability to handle the issues and situations that come my way each day; that I value and respect myself for who I am; and that I am worthy of and deserve happiness.

Without a strong or changing sense of self we will find it difficult to move toward the goals that we dream about. We will struggle to become the people we want to be. Self-esteem is the well spring for a life that is all we hoped it would be. As the value we have for ourselves and respect that we feel for ourselves increase we will find our ability to manage ourselves and the challenges we face will increase as well. This is what my guides helped me to understand. It is why I chose to start this work with "Developing a Positive Self-image." All that I want and all that I will accomplish will come from the value I feel for myself--my self-esteem.

Can we be different?

Re-read the quotation which begins this chapter. When that thought came to me it seemed so clear. What does it mean to you?

EVERYTHING WE DO contributes to our development as people or it works against us becoming the people we can be or would like to be. All that we do directly affects us either positively or negatively. **WE** have the power and the control, the talent and the resources to do for ourselves, each day, what we need to do in order to maintain our developing sense of self. It is imperative that we constantly examine the role **WE** play in what happens to us.

Let's consider behaviour. What do we mean by it? When we hear the word "behaviour" what do we think, how do we feel? Our behaviour (what we do and how we respond) is often based upon our past--what we know to be true from previous experiences, which then become our realities, and the outcomes from past attempts to deal with what we considered important. Our behaviour then represents the sum total of (1) how we think, (2) what we do next (how we respond), (3) how we feel, emotionally, about what we have done, and (4) how we feel physically and mentally after considering our thinking, actions, and feelings--the results of our efforts. Our self-esteem is primarily based upon the results of our attempts to problem solve. If we have not been as successful as we would have liked, perhaps it's time to evaluate our efforts and approach our challenges from a different perspective. Can we do some things differently so that the outcomes will move us closer to our goal of developing a more positive sense of self?

The quality of our existence has to do with how we choose to respond to the issues we face. We play a direct role, every day, in how we feel about who we are. We are responsible for our own self-esteem.

Most developments occur from a process of some kind. Life is a process. Growing up is a process. Solving a puzzle is a process. Developing a positive sense of ourselves is a process. When we **THINK** first, we are automatically slowed down and less likely to react out of an emotional state, anger for instance. Then we can consider what action we will take that will satisfy our need to respond without hurting ourselves or someone else in the process. Now we are likely to feel better about how we went about getting our needs met, how we were able to do what we needed to do to take care of ourselves. The real reward comes when we can go to bed at night and feel good about how we managed our feelings and emotions and how we didn't act before we thought things through first. Can we manage ourselves differently? Yes, we can. However, being open to change is necessary if we are to begin the process. Further development of the skills we need will come once we allow for the possibility of change.

Hope is the key

There is one building block that is essential in the development of self-esteem and that is HOPE. Hope is that feeling that somehow we will be OK, that things will work out for us. We need to feel hopeful that we can, with time and work, become the person we would like to be and have the kind of life we want. I remember being at a seminar some time ago where the facilitator said, "We can do only what we think we can do. We can be only what we think we can be. We can have only what we think we can have. What we do, what we are, what we have all depend upon what we think."

I could see the simplicity in this statement. My self-image and my self-esteem depend upon how I **think** of myself. If I see myself as a decent human being I am likely to act like a decent human being. If I act that way I am likely to feel pretty good about who I am. That would translate into positive self-esteem. If I feel good about who I am, I am likely to be more hopeful. Without hope our spirits suffer or die. I understood that our self-esteem and our spirituality are connected to one another.

H+O+P+E: "a feeling of anticipation that we can be all we want to be."

H--**how** we start being more hopeful by learning new skills that will help develop new outcomes
O--accepting that the **onus** to do what we need to do is always **on us** and not someone else
P--**persistence**--deciding that we will continue to try for as long as it takes (remember that old habits die hard)
E--**execution**--practicing until we get it right and then continue doing it.

What will we need to do?

If we are open to change and are willing to learn new skills, we must accept that it is up to us to pursue what we want, commit to giving it our best effort, and keep trying until we get it right, we will become more hopeful about our ability to succeed. If our old ways have not brought us the success we desired then why continue to do the same things?

We will, each experience our journeys differently. They are unique to us. We will take different paths but we will get to the same place if we keep putting one foot in front of the other, one step at a time. However, I believe there are three key features that are common to all our efforts to feel more positive about who we are and how we define ourselves: maintaining our integrity, being proactive in our daily living and evaluating the validity of our attitudes and perspectives.

A basic travel plan

1. Rules for living

We need to develop some rules, some guidelines, for how we will live our lives. Our rules should reflect our values and principles--what we believe in and to what standards and acts we are prepared to commit ourselves. For example, I value truth, so I try to live by the principle of being honest. I value equality, so I try to be as fair as I can be when dealing with myself and other people. Our self-esteem is strengthened when we choose to live by the rules we deem important. We also maintain our sense of integrity. Integrity results when we defend or maintain our rules for living despite criticism, ridicule, questioning or harassment. It is the spiritual satisfaction we feel when we know we have made the right choice. Integrity goes to the heart of any action we may take. We behave in accordance with what we believe in. We feel good when we know that we have not compromised our ideals and beliefs when it might have been easier to do so or when we might have been judged less harshly by our peers or families.

How do we develop our rules for living? The easiest way is to write down our values--what we believe in, why we feel strongly about them, and what we are prepared to do as a result of understanding them. Then we must think about how we would like to be seen or thought of by people in our community, family, or workplace. Now we must combine the two efforts into a written form. We are creating a blue-print that states how we will live our lives.

My own rules for living statement looks like this: "I know I need to look at how I choose to live my life every day because this day is the only day I have. Yesterday is gone and tomorrow isn't here. It's important for me to consider how my decisions would affect those around me. I will not base my decisions solely on their needs but I will consider how my decisions impact on the relationships I have with them. I will not steal from others. I will try not to hurt other people intentionally either physically, emotionally or spiritually. If I do, I know the faster I make my amends the better I will feel. I will try to treat others as I would have them treat me yet understand and accept that isn't always going to happen. I need to continue doing that for my own benefit, not theirs. I will try to consider my children in all instances, recognizing that they depend on me for their guidance and safety. I will teach them what I know without damaging their spirits. I will try to give something back to the society I live in as often as I can. If I want something, I will earn it and not take it from someone else. I will protect myself, in all manners, from those who would do me harm. I have the ability and the right to choose, every day, how I will live my life. It is mine to govern and I will not let others determine what is right for me. I will try to remain open to new ideas and change."

If we are not willing to make the world an honest place then it is hypocritical for us to teach our children otherwise. How could we say, with any degree of integrity, that honesty is the best policy?

When we develop our rules for living statement and stick with it we continue to create or reinforce our self-esteem, our positive self-image. No one can take our esteem from us. It is not for sale. We can, however, give it away any time we want by not living according to the blue-print we have created. That is our choice. It is important to re-visit our statement from time to time and make any changes in it that are appropriate. It should not be written in stone.

2. Be proactive

We need to be **PROACTIVE** in our daily living experiences as opposed to being reactive. We need to understand that the more active a role we assume in determining the direction our lives will take, the more influence we have over any possible outcomes that could affect us. Do we decide for ourselves or do we let things happen to us because of the decisions that someone else has made?

Steven Covey, author of *The Seven Habits of Highly Effective People*, talks a great deal about being proactive--about the need to do for ourselves and plan our approaches to situations that arise instead of waiting for things to happen to us and then responding. We will always be struggling to keep up with what is going on around us if we are always waiting to see what happens. We develop a "victim's stance" when we allow others to dictate our outcomes for us, when we grant others the opportunity to do our thinking for us and when we don't take responsibility for our own actions. Many people believe that if they don't cause any waves, that if they can stay out of the way and not be noticed they will somehow miss all the "bad stuff" that happens. They develop the philosophy of "out of sight, out of mind."

When we say "I can't" do we mean "I'm afraid to try"? If we never attempt to better ourselves or do something positive for ourselves we will never get ahead. If we don't take ownership for what happens to us, who will? Often, people see proactive people as self-centred because they are always looking out for themselves first. This is simply self-care or doing for me what no other should. It's my life. I need to take care of it and not leave that care to someone else. We expect governments to look after us in our old age while all along it is our responsibility to **PLAN** to take care of ourselves. This is being proactive. Remember that small steps and small goals--attainable goals--will get us there just as quickly.

For example: If I am 30 years of age now and I want to retire at the age of 55 what plans do I need to set in motion, now, so that will happen? Or if I'm going to be short on the rent this month do I wait for the landlord to come to me or do I go to him and explain how I plan to rectify the situation? If I want to finish high school or go to college what do I need to do now to make that happen? Being proactive is about planning ahead by thinking about things and then DOING what I need to do and by taking responsibility for what happens to me. In many cases it doesn't take a great deal of money to be proactive; it takes time, energy, and planning--thought. It seems that those who plan well live happier lives. When I am being proactive, I feel better about myself.

If you don't know where you are going how can you expect to get there?--Basil S. Walsh

3. Attitudes and perspectives

We need to pay attention to our attitudes and perspectives. We often hear people say of others,"Boy, that guy needs an attitude adjustment." Sometimes that is pretty close to the truth. Our attitude is probably the most difficult thing to adjust because we feel so justified in having it just the way it is. It is based on how we see things and what has happened to us in the past. If we have been taken advantage of and hurt in a spiritual or physical way why would we want to be kind or generous to those around us? If we had been abused as children we are likely to see kindness as a way for others to control us or hurt us. Certainly it is something to be wary of. We'll be suspect of those who want to be nice to us. Our attitude becomes one of caution and suspicion. If we believe that to get to the top we have to walk over people it will be difficult to have any meaningful relationships with others.

We believe that our attitude is our edge. We can use our attitude to justify our decisions. We say, "Why does it always have to be me who has to change anyway?" Consequently, we seldom look at the **role WE play** in what happens to us or what doesn't happen to us. It may be more convenient to point the finger at someone else and blame that person for what is happening to us. Some people find comfort in blaming others because it relieves them of the responsibility of taking risks that may be open to criticism. That way we can say we could not have done anything about what happened because it was out of our control.

If we were to define an attitude we could say it was a manner of acting, thinking or feeling that shows our disposition or opinion regarding a belief that we hold. For example: Our attitudes, very often, foster a self-fulfilling prophecy. If I fear being lonely and my attitude is one that demonstrates people can't be trusted, it is likely that I won't trust anyone nor will others trust me. But without trust it is difficult to have a meaningful or intimate relationship. Without that personal connection with others that comes with trust I am likely to feel lonely, the very thing that I feared in the first place.

Our perspectives have more to do with how we see and understand what goes on in the world in relation to ourselves. For example: Do we see the world only as a dangerous place because we were abused or attacked at some time in our lives? Do we choose to see only the worst in human nature and understand that most people are greedy, non-caring, or selfish because that has been our experience? Do we believe that we'll never get ahead unless we take what we can because hard work doesn't really pay off?

The more I choose to see the negative in the world around me the longer I postpone my serenity.

It is imperative that we periodically check our attitudes and perspectives to see if they are still valid. Question them. Ask where they fit in with our rules for living. Is there something that we need to change about how we see our world? Are our attitudes and perspectives moving us closer or further away from our goals? We need to decide how we want to see the world we live in and decide what our role will be in what happens to us.

In my professional capacity I have the opportunity to hear or experience firsthand many stories that continue to fortify me against the doom and gloom people who continually look for the worst that humanity has to offer.

The following story was relayed to me by a colleague. I believe it demonstrates the power we all have within us to make positive choices and how those choices can impact on those around us if we are willing to look at our attitudes and perspectives and challenge them. I'll write it as it was told to me:

In memory of Tom:
"Tom came to the Centre where I work directly from a hospital where he had been admitted as a result of a suicide attempt. He sat in my office with a sad presence, pensively silent. At times his teary eyes would overflow and he would weep softly for brief moments before regaining his composure. Tom was a child of a time when it was not OK for men to cry, especially in front of other men. He apologised for being so emotional. Tom said he needed to talk about his suicide attempt. We had already done the standard personal history stuff, his childhood, life, alcohol use etc. Part of the conversation that followed remains with me to this day.

Tom said: "I remember coming out of the coma in the hospital emergency ward. I remember thinking that because of my behaviour and drinking there was no one left in my life that meant anything to me. All I had left was myself and I had just tried to end that. I realised that living is about making choices and my choices had gotten me where I was at that moment, on a gurney in a hospital emergency room. I had always blamed my drinking on my childhood, my father who had been a heavy drinker, my boss, my wife or somebody, but there I was and nobody else on the gurney except me."

His next line lingers in my memory to this day. He said,"I remember thinking that if I made other choices maybe my life could be different. I never wanted to live more than right at this moment."

Tom did indeed live to make other choices. When he died seven years later of cancer those who attended his funeral filled the largest church in our small city. There is a plaque on a wall of the Centre where I work, not thirty feet from the office where our conversation took place, honouring Tom's memory. Anyone who knew him in those last seven years talks about his kindness and service to others. But then those were his choices, weren't they."--Jim Hanna

Strengths. What strengths?

Whenever I ask someone what strengths they use to work through the troubling times they face they just look at me and shrug. They often reply, "I don't know. I just do it." If we are going to manage ourselves successfully we need to know what strengths we have that we could use to our advantage? Let's think of a time when we dealt successfully with a particular situation or found ourselves having to respond to someone who had been rude or abusive toward us. What did we do? What were we thinking? How can we repeat that success? Many of us have suffered great losses. We have felt the pain of losing a loved one. There were times that we didn't believe we could survive or endure what was happening in our lives but somehow we managed. There have been times of great triumph when we did what we didn't believe was possible. What this indicates is that we all have strengths and inner resources that we depend on to help us through our growing times as well as our times of trial.

Take a few minutes to write down what you believe to be your personal strengths. Include those characteristics or behaviours that you usually rely on to help you cope with what comes your way or the strengths and assets you use to get your needs met.

Use this space if you like.

When you were marking down your strengths, personal characteristics, assets and resources did you consider any of the following?

❐ your friends

❐ your mates

❐ the community you live in and your neighbours

❐ your family

❐ your children

❐ your freedom to choose for yourself

❐ your sight

❐ your sense of smell and touch

❐ your ability to hear and enjoy the sounds of music and nature

❐ your ability to walk and to dance if you like

❐ your health

❐ your ability to learn and to read

❐ your ability to imagine and to dream

Boats, planes, cars and houses are not assets in the true sense. They are acquisitions that we have gained. We can lose them and we can gain them back again. Fortunes are amassed every day, lost and earned again. But once your eyesight is gone, it's gone. Once your health is gone, it's gone. All the money in the world can't change that. You can make yourself more comfortable, true enough, but it's not the same. Our real assets are those which money can't buy. They are usually the ones that we take for granted.

I complained that I had no shoes until I met a man who had no feet. Arabic proverb

It is important for us to focus on our strengths. We are much healthier when we consider our strengths and build on them than when we see our weaknesses and try to fix them. We are more wealthy than we imagined.

What other strengths do we possess?

(Adapted from the work of Jack Canfield, a noted author and President of the Foundation for Self-Esteem)

✎ Put a check next to the strength or characteristic that you feel describes you. Then invite any significant others (children or spouse/partner) to go over the list and check the ones that they think best describe you as well. Often others see us much differently than we see ourselves.

❐ able to take orders
❐ able to give orders
❐ able to take care of self
❐ accepts advice
❐ admires others
❐ affectionate
❐ appreciative
❐ articulate
❐ artistic
❐ assertive
❐ athletic
❐ attractive
❐ bright
❐ brave
❐ businesslike
❐ calm
❐ can be firm
❐ caring
❐ clean
❐ committed
❐ communicates well
❐ compassionate
❐ considerate
❐ cooperative
❐ courteous
❐ creative
❐ daring
❐ dependable
❐ dedicated
❐ diligent
❐ daring
❐ disciplined

- ❐ does what needs to be done
- ❐ doesn't give up
- ❐ eager to get along
- ❐ efficient
- ❐ elegant
- ❐ encourages others
- ❐ enjoys taking care of others
- ❐ fair
- ❐ feeling
- ❐ forceful
- ❐ frank and honest
- ❐ friendly
- ❐ funny
- ❐ generous
- ❐ gets along with others
- ❐ gets things done
- ❐ gives a lot
- ❐ goal setter
- ❐ good cook
- ❐ good dancer
- ❐ good friend
- ❐ good leader
- ❐ good listener
- ❐ good looking
- ❐ good manners
- ❐ graceful
- ❐ grateful
- ❐ good with hands
- ❐ good with words
- ❐ good with details
- ❐ good singer
- ❐ good parent
- ❐ good neighbour
- ❐ happy
- ❐ hard worker
- ❐ healthy
- ❐ helpful
- ❐ handsome
- ❐ honest
- ❐ humorous
- ❐ intelligent
- ❐ inspiring
- ❐ independent
- ❐ keeps agreements
- ❐ kind and reassuring
- ❐ leadership
- ❐ likes responsibility
- ❐ lots of friends
- ❐ makes a difference
- ❐ makes a good impression
- ❐ mathematical
- ❐ mechanical
- ❐ motivates others
- ❐ musical
- ❐ never gives up
- ❐ observant
- ❐ often admired
- ❐ orderly
- ❐ organized
- ❐ on time
- ❐ open
- ❐ patient
- ❐ peaceful
- ❐ physically fit
- ❐ pleasant
- ❐ positive attitude
- ❐ quick learner
- ❐ religious
- ❐ resilient
- ❐ respectful of authority
- ❐ respected by others
- ❐ responsible
- ❐ risk taker
- ❐ self reliant
- ❐ self-confident
- ❐ self-respecting
- ❐ sense of humour
- ❐ sensitive
- ❐ speak other languages
- ❐ spiritual

❒ straightforward and direct
❒ strong
❒ team player
❒ tolerant
❒ trusting
❒ truthful
❒ understanding
❒ unselfish
❒ visionary
❒ warm
❒ well-dressed
❒ spontaneous

Question: How do we use the strengths that we recognize we have? Now what do we do?

There are many actions that we can take. Look at the following suggestions and add to the list. Go over the following suggestions and mark the ideas that appeal to you now. What can you do right now that is doable? Use what you can and leave the rest:
(Adapted from *Self-Esteem and Peak Performance, Steps to Success*, by Jack Canfield)

1. Avoid or limit your involvement with "toxic" people--those who would hold you back or not be supportive.

2. Associate with positive-thinking people who are goal oriented. They can learn from us and we from them.

3. Acknowledge your past successes and the successes of others and talk about them so that you can learn from each other. Success breeds success.

4. Have an attitude of 100 % responsibility for what you do and what happens because of your efforts.

5. Repeat to yourself a positive affirmation such as "I am worthy of success" or "I am a good person who deserves to enjoy life."

6. Don't be afraid to acknowledge your strengths. If you are around positive people, they will see this as a positive act. Remember to acknowledge the strengths of others as well.

7. Ask others for feedback on your actions. Seek constructive criticism from those you respect and trust. Give away what you would like to receive.

8. Decide on what it is you want to do. What is the purpose of what you are doing?

9. Prioritize and focus--be sure to visit and revisit your vision of where you are going or what you want to accomplish. Things change and plans need to be updated. This allows you to accommodate the unexpected because the unexpected can and does happen.

10. Get excited about what it is you want to do. People are more often successful doing things that they enjoy doing.

11. Share your thoughts and your vision with others and allow them to share theirs with you. That way you can support each other. Now you have twice as much energy to draw on.

12. Be sure the goals that you set are attainable--realistic but challenging. There is a Buddhist saying that states "Blessed are the obstacles by which we grow." You will not grow if you are not challenged to do so. Revisit your checklist from time to time to see what new strengths you recognize you can use to help you move toward your goal.

13. Set realistic time-frames for attaining your goals so you can check periodically on your progress. If you don't reach your goal by the time you had marked, look at what happened, decide what needs to be done now and reset the time-frame. Allow extra time for the unexpected and the unforeseen. If you finish early it's a bonus. Setting a time-frame also motivates us to get moving. It's like a contract that we set with ourselves.

14. Ask yourself "what" not "how." You'll figure out the how.

15. Positive self-talk is imperative. When you get up in the morning tell

yourself that this is going to be a good day. If you begin this way the chances are better it will happen this way.

16. Although you have goals that you are working toward, don't overlook what needs to be done today. Look toward the future but live in the day.

17. Allow yourself the opportunity, every day, to daydream. See yourself being successful at whatever you have determined to be or do.

18. Create new outcomes from unsuccessful attempts to achieve your goals. Change the focus of your efforts so that you can see the situation you are approaching from a different perspective. For example: When you see your nonsuccesses as learning experiences instead of failures and use the information you gain to formulate a new plan you move closer to your goal. However, if you don't change anything nothing is likely to change.

19. Commit yourself to "do whatever it takes for as long as it takes." If you are still trying, your goal is getting closer. You do not move closer to what you want when you quit trying to get there.

20. If you need help, ASK for help. If you need information, ASK for information. If you want support, ASK for support. If you need it, ASK for it.

21. Make a poster and hang it in the room where you spend the most time. It says, "Successful people do what they have to do--unsuccessful people do what they want to do." Good habits are just as easy to come by as the bad ones.

22. Self-evaluate and self-monitor. Pay attention to the internal cues such as your feelings and your intuition. Don't be afraid to go with your "guts." Just be sure you have enough hard information to go on.

23. Understand and accept the fact that you will not always make the

right decisions. Evaluate the outcomes of your actions and decide how you could act differently the next time. That's part of the growing process. Mistakes only remain mistakes when you learn nothing from them.

24. Keep a "good feeling" fund. Every time you do something that makes you feel good throw a dollar in a jar. When you have reached a predetermined amount of cash take it out and spend it on yourself. Do something that you would not ordinarily do. Reward yourself for your hard work. It's OK to do that.

25. Expose your mind to positive thoughts, people, books, tapes and videos. These positive thoughts get into your subconscious and will serve to nourish your conscious mind. Never underestimate the power of your subconscious mind. It is the primary source for all of your ideas.

26. Be sure to thank and give credit to those who support you and are there for you, people like your friends, your children and your spouse. Be sure to do it often. Your successes don't come without their help.

27. Remember that "If you help others get to where they want to be they will most likely treat you in kind."

28. Make use of scales or other means to assess your progress.

✎ On a scale of one to ten, one being the lowest measure on the positive self-image scale and ten being the highest on the scale, determine where you would need to be so that you could say, "I feel confident about myself and competent in my abilities." Then mark on the scale where you see yourself at this time. Ask yourself what needs to happen now? What do you have to do to move one number up the scale? Remember that small goals and small steps lead to steady improvement over a period of time. Then go back to the scale one or two months later and mark on the scale where you feel you are at that time. If nothing has changed reconsider what you are doing and formulate another plan. If your mark is higher consider what you have been doing that has contributed to the increase in confidence and continue doing it. Is there anything else you can do?

1___2___3___4___5___6___7___8___9___10___

Take a moment to think about the role **YOU** play in the development and outcomes in your life. Here are some questions for you to consider:

1. What role will you play in the positive outcomes in your life from this time forward? Will it be the role of the thinker? The doer? The listener? The learner? What is one thing that you can do now to improve the outcomes of what you do each day?

2. Recall a time in your life when you felt positive and more confident. What were you doing when you felt this way?

3. What were you thinking?

4. How was your life different?

5. How would people around you know that you were feeling more positive about yourself? What would they recognize? What would they say is different?

6. How will that positive feeling impact on your life? How will your life be different?

7. During the times when you are feeling positive pay attention to who you are with? Where are you and what are you doing that is different? Focus on what is going on during the times when you feel positive. You will notice some things you are doing that are different. Do more of those things more often.

Many of us don't believe that we are deserving people. Perhaps that belief comes from a life where we were not safe--a life where others who were more powerful and influential took advantage of us and helped us learn that we were powerless. Perhaps we believe that we are not deserving because those who were given the opportunity to teach us the things we needed to know, didn't. Perhaps we were never encouraged or allowed to be ourselves. Perhaps those who were supposed to love us and care for us and protect us didn't or couldn't for reasons known only to them. We think if they couldn't love us, maybe there was something wrong with us. Perhaps it comes from a feeling of just being unlucky.

Aren't there those who seem to have all the luck and that everything they do seems to work out for them? But maybe they just work hard at being successful and they BELIEVE that they can succeed. William James said, "Believe that life is worth living, and your belief will help create the fact." Successful people understand that if they persevere, there is a good chance they will come out on top. These people understand the axiom that says, "If it has worked before, continue to do it. If it has not, do something different." They repeat their successes because they repeat what they did to be successful. Success has nothing to do with worthiness or luck.

People are not born "lucky" or "unlucky." We can have the kind of life we want but we have to work for it and not get sidetracked by feelings of hopelessness or anger. We need to look at what other people are doing to be successful (whatever success means to you) and do similar things. We need to be willing to look at ourselves and ask this critical question: "How much of what happens to me is due to how I see the world and how I respond to it?"

Let's look at the things that we do right and do them more often instead of focusing on our faults. That's how successful people continue to be successful. The process of developing a positive self-image begins when we do something positive for ourselves each day. We maintain our positive image by maintaining our integrity and by preserving our principles in the face of criticism or ridicule. Our potential is virtually unlimited and does not depend on anything but our own inner human resources.

We who lived in the concentration camps can remember the men who walked through the huts comforting others, giving away their last piece of bread. They may have been few in number, but they offer sufficient proof that everything can be taken from a man but one thing: The last of his freedoms --to choose one's attitude in any given set of circumstances, to choose one's own way.

--Viktor E. Frankl, *Man's Search for Meaning*

2.

WHERE AM I GOING AND HOW WILL I GET THERE?

WITHOUT ORDER THERE IS CHAOS--Gen. George Patton

Problem solving is one of those human tasks that many of us are able to do each day with an almost automatic or reflexive response. That is, we solve problems with little effort or thought. Which clothes shall I wear to work? What will I have for breakfast since I started my diet yesterday? Which child will get the new running shoes this week or do I wait until they can both get them at the same time? And the list goes on. These are the everyday situations that we face and deal with to get through our days.

But there are other situations that arise that are much more taxing and that require much more internal processing and thought. How am I going to be able to send John and Mary to college? If I can only afford to send one which one will that be? What is the best way to spend my income tax return? The car needs to be repaired but I don't have the money right now. Then there are the more personal problems to deal with: "I feel trapped at work and I know I can't stay there much longer but what do I do if I leave? Where do I go? How can we survive?" Perhaps you just lost your job of 25 years because of downsizing at the company you work for. Now what? Perhaps you are fortunate enough to have earned a great deal of money or you have inherited an estate. Many believe that more money would solve all of our problems. I won't insult anyone's intelligence here and say that is not true. More money would solve a great number of our present problems. We would be able to provide for ourselves and our family's basic needs more easily. But a whole new set of problems would be created. How do I invest this money so that it is protected and how do I make more? Whom do I get to manage it for me? Whom can I trust? We all want to do the best we can with what we have. We want to be seen as competent managers of our lives. Easy to say--not always easy to do.

What I am suggesting here is that no matter your station in life there are problems. The problems differ, true, but are problems nonetheless.

They can be so overwhelming at times that we become stuck and unable to think clearly. Sometimes our lives can feel as though they are out of control and indeed may become chaotic. Chaos creates stress. We can become procrastinators out of fear of making the wrong choice. We become "outcome focused" instead of tackling the issue in a methodical and organized fashion. We worry about what will happen in the worst-case scenario and prepare ourselves for it so that if it happens we won't be surprised. If the result turns out to be less severe or traumatic than we had anticipated then, somehow, we feel relieved that we "dodged a bullet."

We set ourselves up to be unsuccessful when we do this. We become reactive instead of proactive. When we don't have a way of working through our problems our self-esteem suffers because we don't feel as confident or as competent as we would like. We do not grow. We do not move ahead in our lives. So where are we going and how do we get there? When faced with making a decision how do we make the best one we can? First, we need to be open to change.

If change is inevitable, why do people resist change?

Usually when we decide on a particular solution to a problem we face, our lives are affected in some manner. It means that a change or some changes will be made. It is difficult, however, to change attitudes, values and perspectives when, for so long, they have been the basis for all that we have done. Yet the world is changing and our beliefs will be challenged. This does not mean that we will need to re-write our rules for living but it does suggest that we need to be open to change and that change can be a good thing.

When we stop considering possibilities we stop moving forward.

If we look at the bigger picture, we see that, in the last half century or so, we have progressed from the coast of North Carolina, in 1903, where the first motorized flight took place. The Kitty Hawk was propelled to flight for 57 seconds. Less than a hundred years later we are planning to build a space station in outer space. The fantasy shows like Star Trek and Deep Space

Nine are no longer fantasy. We have moved medically from doing amputations to doing micro-surgery and now laser surgery. In some instances we don't even have to cut anyone open anymore to eradicate some inner disease. Amazing. It wasn't that long ago that the work of Guglielmo Marconi led to the invention we know as television and now we have computers that process information so fast the human brain can barely comprehend it. We are developing at such a pace that some people feel that they are being left behind. Many of us get overwhelmed by the rate of change. Some are being displaced by robots that work 24 hours a day seven days a week. How do we deal with that?

There is no question that these bigger scale changes affect us. There is little we are able to do to stop or slow them down.

Looking at things that are closer to home we can see that how we shop for our goods and services is changing. In some cases we don't even have to leave our homes to order food or pay our bills. The cars that we drive are so sophisticated that we cannot fix them ourselves anymore. We have hair for bald people; we have plastic surgery for those who, for their own reasons, try to fight the passing of time. In our daily lives we find it increasingly difficult to hold on to the old ways.

We get comfortable living our lives the same way day in and day out. There is comfort in the sameness of the routine because we can count on it. Our old ways present us with some stability--a sense of security and we will fight to preserve our stability--our comfort zone.

"I'll go kickin' and screamin'"

Many resist the changes that are inevitable out of fear that we won't be able to cope and of fear of the unknown. What will happen to us? How will our lifestyle be affected? Will we be able to provide for our family? Much of what we do and how we respond is fear driven. We become afraid to make a decision because it may be the wrong one. We may be judged by others and held up to ridicule by our peers and friends. We may not have the skills that we need to compete in the workplace. We may feel that we are too old to change or learn new skills, so we fight to hold on to the old ways to preserve our jobs and our way of life. We become threatened by change because it is a foe we cannot fight.

Sometimes we hope that if we carry on as we always have somehow we won't be affected. Sometimes we become frustrated and angry at the changes because they don't make any sense to us. They seem arbitrary. Sometimes we feel threatened by the changes that are happening because we feel helpless to stop them. We become stressed and resentful. "Things were going just fine so why do we need to change anything?" Seldom do we have any input into the change process. It seems that our lives are in the hands of others, whoever they may be. There is a sense of being controlled or of being out of control and so we feel powerless.

On the brighter side, we know that, in many situations, a crisis that is brought about by change can also have hidden opportunities for growth. It can force us to be more proactive in our daily lives. It can force us to learn new skills. Anytime we learn something new, our self-esteem increases. We feel more competent. We become confident in what we do well. Since when was learning anything new such a bad thing anyway? We expand our possibilities when we learn something new.

We become lethargic when we are not challenged. The status quo can sometimes be harmful to our health. When we are not challenged and pushed to be all we can be we suffer both spiritually and mentally. We become stagnant when we are not pressed to think and problem solve. We can grow old before our time--aged by premature comfort. **The challenges that we didn't meet are more likely to be regretted than the ones we did.**

We can learn to manage ourselves and therefore manage change. We have control over how we choose to deal with the changes that are forced upon us as well as those changes that we make voluntarily. If we make no decisions and take no actions there can be no growth. This is a journey of growth and discovery. This is a journey to promote self-change. We can decide to focus our energies on the solutions instead of the problems. We can decide to survive instead of give up or give in.

If we were to view change as something that happens as a natural course of being alive, something to embrace so that we grow as humans instead of something to fear, would that make a difference as to how we went about living our daily lives? If we were to see the changes that happen around us and to us as learning experiences, would we be less stressed and anxious?

Change is a process and so is life

When we consider change as a process we need to look at two distinct systems at work:

1. Our psychological processes
2. Our mechanical processes.

Our psychological processes are at work when we begin to decide to look at things differently. When we are open to new ideas and possibilities we become psychologically prepared for change so the journey becomes much more manageable.

Accepting change and adapting to change involve some insight into what we might expect. We will go through various stages of change beginning with resistance, then denial that changes are coming, maybe even withdrawal and isolation from peers or friends. Anger will certainly be a part of the process. We will ask why things have to change. Why can't "they" just leave things as they were? We are likely to seek a way to postpone the changes we are facing--find a way to hang on just a while longer. When we find that we can't postpone the inevitable we will experience resignation causing depression. But with that comes eventual acceptance of the situation. We will grieve the loss of the old way. This process is the same as the grieving process described by Elisabeth Kubler-Ross in her book *On Death and Dying.*

The outward struggle we have with change reflects the inner struggle we experience regarding the confidence we have in ourselves. If we don't believe we can handle the change, then we probably won't. Without accepting the idea that change may bring us new opportunities we will not take any action that would benefit us. We can easily remain in the anger phase or the bargaining stage or the denial stage, all of which will get us nowhere.

Our mechanical processes are affected when we begin to learn new skills and to take action. We will feel more confident about our abilities to cope with change when we take an active part in the process of change. Information, then, becomes vital. Instead of fearing how impending changes will affect us we need to gain information that will be useful to us in adapting to change.

When changes occur, whether we like them or not and whether we embrace them or not, our lives will be different. There will be new issues for us to deal with and problems to solve. If the office where we work is switching over to a fully computerized system we will need to go to night school to learn about computers. If the company is downsizing we may need to learn how to work more efficiently in teams. If we are having some difficulty relating to our children we may need to enroll in some parenting courses. Accepting change and embracing it is an integral part of problem solving. It will be difficult to work successfully through the issues we face if we are not ready to embrace the changes that are sure to follow.

OK. Now what?

The **key** to problem solving is to have a plan. We need to be able to consider the possibilities that changes may bring and their impact, then to design ways to assimilate the changes into our lives rather than be overcome by them. We need to be organized.

When we have a plan of action our chances of successfully resolving any situation increase dramatically. For as many people as there are in this world there are just as many ways to deal with problems. We will decide on the right way to work through the issues that face us--the way that feels right for us if we are motivated to see and try new things. We all have different styles. Regardless of how we decide to do it the common thread is to have a plan so we can work through the **process**. THINK FIRST--THEN ACT.

Information is great but so is the "how to"

We may have to consider a number of techniques for working through our issues, the obstacles that we face, and the changes we experience. The important thing is to choose the one that works best for you. Combine one or more if you like. If there isn't one mentioned here that you could use look to friends or other people who have been successful. Consider how they did it. What method did they use to work through their issues? Ask about their plan. How similar was their problem to the one you are facing? Whatever works best for you, considering what you are facing, is the best method for the time. Success is only determined after something has been tried. Problem solving is really about your using a combination of skills that you have already learned in a way that has been successful previously. The solutions to our problems are rarely as complicated as we make them. Keep your attempts at solution making as simple as possible. Decide which combination of skills will work best for you, given the circumstances and proceed.

The very first step to problem solving is determining or defining what the problem is. The next step is to decide on a planned response when we feel we have considered the best course of action. Inactivity can cause us spiritual damage, and rash actions can cause us irreparable harm. Here are four types of problem solving techniques to consider:

1. **The "odd man in"** technique invites an unbiased third party to provide feedback on what that observer sees or hears. Perhaps he or she can offer an opinion based on some past successes in similar situations. We are not asking this person to make a decision for us but rather to help us see where we may be stuck or getting side-tracked. Sometimes we can't see the solutions because of our involvement in the issue. Very often the problem is **how** we see the problem. Outside input can be valuable but it has to come from someone we trust.

2. **The "decisional matrix"** technique (See Figure I at the end of this chapter.) For those who like to put things down on paper, or visually organize things, this technique is an excellent way of examining the

pros and cons of possible decisions. As you will see on the form, it gives you an opportunity to observe things from both sides. Often we go to bed trying to sleep but our minds just won't shut down. Thoughts and counter thoughts keep going round and round. We can become tired both physically and mentally. This is the time when we are more likely to make a mistake in judgement.

Using the matrix gives us an opportunity to be more objective and at the same time be able to see our choices so that we can clear our heads. Now we can begin to generate ideas about possible outcomes and what they would mean to us under a variety of situations. By writing things down we clear some space in our heads for new ideas.

When we begin to generate ideas we can ask ourselves what has worked for us before in a similar situation and how we handled things. We can consider times when the situation wasn't an issue for us and ask ourselves what was different then. What was going on for us that isn't going on for us now? It helps us focus on possible solutions or consider where we need to start so that we can work through what is troubling to us now.

3. **Six Steps to Problem Solving.** This method helps to slow down the desire to react spontaneously. When we act or respond out of a feeling state--anger, frustration, hurt, sadness, etc.--we are not as likely to make positive decisions for ourselves.

Step 1. **Is there a problem?**
There isn't a problem or an issue to deal with until **WE** say there is. It means recognizing that we are or have been uncomfortable, feeling at odds with our surroundings, feeling there is chaos in our lives that wasn't there a while ago, that we are feeling challenged or pushed somehow, and whatever other feelings we might experience that we would not consider to be normal. We need to define the problem.

Step 2. **What is going on?**
It will be difficult to begin solving any problems or issues

until we are clear, in our own minds, what the facts are. What has happened? Who is involved? Where did this take place? When did it happen? How extensive is the problem? How did this happen? Whose problem is it, really? Being able to "own the problem" is very important. We can't blame others for our situations. If we don't take responsibility for the problem we won't take responsibility for the solutions. The situation will persist **OR** we may decide that the situation that has presented itself isn't our problem at all. This is, possibly, the most important step of the process. By the time we get finished gathering the information some of the solutions will have presented themselves. Get the facts.

Step 3. **What now?**

Here we begin to generate some ideas. Consider some methods that would help solve the problem. It's important to know what our strengths are and how we can utilize some of our assets. We should build our ideas and solutions around what we do best. Are we good communicators, organizers, or mediators for example? Be creative here. No idea is too crazy at this point. We can rule out the obvious non-workable solutions later. We should try to be as non-judgemental as possible about the solutions put forth. Once our judgements get in the way our clarity suffers. After we have put some ideas together we need to look at them critically and decide if they are feasible and if we can implement them without harming ourselves or others in some way. We may want to consider how the solutions will impact on us. This can be somewhat difficult to do because there is no way of determining how others may respond to our solutions. We may have to go back to gather more information before we can generate any more ideas. Sometimes parts of several different approaches can be used. "When you are laying bricks you don't start with the bricks--you start with the mortar." Generate ideas and then evaluate them.

Step 4. Pick one.

After all is said and done we will need to select a solution which best fits all the criteria. We will need to ask: "If this is our problem how will we handle it in the fairest way possible so that no one, including ourselves, will be intentionally hurt? Do we have all the facts or at least enough information to make an informed decision as to how we will handle or respond to this situation? Have we generated enough discussion so that the choices available to us are varied enough to be thorough?" Once we have satisfied these criteria we need to decide upon an approach and begin to decide how we will implement our plan. When we are considering our plan we need to minimize the negative influences as much as possible such as timing, expense, and those who may try to impede our process. Other questions to ask are Do we have all the resources we need to do this? and Are we as well prepared as we could be? The decision we make will be the best one for the time. That's all we can do.

Step 5. Do it.

Once we have decided on a plan, we must follow through. The thinking is done and now is the time for action. We must put our plan into play and begin to pay attention for any feedback. We continue to assess the outcomes of our plan and look for any new developments that we may need to respond to.

Step 6. How will we know if we were successful?

As with all action plans there has to be an evaluation period. First, we will need to decide for ourselves what success is. Generally it means that we have experienced some relief or sense that things are better or are getting better. We will need to think of some way to evaluate the outcome(s). One way is to look at the outcomes and see how they match up with what we thought might happen. Sometimes the solutions to one problem can lead to another problem. This is often the case when family members or good friends are involved. We need to be aware of this and follow the same procedure we used for the original issue. We may not necessarily use the same plan but we will use the same process. Staying focused on what we need in order to feel less stressed, hassled or resentful will be important.

The value of this exercise is in the evaluation process. That is how we learn about ourselves and our abilities, about what we know and what we need to learn. Being able to problem solve effectively and consistently is a process of trial and error. We were not born with the innate ability to do it right every time. It takes practice and skill to problem solve effectively.

The last approach is very basic and straightforward.

4. **Stairway to Success--**Draw a stairway with six steps, or as many as you may need, leading to a plateau. At the top of the stairway is the goal (solution) that we have considered. The important thing here is to create steps that will move us closer to solving the issue at hand. The actions we take should be those that begin with our goal in mind. The steps should be practical, measurable, and attainable, and should require some effort at learning a new skill. This method, like many others, requires some investigation of facts and information gathering. It also requires that we do a self-evaluation. Do we have the skill necessary to implement this plan? Is there something that we need to do or learn before we can move up to the next step? Break the plan of action down into as many parts as it takes to be successful. We can easily set ourselves up to be unsuccessful if we try to rush this part of the process. Each step accomplished can lead us to another step until we reach the top where we attain the solution to the problem. This method can also be the quickest and easiest way of determining a plan of action. It really does depend on the problem we are dealing with.

Resolving conflict with others

There is another problem that many of us face each day of our lives and that is interacting with other people who play a significant role in our lives--those who we can't just slough off with a shrug. They are more likely to be a family member--a spouse, a child, or a boss for instance. Regardless of who it is there are some basic principles that we can use to help us resolve conflict with others if that is our goal.

1. Look for solutions . . . not for someone or something to blame.

This principle seems to be difficult to adopt for a good number of us. For some reason, we find it more satisfying to blame others for what goes on in our lives: "If you would stop doing this I wouldn't do that." If we are going to be successful at developing techniques that will help us resolve our personal conflicts we need to look for solutions to the issues we face, not try to lay blame for our problems at the feet of someone else. Being proactive (that is, taking responsibility for resolving our issues) allows us to take responsibility for the outcomes as well. It also means not having to respond to the choices others have made. Common choices, common solutions.

2. Focus on the problem . . . not the person.

This principle is similar to the first one. Stay focused on the problem at hand. Resist the urge to bring in any unresolved issues because they will only serve to derail the solution finding process. We need to focus our energies on what the real issues are. People are more likely to work with us if we are not trying to suggest that they are responsible for what is going on with us. It is always helpful to let the other person involved in the situation speak first. This suggests that we are willing to listen to their point of view--how they define the problem. They are more likely to listen to us when we are defining the problem as we see it if they feel they have been heard. Two heads are definitely better and more productive than one. If we alienate the other person we negate any compromise that may be found. WIN/WIN becomes more difficult to attain.

3. Use dialogue . . . not debate.

If we are trying to resolve a difference of opinion or position with someone it is better that we discuss the issues rather than defend our base camps. By debating the issues we are merely trying to prove that our point of view is the only point of view that matters. We are trying to get our opponent to see it our way. If that person is feeling the same way we now have an adversarial situation on our hands, one that is not likely to produce any sort of resolution to the conflict. The other problem with debating the issues, as opposed to using dialogue, is we are not going to hear any possible solutions that are being suggested to us. We are invested in proving that we are right. We are trying to prove that the other person is wrong. How can we be open to any suggestions when we are trying to poke holes in everything the other person is saying? We miss opportunities to learn and to grow when we are not open to the idea that sometimes others can be more right than we are.

4. Try for a win/win solution . . . not a win/lose situation.

A win/win position allows for solutions to be mutually beneficial and mutually satisfying. No one wants to walk away from a disagreement feeling defeated. Those who were involved in the disagreement will feel more committed to the solution agreed upon if they feel that they are positively affected. Win/lose scenarios don't allow for any positive outcomes that involve both parties. When we are more committed to a win/lose scenario, that stance says, "I will have my way and I really don't care what you think about that or how you feel about that." This outcome excludes the other person's rights. It creates an atmosphere of no or low trust and encourages revenge. I'd rather resolve my disagreements at the time they occur and not worry about who is trying to retaliate or get even with me. WIN/WIN is the only way to go. If we each give a little nobody loses.

5. Conflict resolution is a process . . . not a quick fix.

As with all things, there is a process at work here. Conflict resolution needs to allow for thinking time. If it takes an extra day to come to a positive resolution to the conflict, so be it. We are not looking for a quick fix but rather a long-lasting understanding that we can depend on. This mindset also creates an atmosphere of respect and trust for each other. Quick fixes tend to get us where we don't want to be. Quick fixes waste time.

When we consider the resolutions to which we agree we can see that they are not the only answers but rather the best that we could come up with for the time and circumstances that presented themselves. Different situations will require different responses but the process is still the same. THINK and then ACT.

Draw a line and on it mark a scale of 1-10. One (1) indicates "needs work" and ten (10) represents "doing great." Put a mark and the date on the scale that would indicate where you feel you need to be in order for you to feel good about your ability to problem solve.

Where on the scale do you feel you are presently with regards to your ability to problem solve effectively? Put a date at that spot. Now ask yourself what you have to do to move that mark up one number? What's one thing you can do right now? What skill can you develop? Do you need to learn how to communicate differently? Do whatever you need to do, unless of course you are already at ten to which I say "never mind." Go back in a month or two to see where you now are on the scale. Has there been a change? What have you done differently or what have you learned? What's different about you?

1___2___3___4___5___6___7___8___9___10___

Consider the following questions:

1. Can I remember a time when I dealt successfully with similar issues or problems in the past? Do I know someone who has dealt,

successfully, with similar issues in the past? How did that person do it?

2. Can I now use the same skills that were successful in past?

3. Are there particular skills that I need to develop before I attempt to make specific changes in my life?

4. When was a time I felt good about how I handled change in the past? What did I do that was effective and positive?

5. Am I as well prepared as I could be? Do I have a plan that is feasible?

6. How will my life be different when I am able to feel more confident in my abilities to deal with change or to problem solve? What will that mean to me?

7. What would people say about me when I am able to manage change more effectively or to problem solve more effectively? What would they notice that was different?

8. When I can problem solve more effectively how will that change my relationships with others?

9. When I can deal with change more effectively how will that impact my relationships with others?

Problem solving is like doing a jigsaw puzzle. There is a process at work. We may decide to work at the puzzle from the outside in or the inside out. It doesn't matter. What does matter is that we have a plan. As we continue to work according to our plan--as we fit the pieces of our puzzle together--the picture becomes more clear. There is an order to things that needs to be followed so that the chances of success are increased in our favour. We can't jump from A to Z without going through B,C,D,E, etc. Recognizing the need for patience is a key element.

As the quotation says, "Without order there is chaos." We need to feel there is a sense of order in our lives. We need to feel that we are capable of working through the issues that are sure to present themselves in our daily lives. It is true that "order" means different things to different people. Whatever it means to us we need to sense that it is there. There is safety and security in process and order. It helps us feel that we are in control, as much as we can be, of the influence **we** have in our lives. We can be overwhelmed by changes and the uncertainty they present, or we can embrace them as the natural order of life and work to manage them as best we can. To do otherwise invites dissonance within ourselves which leads to stress and discomfort. If we are feeling stressed all of the time and find ourselves constantly challenged, without a plan for dealing with the issues, how else would we expect to feel?

The longer I live, the more I realize the impact of attitude on life. Attitude, to me, is more important than facts. It is more important than the past, than education, than money, than circumstances, than failures, than successes, than what other people think or say or do. It is more important than appearances, giftedness, or skill. It will make or break a company . . . a church . . . a home.

The remarkable thing is that we have a choice every day regarding the attitude we will embrace for that day . . . We cannot change our past . . . We cannot change the fact that people will act in a certain way. We cannot change the inevitable . . . The only thing that we can do is play on the one string we have, and that is our attitude.

I am convinced that life is 10% what happens to me and 90% how I react to it.
And so it is with you . . . We are in charge of our attitudes.

Author unknown

How to use this matrix: For example . . . Quitting smoking

Figure 1

QUITTING SMOKING	
Benefits	**Drawbacks**
Some benefits of not smoking: ■ better health ■ more money ■ role model for my children ■ promotes a cleaner and safer environment for my family	Some drawbacks of not smoking: ■ higher stress levels ■ may become more irritable ■ hassles from my friends

CONTINUING TO SMOKE	
Benefits	**Drawbacks**
Some benefits of continuing to smoke: ■ no withdrawal symptoms ■ relaxes me ■ socially accepted by my peers	Some drawbacks of continuing to smoke: ■ may die from a related disease ■ may alienate my family ■ less money to purchase the things I want ■ is time consuming

We need to be able to look at our decisions from all the angles before we make our choices. Trying to do that in our heads can be difficult at times because our emotions can cloud the facts or circumstances to be considered. It is easier to evaluate the different viewpoints and circumstances when we write them down. We can walk away from them and come back later after we have had a chance to review them. We can add or eliminate points until we feel that we have a clear and subjective picture of the issue and then decide our course of action based on what we believe to be in our own best interests.

Figure 2

MAKING A CHANGE	
Benefits	**Drawbacks**

NOT MAKING A CHANGE	
Benefits	**Drawbacks**

3.

STAYING ON THE ROAD CAN BE TOUGH

WHAT WE DO TO MANAGE OUR STRESS PLAYS A DIRECT ROLE IN WHAT HAPPENS TO US ON OUR JOURNEY TOWARD BEING MORE SPIRITUAL SELVES.

Stress is one of those words that is fast becoming a catch-all for those things that we cannot otherwise explain. We hear, "He is really irritable, so he must be under a lot a stress" or "She looks really tired, so she must be stressed out." What is stress? Where does it come from?

What is it?

There are many definitions of stress. What is stressful for one person may not be experienced as stressful by another. I would define stress to be a mental or physical state of tension that's created when we are required to respond to the demands and pressures relating to our work, families, or any other external sources, as well as those that are internally generated from self-imposed demands, obligations or feelings of inadequacy. The level of stress that we experience is directly related to the belief we hold in our ability to deal with the presenting stressors.

Crisis states and breakdowns occur when we allow our stress to accumulate in us. Our mental and physical well-being is directly affected. Mentally we may exhibit panic and anxiety, anger, frustration, impaired concentration, confusion, poor judgement, and changes in our demeanor which are not normally characteristic of who we are as people. Physically we experience muscle tension, headaches, insomnia, high blood pressure, ulcers, and lower back problems. Stress can be, and often is, a silent killer. It can aggravate a variety of medical problems that may have otherwise not posed any serious health risks. Prolonged stressful experience has been linked to lower immunicological responses, shorter life spans, and increased production of carcinogens--cancer-causing agents. Stress can lead to alcohol and drug abuse, prescription drug abuse, family distress, violence, gambling, food and sex addictions, and even suicide.

Our intellectual, financial, spiritual, social, familial and physical selves can be affected by stress. The good news is that we can learn how to manage our stress effectively so that it does not cripple us or impede our journey toward peace, prosperity, and happiness. Self-management does not have to cost much but it will always require hard work and being open to change.

These are times of great change. Many of us worry about our survival economically and physically. How much of a problem is stress? The International Labour Organization, as quoted from the book *Comprehensive Stress Management*, by Jerrold S. Greenberg, estimates that occupational stress costs industry **200 billion** dollars per year (in the U.S.) for salaries for sick days, costs for hospitalization and out-patient care, and decreased productivity. Businesses pay higher health insurance payments as a result. Absenteeism is on the rise and morale in the workplace is falling like a rock. My suspicion is that there are corresponding figures relating to the Canadian labour force. Many of the foremost causes of death in this country are directly related to stress.

Also mentioned in Greenberg's book, however, is proof that stress-related costs of doing business have been lowered by the implementation of stress-management programs in the workplace.

Is stress always a bad thing?

No. It is not. We need to have some stress in our lives. The objective is not to eliminate all stress from our lives but rather to learn how to manage it appropriately so that the quality of our lives is not negatively affected. Stress can be the driving force to making some positive changes. For example: the working parent is moved to be more efficient because he or she knows that time wasted creates negative stress, so the parent becomes a better planner. The cab driver is stressed by the action of driving in the city but becomes more alert for potential danger and wayward pedestrians.

There is the stress caused by getting married, winning money or coming into an inheritance, the birth of a child, graduation or a promotion at work, and physical exercise that promotes health. These are all examples of positive stress: eustress. Eustress is the type of stress that can promote personal growth--one which encourages optimum performance and leads to an outcome that is both beneficial and enjoyable. Take, for example, professional and amateur athletes who place themselves under tremendous physical and mental stress so they can run a faster mile or swim a faster lap; the student who enters medical school to become the best surgeon he can be; or the law student who dreams of becoming a leading criminal attorney.

The real measure of how stressful a situation is or will be rests on how we see the stressor or stressful situation. If we see hard work as useful and enjoyable--something that we thrive on--we are not likely to be stressed by it. If, however, we see it as being a drudge and boring, as something that we would rather not have to do, we are likely to feel stressed.

The intensity of our stress and the type of stress we experience (positive stress or eustress vs. negative stress) has a great deal to do with how we choose to see the situation or activity we are engaged in.

Where does it come from?

Stress is primarily a man-made thing. Most things that man can make he can unmake.

When I talk to people about their stress, though there are many, many different sources and stressors that they report, I hear one common comment: "It's out there. It's everywhere we go." Those people, places, things, behaviours, attitudes and uncomfortable situations that cause stress are everywhere. They are at our places of work when we wonder how long will we have our jobs. Not managing our time appropriately causes us stress. Having 15 minutes to do a 30-minute job because we couldn't say no to the neighbour. Taking on an extra job at work knowing that we don't have the time to finish the work we have but thinking we'll work it out somehow causes stress. There are stressors in our homes and in our families. Parenting is an extremely stressful undertaking. Is there enough money for college or to pay the mortgage? Not being able to communicate our needs or our expectations is stressful. Not being heard and understood by those around us is stressful. Not getting what we consider to be our basic needs met is stressful. Eating the wrong foods can create stress. There are outside stressors such as air and water pollution, food additives, noise, fear, violence, and anxiety which create or add to our stress. Physicians can, unwittingly, add to our stress by prescribing medications that mask the symptoms of our stress rather than helping to deal with the source of the stress.

Then there are the things that we have absolutely no control over, such as earthquakes, near-miss car accidents, and changes that are thrust upon us with little or no advanced warning. When we find ourselves faced with a situation that resembles an incident from our past, our recollections of how successful we were at dealing with them can cause us anxiety and stress: for example, dealing with an obnoxious person or having to stand up for your rights in the face of criticism by your peers. Seniors are concerned about the standard of living that they may or may not have. Where will they go? Who will be there for them? Will they be a burden to someone? There are stressors at the corner store and the garage and the post office and the tax office and the bank and the government offices and the school yard and the highways and the streets . . . and on and on. No doubt about it, there are stressors out there.

So where does your stress come from? It is very important that you identify your stressors so that you can set about reducing them to manageable levels.

Take a few minutes to complete the following assessment.

STRESS INVENTORY

Please circle the response that most closely represents your feelings for each situation:
1. Never 2. Rarely 3. Not sure 4. Sometimes 5. Always

e.g. 4 (Sometimes) I enjoy being alone.

Home/Social Life (include friends and family of origin here)

_ 1. I feel as though people close to me are judging me and are critical of me.

__2. I feel that there is little or no caring, compassion or understandin in my home.

__3. There is an air of tension and danger in my home.

__4. There seems to be little time for the things that need to be done.

For questions 5, 6 and 7 answer the "R" questions if you ar involved in a romantic or sexual relationship and the "N"question if you are not involved currently in a romantic or sexual relationshi

__5R. My relationship is falling apart.

__5N. Recent relationships have not been satisfying.

__6R. My partner seems to spend more time criticizing me than he/sh does supporting me.

__6N. I feel unwanted and alone.

__7R. My relationship takes more energy than I have to give.

__7N. Not being in a relationship is boring and lonely.

Professional Life

__8. I feel as though I need to give 110 % **constantly** or I will lose m job.

__9. I feel that whatever I do doesn't match the standards I set fo myself.

__10. It is not easy working with other people.

__11. The expectations of constant daily performance can b overwhelming to me.

_12. I don't look forward to going to work each day.

_13. I am physically and mentally exhausted at the end of each working day.

_14. I'm never sure what is expected of me at my place of work.

The Rest of My Life

_15. There a not many people in my life I would call a friend.

_16. The state of my health is constantly on my mind.

_17. The state of my finances is constantly on my mind.

_18. I fear for the safety of those closest to me (children, parents, friends, spouse etc).

_19. I fear walking alone at night.

_20. At night I feel like a prisoner in my own home.

_21. No matter how hard I try I can never seem to get ahead.

_22. The thought/fear of dying is constantly on my mind.

Total the values that you placed beside each situation.
Home/Social (1-7) ___
Professional (8-14) ___
The Rest (15-22) ___
Total _____

Unless the totals are unusually high (average should be about 25 with a maximum of 40) in any one area you may want to look at the balance between the different stations of your life. If one area stands out, you need to pay some attention to it. Go through each category and see how many 5's there are. If there are more 5's in one category than another and the total is high it likely indicates that some kind of changes are warranted. That may mean a change in the type of work you do within the organization or perhaps pursuing a new vocation. It may indicate that some work needs to be done with regard to the relationship you are currently involved in. If you are single it may mean that you need to get out more and socialize, to join a club or a recreational sporting activity of some kind. If you are uncomfortable in the neighbourhood you live in and you fear for your safety, move. The change will do you good.

This exercise is meant to help you recognize potential areas of stress. To reduce our stress we first have to know what it is we are dealing with. So often we get caught up with just living our lives from day to day. It becomes difficult to pin-point why we don't feel well. Everything gets mixed in together so problems at home become problems at work (and vice versa); we have no social life and are bored so we get angry and miserable; when we are frightened or pre-occupied with particular facets of our lives we neglect others.

Enough is enough

But there are other sources of stress around us.

Numerous books, newspaper and magazine articles and just as many businesses, institutions and counselling professionals are telling us that we are sick because of the "toxic" experiences we have suffered at the hands of others, and that we may not know how sick we really are. They encourage us to get in touch with our pasts so that we can rectify the wrong-doings. We are encouraged to step forward and proclaim our grief. Great stress is created in us when we try to do this work before we are ready. Our memories are powerful reminders. Our memories will not go away. But we don't have to *relive* them day after day. We can contract with ourselves to deal with them when the time is right and set them aside for now.

Unfortunately victimhood has become a major industry unto itself. Healers and therapists and clerics have convinced many that the way to the future is through the past. The hunt for the elusive reasons why things went as they did has become a social movement, a quest for some.

We need to ask ourselves what will we do with that information when we have it. How will knowing why things happened as they did make our lives any better? How will that information change what has happened? We could spend our lifetimes searching and seeking out information and answers and never find them. Does that mean we remain damaged or sick? How do we feel when we carry these burdens with us day in and day out? Stress, anger, frustration, tension, anxiety . . .?

I agree that we have to face our "demons." No doubt there at all. Perhaps horrible things happened to us in our childhoods. Perhaps we were neglected or abused. No one deserves to suffer these indignities. Of course, it is good for us to address the issues that trouble us. It is important for us to deal with the issues that stand in the way of our happiness and inner peace--but NOT until we are ready. Let's work on getting better and not on remembering how bad it was. I am not convinced that we have to spend painful time reliving the past in order to deal with it. Nobody is saying that we have to forget what happened to move on but we need to work on accepting that it happened in order to move on. It was painful enough the first time and painful time is usually very stressful time.

When we are able to access and utilize our inner strengths and when, with the help, love and support of those who care for us, we are able to summon the courage it takes to face our issues, THEN we can begin to do the work that needs to be done. That's when the healing process begins. This is part of the spiritual journey we have embarked upon, the inside job.

Sometimes the cure is worse than the illness

As a society, we are obsessed with pathology. For many people the first order of business when they experience stress, anxiousness, or panic is to call a physician and ask for some medication to deal with the symptoms. In the majority of times the physician will prescribe a medication that should relieve or lessen the discomfort. Physicians operate from a medical model which suggests the triumph of chemistry over troublesome physiology.

Certainly, in some situations, there may be a need for some brief or long-term medical intervention. I do not challenge that fact. But the healing systems that most of us operate in do not give any credence to the idea that we have strengths and personal resources that with proper guidance, self or otherwise, can be used to help us work through our issues and do it with a minimum of drugs or none at all. It becomes more difficult to work through our issues when we are medically impaired. We are actually postponing our relief. Do we feel better? I doubt it. Do we feel different? Yes. But different isn't better; it's just different. In most instances, we are no closer to solving our problems than we were before. The same stressors exist. The need for solutions is still there. Our systems, and for the most part our helpers in those systems, are more problem focused than they are solution focused. We need to feel as though we are working on some solutions. Just the feeling of moving ahead creates that "light at the end of the tunnel."

One of the major sources of stress comes from the very systems that we trust to help us.

There's more

The greatest source of stress, for some of us, comes from unmet expectations: those that we have of ourselves, those that others have of us, and those that we have of others. We often place such high expectations on ourselves because we want to prove to others that they were wrong about us or that we are worthy of their trust and support. Sometimes the expectations belong to others and yet we take on the responsibility to somehow make them real or come true. Sometimes we are expected to magically know what others need from us without them ever telling us. Because we don't deliver, they become angry or disappointed with us and we, in turn, own their disappointment. This is certainly the case in our relationships. I think of students who are writing final exams or trying to get into college. I think of parents who want so much for their children and push too hard thinking that they are being helpful or dutiful parents. STRESS. Do we set our goals and standards so high that we or they are destined to be unsuccessful?

Other stressors or factors can be problematic. Lack of time management skills results in our inability to use the time we have, or the time that has been allotted us, in the most effective manner. Our problems with time management may have more to do with not managing ourselves effectively than it does anything else. Having underdeveloped problem solving skills (go back to Chapter 2), or a poor diet coupled with other contributing factors can lead to physical and emotional stress. We need to monitor the amount of nicotine and the amount of caffeine in the coffee, tea, chocolate, and pop that we consume. Too much salt in our diets can, for some, cause higher blood pressure and heart problems. Even the amount of sugar that we use can create stress.

It's always been up to us

When we realize it is possible for us to decide how we will perceive our situations and how we will respond to them, we take a gigantic step toward reducing our stress. Proactive people focus on what they can influence or change. Reactive people focus on what concerns them with little or no energy put toward finding/creating any solutions. The solutions come from us. The solutions to much of what stresses us are within. We become stronger and healthier when we generate our own formulas for success. We may need to learn new skills to help us deal with what comes our way instead of looking for ways to get around it somehow. We may need to search out information or seek the feedback of an unbiased third party so that we can consider an alternate point of view before we make a decision. There may be no easy or pain-free ways to deal with our problems. The best way may be to get right at them so as to meet them head on. We need to utilize our own strengths and surrounding supports so that we can continue to move forward from where we are now and not backtrack into the morass that is our histories.

First things first

We need to know what we are dealing with and how it affects us. The experts tell us that we cannot and should not try to eliminate all stress from our lives. I agree. We need to have a certain amount of stress in our lives because it helps to keep us aware of the need to change and it encourages us to evaluate how we live our lives from day to day. It can alert us to potentially dangerous situations. Sometimes, however, the changes we experience in our day-to-day living can be so subtle that they accumulate within us without our knowing or being aware of their collective influence. How much stress is enough? How much is too much?

Generally speaking when you are having trouble sleeping, if you feel fatigued all the time, when you don't eat right, when you have trouble breathing, when you notice you have a cold that hangs on, or you find that you get sick more often, if you feel as though you don't want to be around anybody, or if you are uncharacteristically short tempered or mean spirited, if you feel confused, anxious, or fearful a great deal of the time, and if you have muscle aches and back aches more than you used to, consider these to be indicators of possible stress loads that are becoming unmanageable.

The **first** step in stress management is to ask ourselves what is different about our lives? Have there been any changes either at home or at work that are financial or social in nature? What are we doing that we weren't doing a while ago? Perhaps we are isolating ourselves or withdrawing from the outside world in an attempt to create a buffer zone between us and whatever stressor is affecting us. The only thing that happens when we isolate or withdraw is we cut ourselves off from the support and feedback networks that we may need to assist us. We could be adding to our stress instead of managing it.

Reducing stress doesn't mean that we have to reduce our outside interests. There is some merit to simplifying our lives. I don't see reducing our interests and simplifying our lives as the same thing. We may need to evaluate the benefits or the efficiency of our current coping strategies. Are we using food, sex, alcohol, drugs, gambling or shopping as a way of trying to cope with ignore, or reduce the impact of stress in our lives? These methods only mask the symptoms of our stress and do nothing to identify or work on the source of the problem. In the end they add to our stress, not reduce it.

There can be a co-relation between trust, whether that is trust in a partner or mate, a friend or a work mate, and stress. It is in our nature to want to trust. It is also in our nature to be suspicious because we need to protect ourselves from emotional and physical pain. If we trust those close to us to be faithful, honest or supportive and they abuse the trust we grant them, the aftermath can be extremely stressful.

Understand that we cannot out-run or out-think stress but we can learn to manage it. Effective stress management requires stress reduction concerning both our physical and mental states.

We manage our stress more effectively when we manage ourselves more effectively.

Consider how the following situations influence your stress levels at the present time:

1. Have you considered the importance of diet/nutrition/exercise?

2. Do you manage your time at work and in your personal life effectively?

3. Do you need to do an attitude check?

4. How are you dealing with job stress?

5. Is there a connection between your trust levels and your stress levels?

DIET AND NUTRITION

It is important for us to understand the connection between what we eat, or don't eat, and the amount of stress we experience. Consider the statement, "We are what we eat." Ingesting the right food may or may not prevent stress but it will enable us to experience lower levels of stress. Proper diet can strengthen our vital systems such as our immune system which wards off diseases, fights cancer and assists our bodies in the fight against bacterial infections so that we heal faster; it can also assist our emotional systems by helping to produce naturally occurring antidepressants and specific brain chemicals which work to reduce hypertension. There are particular foods that assist in the natural production of sedatives and tranquillizers which help us sleep more soundly.

NOTE: before you decide to substitute any food for a medication that has been prescribed to you, please consult with your physician.

Specifically speaking

Let's start with the A vitamin first. It is important because it helps to support our immune system by keeping the microbe-catching membranes of the mouth, respiratory passages and skin intact. It is also essential for the maintenance of healthy bones, eyes and organs. A recent Harvard University study showed a connection between a reduced rate of strokes and reasonable amounts of vitamin A and beta-carotene. You can get vitamin A from eating carrots, spinach, apricots, dried peaches, dark green leafy vegetables, sweet potatoes, pumpkins, beets and mangoes.

The B vitamins are essential to have in our systems because they help provide the body with energy, basically by converting carbohydrates into glucose, which the body burns to produce energy. If we are feeling stressed these vitamins will help maintain our energy levels. Vitamin B6 works against the formation of kidney stones as well. Sources of complex B vitamins are whole grains, blackstrap molasses, organ meats, brewer's yeast, nuts, and brown rice. There are many other sources as well.

When we are under stress the body's immune system become stressed as well. We contract colds more readily when we are stressed. The bodily systems used to fight infection are challenged. Vitamin C is important because it helps to fight bacterial infections and combats muscular weakness. It protects other beneficial nutrients such as thiamine, riboflavin and vitamins A and E from oxidizing more rapidly so that the body gets the maximum effect of what is put into it. As well, it stimulates the energy-producing systems we depend on. Vitamin C assists in tissue repair, helps to heal wounds more quickly and serves as a powerful antioxidant (we'll talk about these in a bit) to protect against asthma, angina and cataracts. It will also help combat fatigue and depression. Some sources of vitamin C are citrus fruits, rose hips, cherries, mangoes, cantaloupe, strawberries, broccoli, tomatoes, cabbage and green peppers, to name a few. Any good health food store will be able to provide you with a list of other sources and additional information.

Vitamin E is a powerful antioxidant that protects the heart and our arteries. It also works to encourage a better flow of oxygen to our braincells, which in turn helps to detoxify our bodies. Medical tests reported in *The New England Journal of Medicine* show a reduced risk of heart disease among regular vitamin E users. Vitamin E can be found in wheat germ oil, vegetable oils, almonds, whole wheat products, meat, eggs, leafy green veggies and whole grain cereals, to name a few.

Calcium is a nutrient, a mineral actually, that is essential in helping us deal with the effects of stress. Diets that are low in milk, milk products and leafy green vegetables don't produce enough calcium in our systems. When we become stressed we get tense. Tense muscles produce higher levels of lactic acid but without enough calcium in our systems to counteract it we feel fatigued, anxious and irritable. Because we may not know why we feel that way we can get angry. Stress also interferes with the bodies ability to absorb calcium, thereby increasing the excretion of calcium, as well as potassium, zinc, copper and magnesium. These minerals are needed in the fight some women wage against the development of osteoporosis.

I mentioned the term "antioxidant." It is a relatively new term to the general public but there has been a reasonable amount of research done to support particular theories concerning the benefits of antioxidants.

Some of the available research indicates that antioxidants are substances that slow down or inhibit the oxidization, destruction or erosion of cell membranes. They also work to prohibit the alteration of cells that encode genetic information in the DNA, thereby slowing or stopping the development of cancer and other illnesses. They occur naturally in the food we eat. It probably wouldn't hurt us to get as much of the food that contains them into our bodies as often as we can. However, we each need to make the decision of what goes into our systems based on what we have investigated for ourselves. This is the essence of self-management.

The following is a partial list of foods known to provide antioxidants:

almonds	apricots	asparagus	berries
broccoli	cabbage	carrots	chili peppers
cumin	fish	garlic	ginger
kale	pink grapefruit	nutmeg	mustard greens
oats	onions	oranges	peanuts
peppermint	sage	sesame seeds	spinach
tomato	watermelon	guava	papaya

I would encourage you to go to your local health food store or library to obtain more information about antioxidants. The sources for the dietary information can be found in the bibliography at the end of this book.

Why don't I just eat vitamin supplements instead?

Multi-vitamin supplements are useful for those who cannot always maintain a regular balanced diet but they should not be a substitute for maintaining a proper diet. Supplements alone would not satisfy all of our bodies' needs. This is especially true for those who are on a crash diet to lose an extra 15 pounds. If you want to help reduce your weight and your stress, eat right. BALANCE is the key. A well-balanced diet can positively affect high blood pressure, ulcers, constipation, dental concerns, obesity, diabetes, indigestion, irritability, anxiety, depression, headaches, fatigue and insomnia.

All of these ailments can cause us stress. Several of them together can cause us great stress. Remember that stress is cumulative. Just think of the amount of stress we can create for ourselves, even before anything traumatic happens, by not eating correctly. We need to eat a variety of foods each day--something from each of the major food groups if possible, but not necessarily large amounts of food each day.

This is not new information but somehow we don't consider the importance of balanced eating. There are four good reasons for paying more attention to what kind of fuel we put into our bodies and why we may need to supplement our diets:

1. This is the age of "fast." We have fast cars, fast planes, fast trains, faster computers, the need to produce more product at a faster rate at work, and fast food. Everything about our lives seems to have sped up to incredible levels. More and more of our food is processed so we get less and less of the naturally occurring nutrients that are necessary for our bodies to work at their peak. Supplementing our diets with good quality vitamins can only work in our favour. Be sure to check with the health store professional and/or your physician before supplementing your current diet. Be sure that any vitamins or multi-vitamins you are planning to take will not be contradictory to any medication you are ingesting.

2. The methods we use to prepare foods often decreases the vitamin content. It is better to steam food than it is to boil it. Frozen foods tend to be more nutritious than canned foods. In any event the benefits of the food we eat are affected by the method we use to prepare them. This may be the time when we need all the help we can get. A good supplement can augment our diet so that we get the nutritional value necessary to enable our bodies to work for us.

3. The quality of our air, water and work environments coupled with the additives in our food has created additional stress for our bodies to deal with by using up the vitamins our bodies would normally use to deal with everyday stress more quickly. The body's immune and support systems are working overtime just to maintain a level of stasis. Any help that we can provide ourselves by way of ingesting supplements could be very useful in the struggle to offset the effects of air, water and food pollution.

4. There are particular groups of people who should seriously consider the use of vitamin supplements: heavy smokers and alcohol consumers who use up valuable vitamins such as vitamin C at increased rates. Those who are recovering from broken bones and serious infections will need to ingest additional vitamins to assist their bodies with the healing process.

Everyone has different needs and will require different types or combinations of vitamins. Consult a health professional for direction. Talk to your physician about the benefits of vitamin therapy. If he/she doesn't know or won't discuss the pros and cons of vitamin supplements, perhaps finding someone who will would be an appropriate course of action. It's your body to manage as you see fit. It's up to you to give it what it needs so that it functions as well as it can.

What about all the stuff we like that isn't good for us?

No one is suggesting that we need to stop eating foods or using substances like alcohol, nicotine, caffeine, salt or sugar. It is, however, important that we become aware of the effects that they have on the body's ability to deal with stress or, indeed, how they contribute to the creation of stress in us.

Alcohol

Perhaps one of the greatest contributors to increased stress levels is alcohol. This is the very drug that people take to reduce their stress levels. Witness the person who comes home at the end of the day and has a drink to relax. It does reduce activity generated by the central nervous system--agreed. There is a calming effect--true. However, the all important levels of Vitamin B are depleted. Those are the ones that help us fight the stresses in our lives. If we are not eating properly to begin with we can see how our stress levels can continue to grow. Better that we find alternate ways of calming ourselves or winding down after a hard day's work than depending on alcohol. There is nothing wrong with a glass of wine or a pint of beer. Remember--we are trying to find ways of reducing our stress not increasing it. As my mother used to say, "Everything in moderation." Good advice.

Nicotine

The common belief is that nicotine helps us to relax, but nicotine speeds up our metabolic rates, thereby using up some of the other vitamins and minerals that are of benefit to us. It also uses up Vitamin C at an increased rate. It is a stimulant. So how does a stimulant help us relax? As I was reading through some information on nicotine I found out that it is also used as an insecticide. Hmmmm. Yummy.

Caffeine

Caffeine is also a stimulant. It also works against our being able to relax. If you drink a great deal of coffee, try not to have a cup at least three hours before the time you plan to retire. There are definite links between caffeine and insomnia. If we are stressed one of the things that we need is good, deep sleep. Without it we become more irritable and edgy so we add to our stress. Caffeine can increase your metabolism, work to create a state of hyper-alertness, and can contribute to an increase in heart rate and blood pressure. All of these conditions add stress to our systems. In large amounts it robs us of Vitamin B. Remember that vitamin B is helpful in combatting anxiety, depression, insomnia and muscular weakness. If stress is already a factor, large doses of caffeine will work against us. Caffeine is found in coffee, chocolate, colas (pop), black tea (regular tea is significantly lower in caffeine), some medications and some diet treatments.

Salt

We are in love with salt. We put it on just about everything we eat. We probably eat 10-15 times what we actually need during any day. Salt has a direct link to higher blood pressure. Salt also helps to retain water in our systems, which can cause swelling. Retaining water means that there is more fluid in the body that the heart has to pump so our kidneys have to work harder to deal with the extra fluid. These conditions add to our physical stress levels. Consider reducing the salt you ingest by using different spices to add flavour to your food, add salt to food after it has been prepared and not during the cooking phase, read labels to see which products have high levels of salt in them, and try to stay away from products such as carbonated drinks and powdered milk products. Salt comes under a variety of names like sodium chloride, monosodium glutamate (MSG), baking powder and baking soda. Try to limit your intake of smoked and nitrate cured foods as well. In excess they may be capable of causing cancer.

Sugar

We often hear about the value of sugar and how it gives us energy. Eating foods that have a high content of refined sugar causes blood sugar levels to increase dramatically. It is the increase in blood sugar levels that gives us an extra boost of energy.

Sugar itself has little valid nutritional value. Diets that are high in refined sugar content can add to anxiety, tension and irritability. To break sugar down the body uses up valuable B complex vitamins. Those are the same B complex vitamins which boost our immune systems and assist in the production of adrenal hormones that help us respond to the stressors we experience. In other words, the more sugar we eat, the more B complex vitamins we use up and the more stress we will experience because we are depleting our system of the very thing we need to fight the stressor. Sort of like a "catch 22," isn't it?

When we are considering our sugar intake we need to read labels on the products we buy. When we read fructose, maltose, lactose, sucrose and sorghum, we are seeing sugar with different names. We also need to be aware of the artificial and low calorie sweeteners. A recent American Cancer Society study of seventy-eight thousand women showed that "users of artificial sweeteners were more likely to put on pounds than nonusers. Sadly, women who used artificial sweeteners gained weight faster."

Pass the burgers and fries

One of the major killers of people today is heart disease. Diets high in fat and cholesterol have been linked to elevated blood pressure and the development of this disease. The higher our blood pressure, the higher our *stress* levels. As the pace of our lives speeds up and we find ourselves having less time to eat properly we have come to depend more on fast food to satisfy our hunger. We are in love with fast food. It is not a secret that fast food is generally higher in cholesterol than the food we prepare at home. If stress is an issue in your life, why not do all you can to lower its effects? Ask your physician to explain the connection between heart disease, high blood pressure, cholesterol and *stress*.

TIPS: If you are considering ways of lowering your blood pressure by minimizing the use of specific drugs, you may want to consider some of the following suggestions. Anytime you decide to reduce your medications in favour of a natural method of maintaining or improving your health, a consultation with your physician is a must. We can never be too well informed:

1. Exercise--either walk, cycle, or jog. Consult with your physician so that you can devise an appropriate program for yourself considering (a) how often to exercise, (b) for how long each time, and (c) how intensely you workout. Be sure to warm up and stretch properly before working out, keep a steady pace while working out, and then cool down gradually before showering. The connection between a proper exercise regimen and lower blood pressure is well documented. If you view exercising as something that is both beneficial and enjoyable rather than something that you have to do, you are more likely to maintain a regular schedule that will provide the maximum benefit.

2. Monitor and reduce the amount of fat and cholesterol you take in and increase the amount of fibre (barley, whole wheat products, oat bran and particular fruits and vegetables) you take in.

3. Eat more fish--once maybe twice a week.

4. Begin to lose those extra pounds and do it slowly. Avoid the "fad" diets and the "get there quick" diets. Those who work steadily at weight reduction are more successful at keeping the weight off than those who "crash" it off. Besides, slow and steady is less dangerous to your health. If high fibre diets create a gas problem, add yogurt to your diet.

5. Cut down on coffee and cigarettes.

6. Make sure that you are getting enough potassium, magnesium, and calcium.
   Potassium--potatoes, pumpkins, grains, nuts, seeds, fruits, veggies.
   Magnesium--raw leafy vegetables, nuts, seafood, cereals.
   Calcium--dark green leafy vegetables, tofu, skim milk, orange juice.

7. Lower the amount of salt you take in. Don't cook with it and add it at the table as well. Try using other spices to make the taste of your

food more interesting and appealing. Experiment. Take a cooking class.

8. Consider taking supplements. Consult with a health care professional first. Time-released tablets or capsules prove to be more efficient. They may cost a bit more but you get more "bang for the buck."

There is life after moderation

I am not suggesting, for a moment, that we stop ingesting all of these things. But if we find ourselves under a great deal of stress it will be good to know that by decreasing our intake of certain foods and by increasing our intake of other types of foods (and supplements) that we can, naturally, help ourselves lower our stress levels. Check with your local health food store for more information on which foods are high in which vitamins and which supplements may be useful. Don't depend upon information that someone gives you who "read a book once." Get information from those you trust who are knowledgeable in the field of nutrition and its effects on stress reduction. There are some well-educated physicians who understand stress and are not willing to prescribe medications first. Drugs are not always the answer. There are those who need medications to function, that's for sure. Some of the stress that we experience may very well respond better to medical interventions. But not *everyone* has to be treated with a magic pill. Shop around for a physician who has some training in stress reduction techniques. You find one just as you would an insurance man or a good investment broker. You interview him or her and know what questions to ask. If the physician won't take the time to answer your questions, maybe that physician is not for you. Then make decisions that are in your best interests based on your own particular circumstances.

The following is a short "Participaction" quiz to see just how healthful YOUR diet is. Give yourself one point for every "A" answer; two points for every "B" answer; three points for every "C" answer; and four points for every "D" answer. Total them up. There is an explanation of the outcomes at the end of the quiz.

1. On average, I eat a serving of vegetables:
   A. Less than once a day
   B. At least once a day
   C. Twice a day
   D. More than twice a day

2. When I'm at a restaurant, and the potatoes being offered are either french fried, mashed or baked I normally choose:
   A. The french fried ones
   B. The mashed ones
   C. The baked ones

3. The breakfast that most closely resembles my usual one is:
   A. A sweet roll and a cup of coffee
   B. Cold, presweetened cereal with milk, a glass of juice and a coffee
   C. Eggs and toast, a glass of juice and a coffee
   D. A natural whole grain cereal (such as oatmeal or granola) with milk and a piece of fresh fruit

4. Following my evening meal, I will have a "junky" dessert (such as cake, pie or ice cream)
   A. Always
   B. Most of the time
   C. Some of the time
   D. Only on my birthday

5. Most of the protein in my diet comes from:
   A. Red meat
   B. Full-fat dairy products (such as whole milk and cheese)
   C. Chicken and fish
   D. A combination of chicken, fish, and a well-planned program of vegetable proteins (from beans, nuts and grains)

6. The refined white sugar in my diet comes from:
   A. What I put in my coffee, put on my cereal, the desserts I eat regularly and the bonbons I munch on nightly
   B. What is hidden in the processed food that I eat
   C. I make a concerted effort to limit refined sugar in my diet

7. If I'm hungry and there is nothing but vending machines around:
   A. I'll have a candy bar
   B. I'll have a pack of crackers
   C. I'll have a bag of peanuts
   D. I won't have anything at all

8. The last time I had something like a Twinkie was:
   A. I am having something like a Twinkie right now
   B. When I was living on a limited budget in college
   C. When I was in grade school
   D. I don't even know what a Twinkie is

9. I eat potato chips and/or pretzels:
   A. Regularly
   B. Only at parties
   C. Never

10. I consider fried and/or greasy foods:
    A. A delicious part of my regular diet
    B. OK to enjoy occasionally
    C. Something to avoid like the plague

Total up the scores and consider the following as reasonable indicators of what your eating habits translate into:

A perfect score would be 36. Congratulations. You have earned the right to go out and have a huge banana split.

A score of 10 means that you have a complete and total disregard for anything that resembles decent eating habits and that starting yesterday to turn things around would not be too soon.

The rest of us fall into one of the following categories:

30-35 Honorably health/diet conscious
25-29 Commendably health/diet conscious
20-24 Acceptably health/diet conscious
15-19 Health *un*conscious
10-14 Reprehensibly health *un*conscious

Diet plays such a huge role in how we think, feel and respond to stressful situations, yet it doesn't take a great deal of money or effort to make a change. It does take a willingness to learn about nutrition and to spend more time preparing our daily meals. Is it possible to experience less stress by managing what we ingest each day? Yes, it is.

The key is **self**-management--it's up to us.

EXERCISE

There is no questioning the value of exercise and the role it plays in stress reduction. Regular exercise which challenges the body results in the manufacture of endorphins and dopamine. These "feel good" chemicals, which are produced naturally in the brain, act in a similar fashion as opiates. They are the chemicals that give us that feeling of being relaxed--of being "stress reduced."

You don't need all kinds of fancy equipment and sexy work-out gear. As a matter of fact, you could be just as fit as the next guy and do it without a home gym. However, if you don't see your efforts as being worthwhile and pleasurable because of the benefits you gain, then the attempt to use exercise as an effective stress reducer will become something to dread. Eventually you will stop doing it. It will seem like work and who wants to work after work?

There is no age limit for exercise. It is never too late. Stress is not something that leaves us or becomes less a factor in our lives the older we get. Using exercise as a way of reducing stress can be a positive factor at any age. One of the keys to maintaining a consistent level of exercise is to develop a program that suits and fits our needs--not by following or tuning in to some program that is on TV or on a video. Yes, we can learn techniques from those sources but we should tailor our exercise programs to suit our schedules and our needs.

Our exercise program, above all else, needs to be fun. Perhaps it will include playing tennis at the community centre or playing some pick-up basketball. Maybe it will include some hiking or walking in the woods. It could mean swimming every other morning with a group of friends or jogging with a neighbour. Our exercise program should include a variety of activities that are designed to improve our cardiovascular systems, muscular systems, and our social systems. If we are involved with other people when we exercise we are more likely to enjoy the activity and do it more often. Otherwise, it can become boring and lonely. We might consider walking with a friend or a group of friends; playing tennis with three others so that it becomes a time to look forward to--a social occasion; join a hiking club and sharing an interest with other people, perhaps some we don't know. It's better to have fun and to play while we workout. This way we get healthier without actually trying to. Couple that with a more conscious effort at reducing salt, sugar, nicotine and caffeine and being sure that our bodies have the proper fuel with which to work and we can cope a great deal more efficiently with our day-to-day stressors.

When our bodies are both physically and mentally healthier we are able to deal with higher levels of stress longer.

Too much too soon!

Note: Before we do anything we need to consult with our physicians to discuss the type of exercise program we should be looking at: what kind of activities, for how long each time, and how often. After we get the OK then we consider how to get started.

The problem for those of us who get enthused about becoming more fit is that we try to do too much too soon and end up tearing muscles or causing some other physical damage. First we have to look at what kind of shape we are in now. If we are really overweight jogging may not be a good idea. Perhaps some walking for short periods would be a better, safer start. If we are really underweight we might want to consider adjusting our diets so that we can add a few pounds. The point is we need to start at the beginning.

1. Assess your current body style and decide on a realistic program that has some reasonable goals. This is why it is so important to work with your physician first and then a professional of some kind. Most YM/YWCAs have trained staff to administer the appropriate tests and help set up a reasonable and realistic exercise plan. You tell them what you have in mind as far as the type of activities you want to participate in and they will help design a program. Be sure to include a variety of activities e.g. swimming, cycling, walking, jogging, hiking, playing golf (walk the course instead of taking the cart if you can), tennis, aerobic dancing, stretching, Tai Chi, etc.

2. Once you have an idea of what it is you want to do be sure that you have the proper footwear (this is not the place to be cheap) and the proper clothing. Cotton is good because it breathes so you don't get overheated. It also absorbs sweat so that your body can feel cooler.

3. Be sure to warm up first. Too many want to get right into it and end up hurting themselves. Becoming more fit and working to reduce stress is not about having it happen overnight. It takes time. What matters most is that we are working in the right direction. We are looking for steady improvement.

4. Easy does it. Don't over-work yourself. The object is not to become Tarzan overnight; it is to work toward becoming healthier. Be sure that you have plenty of liquids around or with you so that you don't get dehydrated.

5. Depending upon where you live you might want to consider the time of day you choose to exercise. If you live in the country, great. Anytime of the day will be fine. If you are in the city it may be better to exercise earlier outside and later inside because of the air pollution and safety.

6. If there are stairs at work, use them instead of the elevator or escalator.

7. According to the *Complete Stress Management Workbook* we should be monitoring our pulse rates. It suggests that "after exercising, rest for five minutes and count your pulse. If the count is above 120 beats per minute, you're doing too much."

8. At the end of your workout take the time to slow down and cool off gradually and then shower.

The documented evidence proves that those who exercise regularly and manage their diets with balance in mind feel better physically, emotionally, and mentally. We look better and we feel better. When we recognize that is happening because of something that we are doing for ourselves, our esteem increases. Our levels of anxiety and depression can be decreased, thereby lessening the stress we experience.

There are other forms of stress reduction that we can consider as well. For instance, progressive muscle relaxation relaxes a particular group of muscles in our bodies and then we move on to another group and so on. Most people generally work from the feet to the head when doing this relaxation technique. Meditation, in its many forms, is also an excellent way of reducing immediate stress.

This information only scratches the surface when it comes to being well-informed about the benefits of nutrition, diet and exercise. There are numerous books on the market that are more specific than I can be here. My purpose was to alert you to the **power** we have in our struggle with stress and to indicate how much we can do to assist ourselves just by managing what we eat and drink and how we choose to exercise.

TIME MANAGEMENT

Time is something we spend. We can decide how to spend it, where to spend it, when to spend it, and how to make more of it.

Would life be any different if there were an extra four hours or even eight hours in the day? I don't believe so. The issue isn't about the amount of time we have; it's about the way we spend it. Great stress is created within us when we don't manage our time appropriately. We fall behind in the tasks that we take on, as the result of some distraction perhaps, and then have a nervous breakdown when we don't complete them as scheduled or expected. Time management is **our** issue to deal with. **We** need to take responsibility for it. Time is a finite commodity.

This is certainly true in a broad sense. As human beings we will only have so much time on this planet before the end of our "time" arrives. How will we choose to spend it? Will we accomplish some of the goals that we had set for ourselves or will we spend our time in ways that were not in our best interests and then be upset or angry or stressed when we don't attain them? As I talk to those growing older, one of the things they mention the most is their sadness and angst over opportunities not pursued or places not seen. Some recognize they should have taken the time to do what some others did. For others it is the unfulfilled dream that is now creating the most stress. As one person said to me, "I don't regret the things I've done. I regret the things that I haven't done."

I don't believe that we waste time. Everything we do spawns an opportunity to learn something so it is not wasted time. However, we may see it as time spent that, in retrospect, was not used as creatively or as usefully as it might have been. We may begin to compare our lives to the lives of our friends or colleagues at work. We may become jealous of what they have or envious of what they have done. We may wonder at how they did it. How much of what happened happened because they are good managers of time?

In a narrower sense we should question how much stress is caused in our day-to-day lives because we didn't get to some place on time or we didn't complete a task on time. As we don't meet our own or others' expectations we push harder.

For many of us the harder we push to catch up, the more mistakes we make. Now we have to spend even more time undoing what we just did and then concern ourselves with the time we lost overall. How much of our stress is due to our lack of self-management skills? When we are able to manage ourselves, good time management skills become a by-product of what we do and how we do it. Easier said than done sometimes, but definitely possible.

Effective self-management means being able to determine which tasks are most important to us and what skills we have available for the task at hand, and recognizing which personal assets and strengths we have that could be applied to the task at hand. Then we must PRIORITIZE, ORGANIZE AND CARRY THROUGH WITH A PLAN OF ACTION.

Determining what is essential and what is not is extremely important. The essentials are those which need our immediate attention. For example: If Junior has just split open his lip while playing, it is obvious that immediate care is necessary. This is an essential time and we make time for this kind of circumstance. But we may also consider time for relaxation as essential because the balance in our lives may be nearly non-existent. Look at what is going on at the time and decide what is essential and what is not.

And so it grows

Can you recognize your particular style?:

1. We zoom from place to place getting caught in traffic jams and end up screaming at some poor unsuspecting guy up ahead. Our blood pressure elevates and we are ready to become road warriors because we are running late for an appointment. We are frustrated by the uncaring people out there who should, by some miracle, understand that we are late. They should just move the hell out of the way and let us through. How dare they get in our way. Don't they know how important this is to us? And so it goes. If we had left for the appointment 30 minutes earlier knowing that it was a 20 minute trip it leaves us 10 minutes to get composed or to account for the unexpected. The unexpected will usually happen. It's Murphy's Law so plan for it. When we get home at the end of the day we are "fried." We are ready to take someone's head off at the first sign of trouble. This is the beginning of the two-martini ritual.

2. There are times when we get so caught up in what we are doing that we don't allow ourselves enough time for the other important people in our lives. We don't give ourselves the time to rest, to regenerate and to evaluate how things are going. Our home life suffers. We never seem to have enough time to get the things done that have to be done. The list of things to do grows. Our partners begin to complain that they never see us or have any time to talk to us about what is important to them. Our relationships suffer.

3. We can become overwhelmed by thinking that we "don't have enough time for . . . " Maybe we haven't prepared ourselves for the task at hand so we don't feel confident that we can do a good job. We put it off; we don't prioritize our tasks and responsibilities either at home or on the job; we are not able to decide or determine the difference between what is important and what is essential; we may spend time on projects, duties or favours for others because we "owed them one." Often these are not what we need to be doing and consequently we get further behind with the tasks that we will eventually have to tackle. Sometimes we just don't want to get started on something because it is not our favourite thing to do so we do the things that we enjoy doing first. Then we don't have time for the others.

4. There are times when we need to be doing things but just don't feel like it. We procrastinate. Maybe we have been physically inactive for a while and we don't have the energy to get going. Perhaps we're not eating right or sleeping well. Perhaps we are just so dogged tired because we have been working long hours trying to catch up with other things and our energy reserves are depleted. No balance. When we get overtired or when we are unorganized we think things to death in an effort to be sure we have all the angles covered. We want to be sure that we have thought of all the things that could go wrong and then come up with the solutions to those things so we'll be prepared. We come up with all the reasons not to get started on something instead of getting on with it so that it is done.

5. Perhaps we say "yes" when we want to say "no" and end up doing

something for which we don't have the time or energy. But we try to fit it in somewhere. Usually we suffer when this happens. We put others' needs ahead of our own and then we get stressed out because our own house is not in order. How many times have we helped Uncle Harry work on his car or fix Aunt Mary's washing machine when all we wanted to do--needed to do--was to make some time for ourselves and our families. Maybe we could have gone fishing with the kids or to a movie with our spouses. Then we get resentful and usually take it out on the ones around us, usually our loved ones.

Stress that is directly related to what we experience is usually the result of one or a combination of the above examples. Of course there are stressors that occur in our lives over which we have absolutely no control, such as the death of someone close to us or the loss of a job because of some bureaucratic decision.

The degree of stress we feel is relative to the importance of the undone task, the severity of the surprise and our belief in our ability to handle it.

Here are some suggestions to consider when you decide that you will manage your time instead of allowing time to manage you:

1. Make up a blank calendar for each month and mark down each appointment, meeting, date or personal engagement, birthday, etc. that you feel is important. Also schedule in time for leisure activities. This is just as important as any time you consider to be "essential" during your day or week. This is how to keep a balance in your life. Put the calendar on the fridge door, in the bathroom or anywhere else that is highly visible so that you will be reminded of what you need to do and when. Check off the activities when they are completed so that by the end of the week you can see what you have accomplished.

2. For those who require a more structured daily approach decide for yourself which are the activities or duties that you consider to be most

important or essential. This works well for those who are in business or work in jobs that require meeting deadlines. Divide your day up into three parts. Write a plan for the day using time from the start of the work day to lunch time; the start of the afternoon to mid-day; and mid-day to the end to the working day. You could use morning, noon and evening if you choose or any other combination that works for your particular working or personal day. You can also break the day down into smaller time frames--whatever works. It's the **process** that counts here. Effective management of any kind involves developing and working through a process.

3. Take a page of blank paper and draw a line down the middle. On one side of the page list all of the activities that are work related that you feel need to be attended to and on the other side list all of the non-work/play activities that are a part of your day. Fix an amount of time to each, leaving some time for flexibility so that your time isn't so strictly regimented that you can't sit and have some fun doing the unexpected. This is just a way of helping you account for your time so that you can be as productive as possible. Remember, it's the time spent trying to catch up that creates stress. The more trouble you have trying to get the essential things done, the more you may need to structure your day in some fashion.

4. Use the "steps to success" method (Chapter 2) to plan an activity or even a whole day. This isn't done with a time-frame in mind but rather is a plan for completion. You stay at one job until it is done. Many of us get started on two or three jobs at once and then get frustrated and leave them all undone or rush to get them all done at once.

5. Learn to say no. How often do we say yes when we want to say no. In the process we put **our** own interests on the back burner so that someone else can get needs or priorities met. There is nothing wrong with being neighbourly or helpful to our friends but not at our own expense. "I need to finish what I'm doing here first. When I get done I'll be happy to come over and give you a hand" works well or "I'm right in the middle of something and can't leave until I get it done. I'll

call you when I'm finished and if you still need a hand I'll come over." We need to pay attention to what is important to us **first**. This is not being selfish or uncaring. This is good personal management and self-care.

6. Sometimes we need to spend time to save time. The old saying "no hurry, no worry" is quite true. If we aren't playing "catch up" and if we have planned appropriately, we are likely to feel less worried about completing the task at hand. Plan to have enough time. Less hurry--less worry--less stress. If you need to be at work at a specific time and you like to take your time in the morning, get up 15-20 minutes earlier than usual. If it takes you 30 minutes to cycle to work, give yourself 40 minutes so that you can enjoy the trip. Often when we are feeling hurried, especially in the morning, we end up taking our anxiousness out on those around us--usually our families, co-workers, fellow travellers, or the boss.

7. When we consider managing our time, understanding the four basic ways that we spend our time will be helpful:

   Type 1 time is time that we spend reacting or responding to some **crisis**, or needing to pay attention to a **deadline** of some kind. These are the activities that require an immediate response. They are the "must do" activities. Perhaps there is a job deadline. Maybe something comes up in our personal lives--a relationship concern or a family member who has been hurt somehow. It could be employment related. The car may have a flat tire and Junior was to be at the ball park five minutes ago. It may be something serious such as a medical emergency. It may be a ringing door bell or telephone. It doesn't matter what it is. It is something that requires our immediate attention.

   Type 2 time is time that we spend **taking care of our needs** central to our mental, emotional, physical and spiritual health. This involves building or maintaining relationships with others--be they our families, work mates, our friends, our neighbours and any others with whom we have meaningful relationships. We spend time planning, thinking, and evaluating, learning and expanding our information and knowledge base.

We also spend time playing because we understand the important role that recreation plays regarding the balance we need in our lives. We regenerate when we recreate. All work and no play makes Jack dead before his time. We put **first things first** when we acknowledge the importance of Type 2 time.

We consider our own needs before the needs and priorities of others. We are governed by what we consider to be important to us. We may lend a helping hand to someone and drop something that we are doing but it will be because we want to and not because we feel we have to so we can please someone else. Managing ourselves in this way enables us to spend time doing the things that we need to do in order to prevent things from becoming Type 1 time activities. Our personal growth takes place during Type 2 time.

Type 3 time is best described as time spent doing things that are **more important to others than to us.** It focuses on the expectations that others have of us. We may spend a great deal of time trying to please others and not succeed. What then? How is our sense of self affected when we are unable to win or gain the acceptance of others? All that happens is they get their needs taken care of and we don't. They get ahead in the game and we are left feeling angry or frustrated or envious. We become spectators in the game of life and not players.

This is the type of time spent when we are impulsive and not focused on ourselves. Spending time in this way does not provide us with any outcomes that are immediately important to us. Do we want to spend our time trying to win the favour of others? Do we want to help others attain what it is **we** are trying to attain? What happens to us and our need for time? Who is there for us? This is, generally, not an effective or productive way to spend our time. If our needs are to be ackowledged or taken care of, it will be up to us to do that for ourselves.

Type 4 time is spent in the pursuit of things that provide very little benefit to us regarding the importance of the outcomes. Activities that just pass time are usually Type 4 activities. When we are involved in Type 4 time activities we generally do things that are fun to do but don't have much relevance to our daily tasks. We spend time just spending time. Type 4 time is also spent by wishing for things that we have no control over at the present time. I call this time the "If only's time" ("If only I had this . . . " or "If only I had done that . . . "). We can develop a terminal case of the "poor me's" when we indulge in this activity. People who are constantly engaged in Type 1 time spend their down time in Type 4 time.

Type 1 time is for the things that we have to tend to and Type 2 time is when we do our developing and growing. Learning to say no to Type 3 and 4 time activities will be necessary if you are to be successful managing yourself. Those who are proactive do well because they utilize their Type 2 time effectively. If we need to create more time for ourselves we can generally find all kinds of it in the Type 3 and 4 time activities.

If you want to do a quick check on your time management skills consider the following questions:

___ 1. Do I often say yes when I want to say no and then have to make choices I would rather not have to make because I have over-committed myself and don't know how to get out?

___ 2. Are my loved ones or those close to me stressed out because of what I do?

___ 3. Do I find that I don't participate in those activities that I find enjoyable because there is always a crisis of some kind to deal with?

___ 4. Am I constantly rushing to finish a project on time either at home, socially, or at work?

___ 5. Do I feel ill at ease most of the time because there is always something for me to do or to check on and never enough time to just sit and relax?

___ 6. Am I always rushing around doing something regardless of its impact on the quality of my life?

Any checkmarks here indicate a need to look at how you spend your time. Step back and look at the impact these scenarios have on your life. How do they add to or detract from your self-esteem? Try to consider more of the Type 2 time activities for balance.

DO AN ATTITUDE CHECK

I spoke of the importance of attitude earlier in the book. When I speak of attitude in this context I mean how we choose to see something (our mindset), and what we are willing to do to get what we want. Generally speaking, our mindsets have been reinforced in us by events that we have either witnessed or participated in, in some way. These experiences are powerful and difficult to challenge. However, once we recognize the impact our attitudes have on our lives we can work to change them.

Positive attitudes leave us open to possibility and change. Negative attitudes close us off from support and outside input.

If, for example, our attitude is one that suggests the world owes us a living and we justify cheating other people because "everyone else does it" we are destined to spiritual bankruptcy. With an attitude like that, we are not open to seeing other perspectives or making positive changes in ourselves. It becomes a self-defeating prophecy.

A hand that is closed is not capable of receiving gifts. A mind that is closed is not capable of receiving gifts either.

What do we mean when we say "I can't"? Do we mean "I won't"? Does it mean that we are fearful of not being successful? Is it better not to try than to be unsuccessful? Saying that we can't do something creates an inner belief, a paradigm, a model of thinking that is very unhealthy. It works to increase our stress levels because it propagates feelings of powerlessness which in turn lessens our self-confidence. It stops us from growing and learning new things. If we are not able to learn new things, we will find it more difficult to deal effectively with our stressors.

Steven Covey, in his book *The 7 Habits of Highly Effective People* suggests the problem is often how we choose to **perceive** the problem itself. If we see the problem as being outside ourselves then we place the solutions to those problems outside ourselves as well. They become external to us instead of internal where WE are in control. When we see control outside our sphere of influence we abdicate responsibility for any decisions concerning possible solutions.

For example, we must not allow our anger to dictate how we respond to a particular situation. Do we say we can't control our anger because other people make us angry so it's their fault I feel as I do? "When they stop making me angry I'll start acting differently." This attitude demonstrates the attitudinal difference between being proactive and reactive.

Proactive vs. reactive

Being proactive means recognizing that an action of some kind needs to happen, that we think things through, decide on a plan of action, then follow through with that plan, evaluate the outcomes and then continue. It means taking responsibility for what happens to us, the outcomes from our decisions, and working to ensure that our best interests are considered but not at the expense of someone else's right to do the same.

Being proactive regarding time management, for example, means that we would allot ourselves enough time to complete the task and allow some extra time for unforeseen circumstances. If there are none, we simply complete the task earlier than expected. If something should happen we have allowed for it and are still able to complete the task as scheduled. It's a win/win situation.

In this case it means doing something for ourselves to help reduce our stress levels. We'll need to take stock of our attitudes and decide which of them stand in the way of reducing our stress and which actually create stress within us.

We can tell if someone is proactive or reactive by the language used. If the speaker says things like "There is nothing that I can do" instead of "Let's check out some options" or "That's the way it is" instead of "I'll need to approach this differently," it is a good bet the speaker is a reactive person. Language acts as a positive self-motivator--an affirmation of sorts which says "I will succeed" and not "I can't succeed."

Reactive people tend to be governed by their emotions. The decisions they make are based on how they feel about something. I'm not suggesting that we all become robots and live our lives with no emotion. But we are likely to make better decisions when we THINK FIRST AND THEN ACT. Proactive people are governed more by their values and their rules for living. Proactive people reach out to take charge of their circumstances. They begin with a goal in mind and then they ask themselves "What do I need to do first to minimize the impact of what is happening " or "What can I do to maximize the opportunity that has presented itself?"

Our stress is reduced when we decide that there is something we can do and then we do it. At this point success should be a secondary thought. Although success is what we all hope for, just the act of doing something that may be beneficial is the important part. It gets us moving. If our action leads to an unsuccessful conclusion then we simply re-evaluate what we did and try again using what we learned to our advantage. Don't repeat the same mistake.

Knowing what we can deal with right now, trying to understand there are things that we can not deal with right now, and using our wisdom to know the difference are keys to effective stress reduction.

Can you identify some of your attitudes that you feel are helpful or positive? Can you identify some that may not be helpful? Take some time to consider them. On a piece of paper draw a centre line the length of the page. On the left side, list the attitudes that you consider important and positive. For example, you may list patience as a positive attitude: "I am more likely to make a good decision if I take my time when making my choices." On the right, side list those attitudes that you recognize may stand in your way of making good decisions. For example, you may list stubbornness as a negative attitude: "I won't listen to anyone else because they don't walk in my shoes. Besides, I'm different."

Which ones get you closer to your goals and which ones seem to hinder or retard your progress?

The question becomes this: "Do our current attitudes stand in the way of our peace (both inner and outer), our prosperity and our happiness?" Was there ever a time when we saw things differently and life seemed to be better? If the answer is yes we need to re-evaluate what we believe to be true and make some changes.

I am always amazed at how we push ourselves over the edge just to see what it would be like and then condemn our choice all the way to the bottom.

We do have choices. We always have choices. We choose how we manage our responses to the situations we face. Our attitudes can keep us from recognizing the choices that we have and they can keep us from realizing our goals.

Roger, Bill and Lucy

One fine summer day I decided it was too nice to be indoors working so I asked my supervisor for the afternoon off. A mental health day was in order. Being the kind and understanding sort, she complied. By one o'clock I was on the first tee waiting to give that golf ball a ride when an elderly gentleman approached to ask if I would like to join him for the round. I find you meet the nicest people on a golf course, so I did not hesitate. It turns out that he was with two other folks. Let's call this man Bill. Bill introduced me to his neighbour Roger and Rogers' wife Lucy. Bill would be a man of 65-70, Roger close to 80 and Lucy about mid 70's. Bill explained to me that Lucy had contracted diabetes some time ago and had lost her left leg to the disease. The unfortunate part, beyond that, was that the medication she was taking created hallucinations. She was not able to be on her own for any length of time. Wherever Roger goes, there goes Lucy. It occurred to me, as our round progressed, that Roger loved her very much.

He was very patient with her, held her, laughed with her and of course allowed her to drive the cart since she could no longer drive the family vehicle on the highways.

I wondered to myself how many of us would be able to look at the situation as Roger did. For many of us, this could easily be a very trying and stressful time and yet Roger had chosen to see the positives in it all. He was with his wife, who seemed to be enjoying herself, and he was out doing what he loved to do the most in his retirement--play golf. Then there is Bill who, as a neighbour, is doing what he can to encourage Roger to get out and stay active. He often gives up a little of his own precious time because he cares about another human being. They have known each other for over 40 years and have been the best of friends for most of it.

The point is people need to stick together. If we were to live our lives like Bill, Roger and Lucy there would be a great deal less stress in our lives. You know it really doesn't take much to look out for one another and to lend a supportive hand. It gets down to people helping other people, so we all can get some of what we need. What a concept! So, I met some nice people, had a great day and I shot a 42 to boot. Honest.

JOB STRESS

What we do to put food on the table can play a large part in the stress we feel each day. Those who enjoy their work would be less stressed by it and vice-versa. If we put job stress together with the other stressors we experience, from poor eating habits to poor sleeping habits, we have a recipe for disaster.

Those of us who are fortunate to have jobs have a different kind of stress to deal with from those of us who don't. No greater--just different.

The following are some ideas to consider when trying to cope with the stress that our jobs create. Dealing with job stress is obviously beneficial. It also provides us with an opportunity to improve our time management skills.

If you:

- ❒ work under deadlines like production quotas, for example, you might want to get involved in some activities that don't involve schedules of any kind. Try playing darts or target shooting. Get involved in some outdoor activity or constructing a model of some kind. Try anything that does not require specific time-frames.

- ❒ work in a repetitive or routine-oriented occupation you might want to look at activities that will challenge your mind as well as your body. Tennis, badminton, golf, bridge, chess, anything that presents a challenge and provides you with some variety in what you do. If you like to read, enjoy some of the classics.

- ❒ work as a member of a team, whether it is management, labour or community-based, you may want to look at spending more time off on your own. It will be important for you to spend quality time with yourself so that you can enjoy your own company. Consider photography as a hobby or some other solitary activity. One-on-one games of some kind where you are not with a group of other people or spending time with your partner enjoying a common interest might be relaxing.

- ❒ work with machinery, understand that noise becomes a factor. Noise pollution (constant banging or whining of machines), although not disturbing at the time, does work to create stress. Nature would be a great place for you to discover the peace and quiet you deserve. Give your ears a break today. You could try anything to do with hiking, being around water (very soothing), rock climbing, sky diving, scuba diving, camping or just going for a quiet drive in the country.

- ❒ work by yourself or in isolation, try being more involved socially. Join a club. Interact with others. Participate in a team sport of some kind. It does not have to be competitive, although it can be if you like. The idea here is to be around other people so that you can laugh and talk about issues that you consider important. We need to feel that we belong somewhere or that we are connected with a group of our peers.

- ❐ work at a job where you don't feel that you are making any kind of contribution, doing some volunteer work could be rewarding. Social agencies are always looking for people to help out. Maybe being a big brother/sister or working with the physically or mentally challenged would be rewarding. Teach a craft or a skill that you may have developed over the years. Give of your time freely. It's the "freely" part that makes it worthwhile.

These other considerations may help to reduce work-related stress:

- ❐ don't be afraid to ask for help.
- ❐ don't get caught up in the gossip that slides around your work-place. Be sure you are working with facts that you know to be true.
- ❐ learn to delegate. You don't have to do it all.
- ❐ be sure that you communicate your needs clearly to those you work with.
- ❐ develop a couple of friendships at work so that you have someone to share your ideas and concerns with. This way your stress doesn't stay bottled up inside.
- ❐ leave home a bit early so that you can take the scenic route to work. If there is no scenic route, at least you won't be rushed to get there.
- ❐ get outside as often as you can. Take a walk at lunch time instead of sitting around in a stuffy lunch room.

TRUST AND STRESS

In the literature that I have read regarding stress and its creation I have seen little that would connect trust, or the lack of it, to stress.

I recently travelled to a small village in Maine called Ogunquit that has one of the most beautiful beaches that I have ever seen. This day while walking along the shore I realized how peaceful and relaxed I was--not because of the solitude but because of the safety I felt. It is a place where there is no visual violence. I could see no graffiti, broken bottles or run-down buildings. I encountered no ill-mannered and disrespectful children and teenagers who seemed to feel it necessary, especially around adults, to impress us with very limited vocabularies better suited for a locker room. (To be fair, there were lots of kids around who seemed very respectful of others' valuables, property and auditory freedom.) I saw no apparent vandalism and felt no hint of danger as I walked alone. I experienced a sense of trust in that environment. I realized how stress-less I felt.

For me, there is a connection between the stress I feel and the amount of trust I experience, whether that trust is of the people I choose to have around me, the places I find myself in, the relationships I share with others, or even the governmental system that dictates how I live my life each day. There is a correlation between my spiritual, mental, emotional and physical safety and the stress I experience. I can reduce the stress I feel by putting myself around people I have chosen to trust and in places that offer me safety. These are choices that I can make. I can, to a large degree, manage the level of stress I experience.

In a nutshell

When we think about stress we need to think in terms of what **we** can do to manage it more effectively so that it doesn't manage us. In no particular order, let's consider some choices:

1. Be sure to eat right, sleep well and exercise regularly. This advice sounds simple but it's very effective. Each of us has a responsibility to give our body what it needs so that it can perform for us. It will take care of us if we take care of it.

2. Expect the unexpected to happen--because usually it will. Schedule

your time so that you have some flexibility. That way if you need some extra time to complete something or to go somewhere, you have it--stress free.

3. Build in Type 2 time as if it were Type 1 time. It is that important. Plan to take time for yourself as a part of your day. Investors will often tell their clients that they should put away 10-15% of their wages every week and to consider the savings like any other expense. Time is the same. Put aside time for yourself and consider it just as you would any other Type 1 activity. **Balance is the key. Time for me, time for them, and time for us.**

4. Develop some basic decision-making skills to help prioritize goals and plans for using your time. (The decisional matrix in Chapter 2 is an excellent tool for doing this kind of work.)

Procrastination is the thief of time.--Edward Young

5. Be sure what you decide to be important is important to **you**, first and foremost, and not someone else. Decide which of your needs are more important than others. Don't neglect others or discount them in the process. ORGANIZE--PRIORITIZE--CARRY OUT THE PLAN.

6. Do an attitude check. Do you need to re-evaluate the validity of some of your belief systems? They may be standing between you and your happiness.

7. Make sure that your job stress doesn't dictate how you spend your free time. Build in time for relaxation. Make time for some yoga, meditation or a massage. Treat yourself. You deserve it.

8. Be certain that the people you choose to have around you and the situations wherein you spend your time are trustful and safe.

9. Identify the things that create stress in you. Decide which ones are

the most common stressors and decide how to lessen their impact on your life. One at a time.

10. The stress you experience may be connected to some medical problem, so don't discount that possibility. Shop around for a practitioner who understands wellness and holistic approaches to treatment and not someone who automatically suggests a magic pill. Medication may be necessary but not mandatory. Become informed. Knowledge is a powerful tool.

11. Set realistic goals for yourself. Don't let others' expectations of you, or for you, dictate how you spend your life. They have their own life to live. This one is yours.

Draw a horizontal line and on it mark a scale of 1-10. On the left end, put a 1 to represent "needs work" and mark a 10 on the right end to represent "as good as it could be." Now put a mark and the date on the line where you believe you would need to be to feel that you are managing your stress effectively (Think about what your life will be like when you feel what you consider to be minimal stress). Now put a mark and the date on the line where you feel you are right now. What is one activity, skill, or strategy that you could use or learn that would help to move your mark up the scale one number? Repeat this exercise a month from now. What has changed? If your mark has gone up think about what you did to create that change. If it has not, re-evaluate your approach, make some adjustments and try again.

1___2___3___4___5___6___7___8___9___10___

Consider the following questions:

1. Can you remember a time when you were not as stressed or feeling as overwhelmed by what was going on around you? What were you doing then? What were you thinking? What was different for you then?

2. How did you deal effectively with stress in the past? Could you use some of the same skills today? What you did then may be just as effective today.

3. What would a less stressful life feel like for you? How would you describe it? (You have to know what it is you are after and what it is you are trying to re-create. Without that idea it will be hard to know where you are going and when you have arrived).

4. How will your life be different when you feel less stressed? How will you know when you have reached your goal of having less stress in your life? What will that mean to you?

5. What are you willing to do to reduce the stress in your life?

6. What will other people notice about you when you are less stressed?

"The beat goes on"

We began our journey by emphasizing the need to understand more about ourselves and the strengths that we have. Which of our strengths can be used, right now, to help manage our stress?

Recognizing our strengths and utilizing them produces the hope we need to progress along the road we have chosen for ourselves. We are learning that we are much more than we believed. As we become more confident and we see ourselves more competent to deal with what comes our way we will find that situations that were stressful are less stressful or are no longer an issue for us at all.

We now have some methods we can use to decide on the best course of action to take when controversy appears. We can take our time to decide how to proceed in a systematic, rational way. Success will come more frequently when we stop to plan and think our way through the issues that present themselves. Somewhere I read that we don't plan to fail but rather we fail to plan. Successful people stop--think--plan--act--evaluate the outcomes--and proceed again. Will we stop making mistakes? No, we won't. But we are likely to make fewer of them. We can learn from those mistakes and use the information to produce an even better plan to overcome our difficulties or to prioritize our thoughts and issues.

We also have more fuel for our trip now that the thief of our energy--stress--is less an issue. Staying on the road can be tough at the best of times but if we manage this part of the trip effectively we will travel far. Stress can be the roadblock to our success. Focus on what is possible and not on what is not. Focus on solutions and not on the problems. It's the only way to travel.

"I never knew I could just claim happiness, at any time, as my birthright and not be limited by the condemning evidence of my own personal history and past. That awareness, which I previously resisted as preposterous, has been a blessing and changed my life profoundly, allowing me in my own imperfect way to be so much more loving, peaceful and useful to myself and all those I touch".

Barry Neil Kaufman, *Happiness is a Choice*

Much of what we need to do to relieve our stress involves telling other people how we feel about things, how we feel about the way they treat us, and what we need from them. How do we claim, or re-claim, our rights without hurting them or ourselves in the process? How do we resolve our conflicts, state our rights and clarify our beliefs without feeling guilty in the process? Becoming more assertive in our day-to-day living experiences is the next step in our spiritual evolution.

4.

HOW DO I TELL HIM I THINK WE ARE LOST?

IT IS DIFFICULT TO SHAKE HANDS WITH A CLOSED FIST. --Indira Ghandi

Being assertive is a characteristic that some view as being bossy or self-centered. We often hear people say things like "who does he think he is?" or "she sure is rude" when someone is trying to be assertive. It seems whenever people speak up for themselves they are considered pushy or better than others. Add the gender issue and you often get "She's a real bitch" for a woman who speaks up for herself and yet men who are assertive are considered to be very business-like or self-assured.

It is no wonder that people have a tough time being assertive. How difficult is it to tell others that you disagree with them? Most of us want to be seen in a positive way by our fellow travellers. Most of us will do whatever we feel we need to in order to make that happen even if it means putting our needs aside for the needs of others. We want to be accepted by those around us. We would like to be spoken of in positive terms by those we admire or those we see as successful. It is important for us to be seen as someone who is nice, whatever "nice" means. The idea that we must be all things to all people satisfies our need to belong somewhere, but at what price? I feel the price we pay, sometimes, is far too high. There are other ways to get that need met without putting aside what is important to us.

What is assertiveness? There are many manifestations but the basic principles are the same. Assertiveness means that "I am able to speak my mind about how I feel, what I want, what I need, what is acceptable to me as a human being and what is not, without feeling guilty or apologizing in anyway. I do this, while always respecting the rights of others to do the same thing without criticism or judgement." Being assertive means that we take care of ourselves, that we put ourselves and our needs first, at no one else's expense. This simply demonstrates self-care. Being assertive helps us claim our right to relax, to be as stress free as we can be, and to enjoy the kind of life to which we are all entitled.

Some general beliefs prevail that the only way to get ahead or to get our needs met is to be aggressive--to take, demand or intimidate. Some believe that only the strong survive and to be strong we have to be aggressive.

Some are able to take what they want from others and they probably feel pretty good about it. They are not going to buy into the idea that you can get your power needs met by being assertive.

I have been accused of being an idealist but I believe that the majority of people are decent human beings who want to stand up for themselves, get their needs met and, coincidentally, offer the same opportunity to others. If we could do this, our mutual environments would become more peaceful, assured and safe. Consider people who buy guns to protect themselves from those who buy guns. The aggressors use them to take from or to intimidate others. They do so to get some need met whether it is a need to exert power, to survive or to promote a sense of belonging with other like-minded people, such as members of a gang. If there were no guns, would there be as much violence? Maybe, but maybe not. Would innocent people, those people who kill or maim others in self-defence or out of a sense of fear, be as likely to hurt someone else? Probably not. Would the aggressor be as aggressive if he or she had to face somebody with just a pair of hands? It's doubtful. How does the aggressor get his or her needs met without being aggressive?

Being assertive is not just a way of existing. It is also a way of thinking and living. It is a mindset that helps us get our basic needs met as often as we can so that we don't feel we have to take from or intimidate others to achieve them. Aggression and intimidation, unless they are used for protection or to promote one's safety, are lazy ways of meeting one's needs. Anybody can be aggressive but it takes time, effort and skill to be assertive. If we want our children to feel safer, more confident in themselves, and self-sustained we will need to demonstrate the skills by which that can happen. They learn from watching us.

Aggression tends to make people tentative. If we are the recipient of aggressive behaviour we are likely to put a great deal of our time and energy into being self-protective rather than promoting our own best interests. If, for instance, we are the partner of someone who is physically, emotionally, verbally or mentally abusing us we are likely thinking in terms of how we can prevent or avoid any more abuse. Eventually we may act, out of fear, in a way that promotes our best interests but it is not likely to be our first response. What needs are being served or met when someone resorts to aggressive behaviour as a means to an end? If we are the aggressor what are we trying to attain?

We don't grow spiritually or mentally when we are in a reactive or tentative state of mind.

Nobody can make you inferior without your consent.
--EleanorRoosevelt

What needs? Whose needs? My needs.

What are our needs anyway? What do I mean when I talk about getting our needs met. Do you have any idea what yours are?

Very often, when people come into my office, they say: "If only I knew why I do the things I do life would be so much different for me. I would have some answers to things that have troubled me for such a long time." I'm not convinced we need to know the answer to this question. I'm not sure that the answer would be useful to what is relevant for us right now. We need to learn how to deal with what is in front of us at this moment because it is the only moment we have. When we have the time to spend we can go looking for answers. But for the sake of discussion let's consider the statement above.

We will do what we think we need to do in order to attain some or all of five basic human needs. This is not new information. It stems from the work of Dr. William Glasser, a psychiatrist responsible for the development of Reality Therapy. The principles centred in Reality Therapy suggest that we choose our behaviour and are therefore responsible, not only for what we are doing, but also for how we think and feel.

I interpret this information to say that we will do what we feel we have to do, whether we are concerned about the outcomes of our behaviour or not, in order to satisfy one or a combination of these basic needs. Simply put, we will take care of ourselves first and concern ourselves with the outcomes of our activities later. How we decide to meet these needs governs how we feel about ourselves and is the basis for our positive or negative self-image. The course of our lives is directly related to our thinking and our doing. We can assume the responsibility of managing our lives anytime we want. When we accept that responsibility we put ourselves in a position of direct control over what we do to get our needs met and therefore the outcomes of those efforts. **If we don't like what is happening to us, we need to do something different.**

We all have the same five basic needs as people:

1. We want to be seen as being good at something. We want recognition for a particular talent we may have developed. It is important to be appreciated for a particular skill that may set us apart from the accomplishments of others. It is important to us that others see us as successful in some way. Some are able to find this recognition as athletes, actors or artists. Others may be seen as good parents or astute business people, capable fire fighters or competent police detectives.

   Others will become skilled at car theft or forgery. Some will develop a reputation as con artists. Even being able to collect bad debts is a vocation that some are good at. I'm not advocating these talents be utilized. We will strive to be seen as proficient at something, so that we become recognized, known by others, and we hope accepted.

2. We all strive to be accepted somewhere by someone or a group of someones. We want to be loved and we want to feel a sense of importance, that we have value, that our presence has meaning, and that we matter to someone who understands us and accepts us for the fallible human beings that we are. It is important for us to feel that we belong. Look at how hard children work to be a part of the greater whole. Witness the devastation of family members that goes along with the unit breaking up or falling apart. What do we feel

like when we are at work and our workmates don't include us in the "loop"? How do we feel when we find out that we are the brunt of a joke at the office? We will change who we are or compromise our value system to feel that we belong somewhere. We do this by joining in the group that discriminates against another worker or tells inappropriate jokes knowing and feeling that it isn't right. But we'll do it because we want to fit in.

As I work with couples in their recoveries the topic of abuse usually comes up. Many have said they abused their partners out of a sense of fear, that they believed the only way to keep their partners with them was to threaten them physically or mentally. They spoke of the fear of being alone and of not being able to intereact with their partners or their families. In these cases it was because of their alcohol and/or drug use. They were caught in the cycle of using substances and it was destroying the trust and security in their relationships and their homes.

They began to wonder how much longer their partners would put up with their activities so they began to abuse them in some fashion to encourage them to stay. The partners often stayed out of fear for their safety or the safety of their children. Often, both partners were abusing each other in some way. The men tended to be physical. The women tended to use a more psychological approach focusing on their mate's inadequacies as a parent, provider or sexual partner.

If we look at street gangs which, in many cases, provide more of a family environment than many of the members have ever experienced, we see a sense of community, common purpose and togetherness. They work for and with each other just like a family is supposed to. Legally, when we think of the natural outcomes to some of their activities, this makes no sense to us but socially it makes perfect sense. We all need to feel that we belong somewhere and we will do what we need to do to achieve that state.

3. We need to be able to engage in activities that are enjoyable, that we consider worthwhile, that have some value to us, and that

provide us with a sense of excitement, stimulation or relaxation. We may enjoy hang gliding or scuba diving. We may try mountain climbing or white water rafting. People around us may not understand why we do certain things or choose certain activities. They may put forth particular arguments to us or impose sanctions on us for our choices. Being carefree means that we will do them anyway because we feel that they are important to us. Being carefree does not necessarily mean being careless.

4. We need to feel that we are free to make our own decisions, without having to justify them. This is a must for most of us. We need to feel that we are competent enough and able to decide what is in our own best interests. This is not to say that we do not take other information into account, but we need to feel free to decide what we want to do with that information. We need to feel free to do what we want and to do it when we want. This includes knowing that we alone are in control of our own destiny.

When I think of bulimic and anorexic people I wonder how much of their behaviour is due to this need, somehow, being met. They are in control of what goes into their bodies, how much goes in and when it comes out. This may be the only decision that they feel they can make that can't be taken away from them.

It means being in command and control of what happens to us or what we are doing at any given time.

5. This need entails the very basics of existence: being able to get enough food, shelter, clothing, warmth and medical attention. These are the needs that we have to have in place before much else can happen. These are the needs that, in my opinion, will become more difficult to meet for a greater number of people in the years to come. As our political system makes the tough decisions regarding fiscal reality, the social safety net is slowly being disassembled without adequate alternate provisions being in place. People will do whatever they have to do to ensure their basic needs are met for themselves and particularly for their families.

> Governments at all levels are collectively insane if they believe that people will not engage in anti-social behaviour to get these needs met. The primary reason that domestic governments exist should be to ensure that **everyone's** basic needs are met, or that the opportunity to do so is possible without exception. There can be no excuses. Denying legitimate opportunities to ensure a basic standard of living promotes aggressive behaviour. We cannot expect people to live within the norms of society unless they are able to obtain and maintain the basics which in turn help to promote a sense of dignity.
>
> I have always believed that societies will be judged by how they care for those who are less fortunate. How do we, as a society, want to be seen?

When each one of us stops to think about someone we know who has become troubled or troublesome let's consider what is going on in his or her life with regards to these five needs. Which ones aren't being met? When we find that we are stressed or angry or tired, which one of our needs isn't being met? What do we need to do to meet that need?

This part of our journey is about developing more assertive skills--working to get **OUR** needs met without having to resort to aggressive behaviour to do it. We are also trying to learn how to deal effectively with others who are aggressive towards us. It may not always be possible.

There will be situations when being assertive just won't be appropriate. If you are being threatened or physically abused, trying to assert yourself may only serve to antagonize an aggressor even more. Withdrawing may be the best approach at a time like this. Part of learning to be more assertive is knowing or recognizing when not to be.

Other benefits accrue when we learn to be more assertive: our self-esteem will be positively affected; we may be less angry, depressed or resentful, especially towards others who are important to us; and we are likely to experience less anxiety especially in situations that we judge to be unfair or unjust.

Look again!

At the beginning of our journey I stated that I wanted to challenge your belief systems. I wanted you to think about how you manage your life now and how you could do it differently if you were to consider some new information. Consider some of the traditional beliefs about assertiveness.

1. **Some would say:** If you think about yourself first you are being selfish and self-centered.
   Consider this: You have every right to put your needs ahead of those of others provided you don't negate the rights of others to do the same.

2. **Some would say:** If you don't think that you can do it right don't do it at all.
   Consider this: You have the right to make mistakes. As a matter of fact, making mistakes helps us to learn how to do it right. We weren't born with a manual attached to our back sides on how to do it right. We learn from our efforts. Then we evaluate our efforts and decide how we could do it differently the next time.

3. **Some would say:** We are not supposed to burden others with our problems. They have better things to do with their time than to listen to our issues or concerns.
   Consider this: You have the right to ask for assistance and support. You may not get it but you sure have the right to ask for it. This is often the time when you find out who your true friends are.

4. **Some would say:** It's not a good idea to create waves. It is always better to go with what is happening even if it doesn't suit your needs.
   Consider this: You have the right to challenge others' ideas of what is good for you as long as you don't negate their right to do the same. Try negotiating for a compromise.

5. **Some would say:** Other people don't want to hear that you are feeling bad or hurting or that you are having a hard time.

Consider this: You have the right to express how you feel whether that is about pain or sadness or any other uncomfortable emotion. Holding things inside increases the risk of intestinal problems and heart problems, and adds considerably to your stress. We need to be able to express our concerns openly without criticism or judgement.

6. **Some would say:** Asking questions or being inquisitive leads people to believe that you are stupid or dumb. Therefore, you should remain quiet or passive with the hopes that others will assume you agree or that you accept what is being put forth.
Consider this: You have the right and the obligation to ask for clarification on any issue you consider to be important so that you can make an informed decision based on your own set of personal values. You do not have to accept anything at face value.

7. **Some would say:** You should be more flexible and be willing to re-think your position on things. Questioning and confronting others is not acceptable and shows bad manners.
Consider this: You have the right to challenge what you believe to be unfair treatment or judgement by others. Nowhere is it written that you have to be a door mat for anyone. Our self-esteem takes a beating when we let others dictate our thoughts and actions.

8. **Some would say:** You should always pay close attention to what other people have to say, especially if they are in a position of power or authority. They didn't get there by being stupid so we need to follow their direction.
Consider this: It is usually a good idea to listen to people who have been successful at something that you consider to be important. That is how you can learn new skills. There is no point in re-inventing the wheel. However, you **always** have the right to your own opinions and beliefs. You can take some or any of the information that is presented and adapt it to your own circumstances. You don't have to play follow the leader.

9. **Some would say:** You should always be decisive and when you have decided on a course of action follow the plan to the end.

How do I tell him I think we are lost?

Consider this: You have the right to evaluate your actions at any time and make adjustments as they are warranted. Evaluating what we do enables us to learn. It is OK to change your mind if you believe the outcomes would be better in the end. Follow your intuition for it is probably right more often than not.

10. **Some would say:** It is being responsible and polite to follow the advice of others if they take the time to give it to you. Anything else would be rude.
Consider this: You have the right to decide for yourself whose advice you will consider, if any at all. You are the only one who lives in the shoes you wear. No one has the right to tell you how to live your life and expect you to do it. If they try, dump them.

11. **Some would say:** It is considered bad taste to be openly pleased about something that you have done well. For the most part people don't like others who appear to be self-important or braggarts. Be modest about your accomplishments.
Consider this: You have the right to receive the recognition you deserve for a job well done. If others have a tough time with that, that is their problem not yours. I don't believe we should flaunt our successes but it's OK to feel openly proud of what you have done and how you have done it. To feel that we are good at something and be recognized for it is one of our basic human needs.

12. **Some would say:** If you don't look after the needs of others they won't look after yours when you need them.
Consider this: You are the only one responsible for your needs. You have the right to say no when saying yes is not in your best interests (remember that part in the time management section). Friends are those who don't put any conditions on their friendship. They give unconditionally knowing that if they need you, you will be there for them just as they would be there for you. It is not a matter of "I'll do this for you but I expect that you will do this for me." That is not friendship but a business arrangement.

13. **Some would say:** If you turn down an invitation to join with other

people, they will think that you are strange or that you don't like their company. They may even think you are being judgemental.
Consider this: You have the right to decide how, when and with whom you will spend your time. If solitude is what you need, take time for you alone. It's OK to say: "Thanks for the invitation but I need some time to myself. Can I call you tomorrow?"

14. **Some would say:** If you don't have a good reason for what you do or how you feel, something is wrong with you. It is important to show that you are always in control of yourself.
Consider this: You don't have to justify yourself to anyone. You have the right to act, feel or demonstrate your feelings whenever, as long as you are not infringing on someone else's rights, freedoms or space. They, as well, have the right to respond to you the way they see fit, provided they are not abusive in any way.

15. **Some would say:** You should always jump in to help someone who is in trouble. That's what friends are for. After all, they would do the same for you, wouldn't they?
Consider this: You have the right not to accept or assume responsibility for others' problems. Often when we jump in to ease the burden of someone's problem(s) we rob them of the opportunity to learn a new skill or develop a personal resource that would be useful to them the next time they found themselves in a similar situation. That is not to say we never help out or lend a helping hand. It is to say that we need to let others take responsibility for their own solutions. Being supportive and owning someone's issues are different situations.

16. **Some would say:** You should always try to be aware of how others are feeling so that you can help them through their difficult time even if they are not able to tell you what they need.
Consider this: You have the obligation not to assume you know what someone else needs. You have the right to wait until others are clear about how they feel and what they need before you decide whether or not you can help.

How do I tell him I think we are lost?

There are many other basic rights and freedoms to which we are entitled. We have the right to be assertive with others so that we can get our needs met and they have the same right to be assertive with us. No one knows us better than we know ourselves. Who knows better what we need, when we need it, and how that should happen for us? We have the right to decide and negotiate our way through life. This life is ours and ours alone.

> **The art of being wise is knowing what to overlook.**
> **--William James**

We take a risk every time we make a decision and follow that with an action of some kind. That risk is to our self-esteem. It is the same with being assertive. Each time we assert ourselves we take the risk of being negated, criticised, judged or condemned. Each of these forms a direct assault on our self-esteem. If we don't assert ourselves the outcomes of **that** decision can be more devastating. We will always consider the best interests of others and seldom our own. There can be no spiritual growth without recognizing our right to satisfy what we consider to be our own best interests. It is this consideration that enables us to begin the process of change that is vital to our spiritual and emotional growth.

Until we decide to work in our own best interests we will continue to work in the best interests of others. Better to take the risk.

How people work to get their needs met

We all know folks who appear to be patient and congenial at the office but are impatient and demanding away from work. There are others who are very aggressive in public but are very quiet at home. We assume different roles at different times depending on the situation that presents itself. We will act or respond differently when we assume the role of a parent, for instance, or the role of a consumer, an employee or a teacher. Depending on the role that we assume, we will need to decide for ourselves the "whens" and the "wheres" for being assertive.

I believe most of us would choose to be assertive if we felt we had the skills to do so and if we could get by the old tapes that play in our heads. Those tapes are the beliefs that we have developed over the years that govern our thoughts and actions. They are based on what we have been taught by our parents, neighbours, friends, relatives and teachers. They are the forming grounds for our values and our principles.

There are four basic approaches that people will employ, either consciously or unconsciously, to get their needs met. They may, in fact, be completely unaware of what they are doing. All they know is what they are doing helps them get some need met and that is their goal. Some get very creative and use combinations of approaches depending on the circumstances they are faced with.

Passive people

- Passive people avoid conflict at all costs. They will usually negate their own needs and allow others to choose for them. They go along to get along.

- They generally feel frustrated, resentful, anxious, hurt and less deserving than those around them.

- Very seldom are their relationships with others fulfilling or pleasant since they do not get their personal and emotional needs met. They are often the victims of other people.

- Those who are around passive people generally feel irritated and sorry for them.

- Passive people will make sure that everyone else is OK whether they themselves are or not.

Aggressive people

- Aggressive people don't consider the needs or feelings of those around them. They attempt to get their needs met by forcing their views on others. They will at times single out those who haven't established clear boundaries of acceptable behaviour by others. The aggressor might use bullying tactics with these people to meet their own needs. At other times they use more subtle behaviour. When discussing a topic, especially in a crowd, they will not acknowledge someone else's opinions. They could try to discredit the person by discrediting that person's point of view.

- They feel that they are better than others. There is an edge to them that says, "Don't even think about challenging me." Although they may feel some guilt about their behaviour they would never show that in public.

- Aggressive people don't often have many close friendships because they turn on those who may disagree with them or openly challenge them. They generally get ahead at the expense of others.

- Those around them usually feel defensive and angry, embarrassed or resentful.

- Aggressive people only care about how they are doing. They care little about how anyone else is doing. They tend to be self-centered in their approach. They will work to keep others down so they can excel.

Passive-aggressive people

- This group of people are seen as chameleons in that they are not often as they appear. Their method of getting their needs met tends to be indirect, covert almost. They usually don't confront issues head on but rather choose to act behind closed doors. They will go with the flow of things but will complain or object most of the way.

- Passive-aggressive people use sarcasm and innuendo as tools to make their objections, especially in front of others. They may resort to starting rumours about someone they cannot confront or of whom they are envious or jealous.

- Passive-aggressive people will find a way to get even. In their minds they are justified in gaining a measure of revenge.

- They seldom attain their goals and this failing tends to fuel their justification for their behaviour. The relationships that they are able to establish don't do well for long and usually fall apart or at least are not rewarding.

- Those around passive-aggressive people feel confused and frustrated. We all want to believe in the good we see in people so the confusion comes from their polarized behaviour. They say this but do that.

- Those who find themselves around passive-aggressive people often feel as if they are being used or manipulated somehow.

- In the end we find that these people are not doing very well and neither are those around them.

Assertive people

- This is who most of us would like to be. Assertive people find little difficulty in being honest and straightforward. They do not force their opinions on others but they are able to state clearly where they stand on most issues and why. Assertive people are not challenged to compromise but rather will do so if they can see how both sides can benefit from a decision. They will not sacrifice the rights of others to forward their own agendas.

- Assertive people are more likely to observe the boundaries of others while helping others understand theirs.

- Assertive people usually feel good about themselves and how they go about their business. It generally shows by way of a confident and self-assured manner.

- Assertive people are more likely to achieve their goals without discouraging others from doing the same.

- Relationships tend to be more fulfilling and longer lasting.

- Other people seem to enjoy the company of assertive people feeling more at ease, valued and respected for who they are and for what they are trying to accomplish. Assertive people would probably pitch in to help others get ahead as well.

- These folks look at life and say, "I'm doing OK today and I hope you are too."

I was just born that way!

During times of stress or challenge we often revert to old behaviours and programmed responses that served us in the past. Maybe we don't know any other way. Maybe we were never helped to understand how things could be any different. There are several possible sociological reasons why we behave the way we do.

There is the argument of nature vs. nurture. The nature side says that we are born with certain behavioural traits or characteristics that predetermine how we will react or respond in a particular situation. I often hear this when my clients are trying to explain why they drink or use drugs: "This runs in my family," or "I, like my father, have an addictive personality." The nurture point of view suggests how we were brought up and what we were taught have a more direct impact on how we react or respond.

Some understand that males are socialized differently than females. From the time boys can walk and talk we are told that we need to be strong and to be outgoing and demonstrative. If we are to have what we want we need to go after it and show no sign of weakness. Don't back down and never let the other guy know that you are frightened.

Girls are more likely encouraged to be quiet, polite and courteous. Girls who are seen as assertive are considered to be unladylike; therefore, their behaviour is unacceptable. Children who are outspoken are seen as being precocious. Of course this is nonsense but unfortunately, even in the 90's, this mindset won't die. We mistake passivity for being mannerly, well adjusted and generous. As parents we discourage the development of assertiveness in our children when we mistake their efforts at being assertive as being disrespectful.

Other thoughts

Non-assertive people may be hesitant to make a decision or assert themselves because they are afraid of the criticism that will follow. Not making a decision is often better than making one that could be wrong. "If I don't decide, I can't be wrong. I can't be rejected, criticised or labelled."

They may also believe that they are not worthy or important enough for anyone to listen to or respect. Some people believe they don't have the right to tell someone else what they need or want.

Conversely, there are people who feel so insecure that they act out in very aggressive ways. By intimidating others they can perhaps protect themselves from whatever it is they fear. They must appear strong so people will be less likely to challenge them. For many, the best defence is a good offence. We would notice aggressive language, aggressive body language or demonstrations of physical strength. If they had been victims of aggressive behaviour they would learn that being aggressive does get results, so why not use it too?

Only strong people can check their aggressive tendencies and opt for an assertive approach to getting their needs met. Aggressive behaviour works, but only in the short term. Others will find ways to "get even" whether in a passive sense or returned aggressive behaviour. In either case the aggressor becomes lonely and isolated. Think of those around you who are very aggressive. Would you really want their lives? Think of what others say about them behind their backs. Would you really want them saying the same about you?

Being assertive is a learned skill and as with all skill development it takes time, practice and effort.

What I am is good enough if I would only be it openly.
--Carl Rogers

The reason for learning how to be more assertive is not about getting other people to do what we want them to do; it's about getting our needs met in a way that doesn't negate the rights of others to do the same. It's not about manipulating words or people. **It is not about them. It is about us.** It's a way for us to develop a more positive sense of ourselves. It's about developing more self-esteem--a sense of self-value and self-worth. Being assertive can mean that we walk down a busy street and meet other peoples' glances eye to eye instead of watching the cracks in the sidewalk as we go our way. It can mean that our body language says we are more confident today than we were yesterday. Being assertive is about clearly stating our feelings and thoughts .

One theory on communicating suggests that the effort to communicate is based on 50% body language (how we present ourselves), 40% voice (tone and inflection) and 10% words (the message).

If you are practising being assertive in appropriate situations, be sure that your body language and the tone of your voice match the words and the meaning you are trying to convey or the message you want to be heard. For example, if you are trying to tell someone how much you love him or her while in the midst of an angry outburst, your words are not likely to match your actions. It is unlikely that you will be believed. How could you be?

Being heard and feeling that you have been understood are what communicating is all about. Try to remember a time when you had something important to say but you didn't believe that you were heard or understood. How did you feel? Did you become frustrated or angry? Was it because your tone of voice was at odds with what you were trying to say?

Resentment keeps our hands closed in a fist and our spirit closed to what is good around us.

There are other issues to consider as well when we are trying to communicate our thoughts and feelings to others. We need to think about other people's customs and culture. In some native cultures direct eye contact, until a sense of trust is developed, is avoided and should not be expected. Some European cultures hold the belief that, unless you are open and straightforward from the first time you meet, you may have something to hide, you may be dishonest or you may be untrustworthy. North Americans would tend to be reserved at a first meeting with someone. In the Far East observing honour and tradition are primary concerns in any face-to-face interaction. In many tribal cultures only the men speak or represent their families or villages. To do otherwise is considered a slight.

We need to understand that other people have different safety zones. When we get too close they may consider our behaviour a threat, even though that is not our intention, and may react aggressively, believing that they have been physically challenged.

There is much to consider when attempting to be assertive. It doesn't mean we shouldn't try. It means that we need to be aware of other people's needs as well as our own.

What do we do now?

It will be difficult for us to do the things we need to do to continue our program for personal growth unless we feel good about ourselves or unless we are working on developing that positive sense of who we are. So the first part of our journey is about getting stronger: working to feel better about who we are and where we are going, and recognizing that we have personal resources and strengths that will help get us there. However, there has to be a desire and a decision to change BEFORE anything can happen. We may not know what to do or how to do it but we must decide to consider new approaches and techniques before we can learn anything new. The same holds true when trying to be more assertive.

A strong connection exists between being assertive and thinking of ourselves in positive terms. We will find it easier to be assertive when we are able to do the following:

❒ Accept that we have strengths and resources just like everyone else and that we were born no differently. Positive self-talk is critical. We won't get stronger by saying we are stupid or useless. If we are always around negative people in negative places doing negative things, how would that affect us? What would you expect to feel? The same depends on our using self-talk that is positive. It focuses us in a way that encourages us to learn and move forward.

> E.g. Say: "What can I do differently so that the next time the outcome will be more positive," NOT "Boy that was just pure stupidity on my part. I'll never try that again." It seems like a small thing but if you put enough negatives together throughout the day how would you expect to feel at the end of it?

No man ever gained an inch by stepping backward.

- ❒ See that our needs are just as important as anyone else's needs and that it is OK to ensure that they are respected and understood by other people. We are then able to move toward claiming our own rights. We can also help others reclaim their rights by granting them the dignity and respect that they deserve but not at our expense.

- ❒ State clearly what our rights and needs are so there is no misunderstanding about what it is we are trying to say.

- ❒ Accept the responsibility for the outcomes, whether they be pro or con, and try to see our activities as **learning experiences** rather than personal failures. We are the products of our experiences. If we use those experiences to our advantage by accepting them as lessons learned, then we grow by self-evaluation not self-depletion.

- ❒ Accept the responsibility for how we feel and why we feel that way. We need to understand that we are not responsible for the feelings of others. When we try to assume responsibility for other people's feelings or when we feel that it is up to us to, somehow, make other people happy, two things happen:

1. We will cease to consider ourselves and our needs as the most important thing because we will be concerned about how our

activities will affect others. As long as what we do is not designed to intentionally hurt, disregard, embarrass, intimidate or disenfranchise anyone else, we need to do all that we can to ensure our own rights, wants and freedoms are protected.

For example, someone you drive to work smokes in your car. You do not smoke and you do not like the smell it leaves in your car or on your clothes. You have the right to say to that person, "If you could have your smoke just before I pick you up I'd really appreciate it." If that person chooses to be upset by your suggestion that is his or her problem not yours. DON'T TAKE IT ON.

2. We deprive others of the opportunity to learn how to deal with their own issues. We don't have the right to do that. When we take responsibility for what happens in our lives, so will they. That way we all get what we need. Being supportive is different from being protective or sympathetic.

❒ Consider the importance of our needs and try to negotiate our way toward win/win solutions. For a win/win outcome both parties need to walk away from a situation feeling that they were heard, understood and that they did not come out second best. They may have compromised but they got some of what they wanted or needed and so did we. This may not always happen but if that is the spirit of your discussion then you have done all you can to work toward a positive outcome.

What do we have so far?

1. One thing is for sure. Not everybody will be thrilled by our attempts to develop a new skill. This one especially. Our new assertiveness means that they will have to find other ways of dealing with us. We often force others to change how they do their business when we change how we do ours. Remember that people resist change. Some could exert pressure on us not to change. Stay the course. If we are deciding to change our lives for the better how can that be a bad thing?

How do I tell him I think we are lost?

2. Whenever we are developing a new skill we need to practice in situations that are of low risk to us. Not every situation we find ourselves in will lend itself to our being assertive. Part of learning a new skill or technique is to know when, where and how to use it. This part is extremely important. If you don't feel that you can be assertive in a certain situation, don't try to be. Pick and choose your spots--on your time.

Travel at your own speed. Life is not a race; it's an experience.

3. You may find you won't always be as successful at being assertive as you might have liked. It may not always feel good to be assertive. At times, you will experience some feelings of guilt. At times it may seem easier to just let it slide. Compromise is one thing but giving in is another. It is OK to let things slide if our self-esteem isn't compromised in the process. Otherwise we need to let people know what is acceptable to us and what is not.

4. Being assertive will not always get us what we need or what we want. What it will do, though, is give us the feeling that we did what needed to be done and that we stood up for ourselves. That, in itself, is very satisfying. As long as we are trying to take care of our needs we are doing something positive--we are winning.

5. Be sure to consider non-successes as learning experiences. Evaluate the outcomes so that we can see what we need to do differently if, or when, a similar situation presents itself. Be sure to examine our successes, as well, to see what we did and how we did it, so that we can do more of that in the future.

When I was young and free and my imagination had no limits, I dreamed of changing the world. As I grew older and wiser, I discovered the world would not change, so I shortened my sights somewhat and decided to change only my country. But it, too, seemed immovable. As I grew into my twilight years, in one last desperate attempt, I settled for changing only my family, those closest to me, but alas, they would have none of it. And now as I lie on my deathbed, I suddenly realize: if I had only changed myself first, then by example I would have changed my family. From their inspiration and encouragement, I would then have been able to better my country and, who knows, I may have even changed the world.--Anonymous

The work begins with us. It has always been that way. If nothing changes, well then, nothing changes. If we want our lives to be different we need to do all we can to make it that way. The choice concerning our direction continues to be ours.

To repeat, we will not be able to sway people to our way of thinking by being assertive. The best we can hope for, in the majority of situations, is that we will be heard and understood. That is the real goal of being assertive: to state clearly what we feel we need in any particular situation without negating the rights of others. There will be those who will resist our attempts at getting our thoughts and feelings stated openly and clearly. The one constant in being assertive is remaining assertive. Be consistent in your approach.

Here are some methods we can use in situations where someone resists our right to be assertive:

❒ Continue to repeat our thoughts and feelings clearly and consistently. If we believe in our position we don't have to defend it or debate it but just work to maintain it.

❒ It's OK to say, "I think I understand what it is you are trying to say to me but I don't agree." That way we acknowledge that others are entitled to their opinion without judging them or their ideas and thoughts. We are entitled to the same consideration. In this case our opinions simply differ. Nobody loses anything when each side acknowledges the other's point of view. It will be more difficult for them to wear us down by continuing the discussion.

- ❒ When we are dealing with resistant people or with those who would try to convince us that we don't have the right to think or feel a certain way it is necessary for us to state how important our position is and how strongly we feel about what we are saying. We all know those who say, "You must be stupid to think like that" so our response might be this: "I believe it is possible to see this from more than one perspective. I stand by the way I see this one."

- ❒ If the discussion continues we may have to work hard to keep our main point central to the situation. We may need to say, "I understand that you feel as strongly about this as I do but the point here is . . . " Continuing to stay focused on the issue is the key to this technique. We have to let the remarks go that would lead us to an argument or into another direction. In the heat of a discussion we may jump at the chance for recriminations. The person we are dealing with may become frustrated and get into name calling or sarcasm. These tactics are used to take us away from our initial thoughts. Stay focused. Consistency is our ally. Restate your position: "I am not being stubborn. I believe these points are valid. We can agree to disagree if you like."

- ❒ We can suggest joining together to find a solution that is suitable for both parties. We can discuss areas of agreement. We can ask: "How can we both get some of what we need? What would be important for you?" We thus leave the door open for suggestions. This provides a way for both parties to walk away from the discussion to consider alternatives. We help to create a win/win situation, at least for the moment.

The toughest situations to be assertive in are those in which we have been criticized in some way. Our natural response is to defend ourselves, "to get back in the other guy's face." But being able to defuse conflict is just as important as learning any other part of this skill-building process. In the song "The Gambler" Kenny Rogers sang, "You have to know when to hold 'em and know when to fold 'em'." Good advice. Pick and choose the time to take a stand. Not every situation needs to be defended.

We will, from time to time, make mistakes or do things that other people will not find amusing or pleasant. That does not make us bad people. It does make us human. We need to accept that we are not perfect beings. Don't make excuses but do make any apologies that may be appropriate. Live with it and move on.

There may well be times when criticism is warranted. That does not mean that we should accept verbal abuse from anyone but simply admitting that we are wrong may be the best thing to do to defuse a potential argument. For example:

Comment: "It seems that everywhere I go there you are. Anytime I need some down time or I stop in a hurry you bump into me".
Resonse: "You're right. I didn't realize that I was crowding you. I need to allow you some space." The criticism is justified so just admit it and move on. There is no harm in recognizing an activity that distresses others. Be pleased they have pointed it out so you can stop doing it.

Comment: "You said that you would have the job done by tonight. I can see that is not going to happen."
Response: "You're right. I did say that."

Once spoken, our words become weapons that destroy or assets that build and create. In either case they can never be retrieved.

There will be times when we have done our best on a project or an assignment of some kind, whether at work or at home, but it does not meet the expectations of a supervisor, friend or relative.
Comment: "I am not happy with the way this turned out."

How do I tell him I think we are lost?

Response: "What part of the job are you unhappy with?" or "Tell me which part of the job you are not pleased with."

This response asks the commenter to be more specific about the complaint so that you have a better idea of what it is you are dealing with.

Easy to say--hard to do. It takes practice. If we are trying to be more assertive and to observe the rights of others in the process, we need to be able to respond in ways that allow for discussion and resolution. "Up yours. Do it yourself the next time, you ingrate" would not be appropriate. That response will make it difficult to continue any kind of relationship until apologies are made or an amendment of some kind is made.

To admit that I have been in the wrong is but saying that I am wiser today than I was yesterday.--Allan Picket, From *Believing in Myself*.

It's OK to say no

Equally important is developing the skill to say no when it is in our best interest to do so. The word is simple enough to pronounce yet so very difficult to say.

We may often say yes when we really want to say no. Being assertive means that you don't have to apologize for asking for what you want. Sometimes saying no is getting what you want. It means that, right at this moment, your needs are more important. Perhaps you have decided to spend the afternoon with your child or your partner. A friend calls and needs you to come over to help him do something. In the scheme of things, which is more important--your family or your friend? It shouldn't get down to making that decision but sometimes it does.

That's why saying no can be difficult. It often involves a choice that puts us either first or last.

There are three different ways to say no. We will not find a particular way to say no all the time since the situations that we may find ourselves in will differ greatly. What we can do is understand that it is OK for us to say no to those who would have us put their needs ahead of our own. If the word is uncomfortable to say, find a phrase or a gesture that says no.

1. We could say no without discussing or explaining our decision. If we needed to help someone understand that we were not in favour of getting involved in an activity that was against our better judgement, or that compromised our integrity--our value system--sometimes a simple no says it all. We would be more likely to use this style with someone we didn't know well or someone who was being very pushy or directive or perhaps someone who was trying to leave us with no apparent way out by cornering us.

   E.g. A resident in your neighbourhood is trying to rally other residents to confront your next door neighbour over an issue that really doesn't concern them or you. You feel that his/her motives are more personal than they are connected with the issue.

   Response: "I'm not interested in joining you."

   You have not exactly said the word no but you have made your feelings known that you are not interested. You haven't spent any time or words explaining your decision. It's short, sweet and to the point. It leaves little room for comment or negotiation. This style is less concerned with maintaining friendships and more concerned with helping people understand our boundaries.

2. You could say no but feel compelled to explain, clarify or justify your decision. This is a style that is used so we don't rock the boat or have anyone angry with us because we didn't go along with the group. This style is used more often by fence-sitters. It is a more passive style.

   Response: "Unfortunately I won't be able to go along with the group today because I promised the kids that I would take them to the mall. I really don't like to make promises to them and then not keep them. Perhaps, if I had known earlier in the day that you were getting together

How do I tell him I think we are lost?

I could have made other arrangements but it is too late now."

There really is no need to go on and on about a decision that you have made. The more you try to explain your decision the more it appears exactly what it is--an excuse to avoid something. It does not convey conviction. It does not convey a sense of what you stand for or believe in.

3. We could be assertive in our response and say clearly that we don't agree with what is happening and that we don't want to be a part of it. We can say this in a manner that is friendly but clear.

   Response: "I don't see that as an issue for me to go to him about. You'll have to go ahead without me."

   We have been very clear that we don't intend to go along with the group. We have not suggested that they are wrong in any way nor have we made any judgements about what they're doing. This is not an issue that concerns us.

Saying no is about doing the things that we feel are in our best interests. If those around us will be upset because we haven't gone along with them or haven't supported them regardless of how we feel, perhaps we need to re-evaluate our relationship with them. The people we associate with need to allow us to be who we want to be and to grant us the opportunity to make our own choices without guilt, fear, or condemnation. There may be times when saying no may jeopardize your standing with your boss. You have to decide which battles you want to fight and when. How important are they? There will be times when your best interests may be better served by **not** being assertive. You have the control. You decide for yourself. You pick and choose the times when you will be assertive. Part of the learning process is knowing when to use your new skill and when not to.

The "broken record technique"

We can also consider the "broken record" technique if we are dedicated to a decision that we have made and want to remain steadfast despite outside pressures. Some people around us may not like the decision or the course of action we have chosen because they feel threatened or provoked and so may try to influence our decisions in some way.

When we are part of a group that has some history together or has become close, our decisions and our behaviours ultimately affect them to some degree. When we decide to change some aspect of our lifestyle our decision affects those around us. They may be saddened knowing that we won't be a part of the Friday night poker game anymore or that we will not be with them every Wednesday evening after work for tennis or golf or whatever else the activity may be. Our decision may very well force others to evaluate their own behaviours and they may be uncomfortable doing that.

For example: Bob has decided that he is going to quit using alcohol for a while because he has recognized that it is tougher for him to get up in the morning, it takes him longer to get mentally prepared for the day, it has begun to affect the way he does his job, and his wife has begun to complain about his lack of participation in family activities. He decides to stop drinking for a period of 30 days to see if, by not drinking, he thinks and feels differently. When he tells his friends they begin to argue that he doesn't drink anymore than they do and they are all right. He persists in his decision and they apply more pressure because they don't want to lose a friend and a drinking buddy.

It may also mean that some of the group may have to look at the amount of alcohol they have been consuming. Some in the group may have been thinking, to themselves, they drink too much and now are forced to evaluate their own behaviour. If they can keep Bob using alcohol, they can postpone having to consider their own use.

Here is a possible scenario that involves Bob and his decision to stop drinking and how the broken record technique can be used: It's a hot summer day and Bob is at a friend's house for a neighbourhood back yard barbeque. A buddy, Jerry, comes up to him with a cold beer in his hand and offers it in front of some other people. Bob has made a commitment to himself and others not to use alcohol for 30 days. How does he decline gracefully?

How do I tell him I think we are lost?

Jerry: "Hey Bob, I'm glad you could make it. I didn't know if you were still attending these things. When I saw you come in I took the liberty of getting you a cool one."

Bob: "Thanks for the offer, Jerry, but I think I'll have a pop instead." (Bob hopes that Jerry will pick up on the fact that he is trying to maintain his decision.)

Jerry: "But this one's got your name on it. If you listen real hard you can hear it calling you."

Bob: "I appreciate the thought but I don't feel like having a beer today. If you're going that way, though, a pop would be great."

Jerry: "Come on, buddy. It's so hot a cool one would slide right down the sides."

Bob: "Well, it sounds good but I would prefer to have a cool pop right now. Ginger ale if you got it."

Jerry: "Are you sure I can't interest you in one?"

Bob: "Yeh, I'm sure. Thanks anyway."

This technique helps us to stay focused on our decision without getting angry at the other guy. We are able to say no without jeopardizing our relationship with our friend. At the same time we are able to deal effectively with a possibly embarrassing situation and the pressure to set aside our decision in front of others. The key is to use strong, decisive phrases like "I will . . . ", "I want . . . ", "I will not . . . ", "I do not want to . . .", and "I'm still not interested, thank you." It works and it works well.

Working to win/win

In win/win situations both parties see the outcome as mutually beneficial. They both agree to work toward an outcome that provides each with **some** of what they need. They discuss their common ground, deciding to build from there instead of focusing on how far apart they are.

The following is a method that can be used to that end. One of the things that we want to do is to assert ourselves in a way that is clear but doesn't criticize or challenge the other person. Assertiveness is about us getting what we need at no one else's expense. The **D.E.S.C.** model helps us to do that and it is easy to use.

The **D.E.S.C.** Model

D escribe the situation
E xpress your feelings
S pecify what you need
C hoose a positive outcome

When we are being assertive let's try to avoid using words like "you," "why"and "but" as much as possible. Used in situations where there are differences, these words often connote blame or responsibility of some kind. When these words are used in this context there is an almost automatic response to defend oneself. Arguments usually follow. When we are trying to enlist the assistance of someone else, the last thing we want to be doing is make them feel challenged or defensive. The D.E.S.C. model first helps us to explain how we see a particular situation, helps us to express our feelings about it, and then asks for a mutual solution.

Situation: You are a parent who is becoming increasingly frustrated with your attempts to get your daughter to put her dirty clothes in the laundry basket. You have lectured, threatened, and yelled but nothing has worked.

D. Describe the situation that has presented itself and try to do so using words that are descriptive rather than labelling. **"I have been finding**

dirty laundry all over the place again." You haven't gotten into name calling or labelling. You have simply stated your observations.

E. Express your feelings because of your observations. Don't say, "You make me feel . . . " but **"I feel angry, resentful and not heard when there is dirty laundry left all over the room. When I have to gather it up it adds to the amount of work I do each week."** We simply want the other person to know how we are feeling about what is happening and how that affects us.

S. Specify what you need from the other person or what you would prefer to see happen. **"I would appreciate it if all the dirty laundry was kept in the closet basket. Is that a possibility?"** We are asking the other person to join us in finding a solution to the situation. Others will be more compliant to our needs if they feel that they are part of the solution and not the source of the problem.

C. Choose or suggest a positive outcome that would occur if they worked with us. **"That way when it comes time to do the laundry all of the clothes will get cleaned."** The suggestion is that the clothes will not be washed if they aren't where they are supposed to be. There is no challenge put forward. Your daughter begins to understand that if she doesn't put her clothes in the basket they will not be clean when she needs them.

That said, when you decide on a possible outcome be prepared to carry through with **not** doing the clothes if they are not in the basket. This is the crucial part of this method. If you don't allow the clothes to stay dirty if they are not in the basket your attempts at gaining support or assistance will be fruitless. There will be no reason for them to assist you if you will do the extra work anyway. The outcomes need to reflect the activity. No help--no clean clothes.

Tips for being assertive:

1. Always maintain direct eye contact. The impact of your statements will be less believable if you cannot maintain eye contact.

2. Be sure that you are maintaining erect body posture. You want to be seen as self-assured and meaningful when you are trying to be clear about the importance of your message. There needs to be consistency in your presentation. Your body language, the tone of your voice and the message you want to send need to be congruous.

3. Speak clearly and audibly. People will be more inclined to listen to you if you are not yelling at them or if they are not straining to hear what it is you are trying to say. Speaking in a controlled manner indicates self-assurance and emotional self-control.

4. Don't whine. Whining means trying to push a great deal of emotion through a small hole. Use a vocal tone that is easy to listen to. Nobody will listen for long if you are whining. Whining does not suggest sincerity; it suggests that you are on the edge of losing some of your emotional control. This often makes other people uncomfortable.

5. Make use of facial expressions and hand movements that help you to emphasize the importance of the message that you are trying to deliver. I'm not suggesting that you flail your arms about like a wild person. Simple hand movements that may indicate sincerity or importance can be helpful in expressing what your words may not.

Why change anyway?

Changing from one mode of thinking or doing to another may be difficult, especially if a particular method seems to work. The actions we initially take may help us feel good for the short term but we need to consider the long-term ramifications if we are going to act in our own best interests.

In my work as an Addictions Counsellor I find the most difficult part of my job is to help my clients accept the idea that they need to look at how they resolve their issues. If what they are doing serves to complicate or nullify any positive solutions or growth, they will need to consider some alternatives. I am asking my clients to give up their current way of getting their needs met--one that, for the most part, they feel, works very nicely for them. It really doesn't sound like much of a bargain to them, but that is exactly what has to happen if they are to begin to experience any positive self-esteem or spiritual freedom.

For example: a client of mine was so angry about a recent divorce that he quit a high-paying job and went on government assistance because he didn't want to give his ex-wife any support money. Talk about cutting off your nose to spite your face! But he felt very justified doing this. It satisfied his need for revenge. He didn't consider what this would do to his own standard of living--he didn't care. He was prepared to sacrifice his own happiness so that she wouldn't get a dime from him. The only way that he will regain any semblance of peace and begin to move on in his life is to give up the desire for revenge. As long as this person continues in this pursuit he allows his ex-wife to "rent space in his head." He will never get past this experience. He will constantly be reminded of the pain and anger every day. This activity and mindset is a spirit killer. He needs to understand that, for every day he continues hating her, she is still punishing him. The thing is, he can put a stop to it any time he wants.

Where does the incentive to change come from? Before people will make changes they have to see the benefit for them of making the change. The same is true, for instance, when we consider making the decision to change from being passive to being assertive. If being passive has been our approach to getting our needs met in the past and it has worked for us, why would we want to change it now?

A primary reason is that by learning how to be more assertive in order to get our needs met, we begin to develop a more positive sense of self. Our positive self-image is one thing we cannot buy. We have to develop it and we cannot develop it if we are unable or unwilling to stand up for what we believe is right for us and for those around us. Seeking a positive sense of self is one of the most powerful driving forces that we will ever experience as humans. It is the one thing that is common to us all. We want to FEEL that we matter to those we deem as being important to us.

Passivity can be just as powerful as aggressiveness. Strange as it may sound being passive can be an awesome weapon in the hands of a professional. I'm not talking about getting material possessions. I'm talking about finding a way whereby others can be manipulated into helping us meet our needs and, in some cases, without their even knowing it. There are many benefits to being passive but there are drawbacks also. We can decide for ourselves which we prefer by doing a matrix.

For example: If you don't want to take the responsibility for making plans or for making a decision, the easiest thing to do is to be passive about it, to show no interest. It is likely someone who has passion for the task will jump into the situation and take charge for you. People learn not to count on us when we are passive. What is more important, you can never be criticized for making a poor decision if you never make a decision in the first place.

Consider the following matrix. It is based on information provided in *Volume 6, Discovering Life Skills,* a series produced by the YWCA. You can use this format to determine the pros and cons of becoming or remaining passive, passive-aggressive, aggressive or assertive. It is always easier to make decisions when we can see the pros and the cons laid out before us. All this requires is your honesty (looking within yourself for the real answers) and a willingness to change. For those who need to have some explanation for their behaviour, using a matrix is an excellent way of arriving at that understanding without spending a great deal of time. Again it requires an honest approach.

Positives for remaining passive	**Negatives for remaining passive**
It can provide protection from other more aggressive people. Passivity allows us to stay in the shadows so we are not perceived to be threats to other people's agendas.	We lose our independence. We become followers instead of leaders.

Positives for remaining passive	Negatives for remaining passive
We may be seen as conforming to the ideas or wishes of others. We could be seen as part of the team which would provide a sense of belonging.	We forfeit our rights and power to think and make decisions for ourselves based on what we believe are our own best interests.
Remaining passive allows us to maintain a behaviour pattern that is known to us. Most people who have been discouraged from making decisions would likely become more passive in their day-to-day lives.	We would not have honesty in our human relationships since we are unable to state clearly what we need and what we want from the other person or people. This is not fair to them either because they believe you are being up-front with them. They have a right to your honesty.
By remaining passive we can avoid taking responsibility for decision making or initiating plans of action.	We do not gain the respect of others. That respect is a vital part of developing a positive sense of self.
Maybe the most important positive would be that we could avoid being **rejected** for our activities, of having **others angry at us for disagreeing** with them or taking an independent stand, and being able to **avoid conflict** of any kind.	It becomes difficult to control our emotions if we deny our right to express them at appropriate times. We find ourselves blowing up at things that would not normally command that response.
	We become more stressed and less relaxed. Our tension and disappointment is turned inwards and that always leads to health problems.

Positives for remaining passive	Negatives for remaining passive
	We do not experience the satisfaction of developing new plans and initiating them. We lose the opportunity to think for ourselves and to use our ingenuity to make positive contributions to our lives. We also miss the opportunity to positively influence others.
	We are unable to be clear to others what we will accept from them, what they can expect from us and what they cannot expect from us. We are unable to establish any personal boundaries with regard to the quality of our own lives when we are being passive.

There are other pros and cons that could have been listed. Take the time to add them to this list based on what you recognize about yourself.

Where are we now?

Draw a horizontal line and on it mark a scale of 1-10. On the left end put a 1to represent "needs work" and on the other end of the line put a 10 to represent "as good as it could be." Now consider for a moment where on this line you would need to be in order for you to feel confident and comfortable in your ability to make your feelings, thoughts, wants, and needs known to other people without negating their right to do the same? Put a mark and the date on the line that would represent that place. Now put a mark and the date on the line that would represent how assertive you feel you are right now. What can you do or begin to do now that would help move your mark up the scale one number? What skills can you use? What

How do I tell him I think we are lost?

do you need to learn? Where can you go to learn? If you are already at the mark where you are comfortable what do you have to do to maintain this level of confidence ?

1___2___3___4___5___6___7___8___9___10___

Our positive solutions are within

The solutions to our problems lie within us. They also lie in the past successes that we have experienced.

However, before we can begin to make any changes in our behaviour we need to determine what benefits, if any, are likely to result. We will generate the motivation to change when we recognize how we will be positively affected by any changes we make. If there is a need to change, a desire to change, and the appropriate effort put forth to change we can develop the assertiveness skills that are necessary for us to advocate for what we believe to be our own best interests. We can do that without detering others from doing the same. When we become more assertive we strengthen our self-esteem.

Ask yourself the following questions:

1. When you think of a time when you felt good about how you handled a situation in an assertive way, what skills did you use? How did you do that? Could you do that again in a similar situation?

2. Do you know others whom you consider to be assertive people? What do you like about them? How could you be more like them?

3. When you are more assertive what difference will that make to your life? How would your life look to you then?

4. What are you thinking about that is different and what are you doing that is different when you are being assertive?

5. What current situations are safe enough for you to practice being assertive?

6. When you become more assertive, what would people who know you say was different about you?

7. What statements or words could you use that would demonstrate your decision to be more assertive? If you used words like "I will" instead of "Maybe" and "I can" instead of "I'll try" would that be different for you? Add other phrases and words to the list that you are currently using or that you will use that demonstrate assertiveness.

Assertiveness is a choice we make

When we consider the idea that we are "depressing ourselves" and "angering ourselves" we take a giant step toward taking control of how we feel--control over our emotions. **We can choose to manage ourselves. It's an inside job.** We are not helpless. Our feelings are not governed by outside forces but rather by how we choose to interpret those forces. We decide what impact they will have on us.

Being assertive is a choice we make. It must become a way of thinking and living, a concept if you like. We are not born assertive. Assertiveness is a skill that is developed over a period of time. Our belief in the importance of being assertive is reinforced when we are successful at stating, maintaining, and protecting what we feel are our rights. The more we attempt to be assertive and the more successful we are at being assertive the more likely we are to continue with the approach. We need to think in assertive terms with regard to how we participate in our daily lives and what we will accept from others. If, however, we are not acting assertively, we will never adopt an assertive lifestyle. We have to DO (be assertive) consistently before we can BECOME assertive people. Then it becomes a mindset. Then we are well on our way to becoming full participants in day-to-day living.

If we walk around with "a closed fist," as the quote on page 94 says, we are not open to try new things or to look at things differently. We cannot embrace the world and all it has to offer. We become closed to new ideas and self-evaluation. The process of self-evaluation stimulates learning and nurtures growth. Aggressive and passive people don't grow by their behaviour; they simply exist. They remain stagnant as human beings because there is no opportunity to learn and no opportunity to develop a positive sense of self.

Greeting the world with a "closed fist" is a self-defeating activity. This is one of the many reasons that anger and revenge are self-perpetuating. We get angry because we **are** angry and yet we are unable, so we think, to get out of the rut. What keeps us there? How do we work through the urge to be angry or hurtful? How do we NOT respond to what our feelings are telling us to do?

5.

IT IS EASIER TO STAY LOST THAN ASK FOR DIRECTIONS

THOSE WHO WOULD BE UNSUCCESSFUL DO WHAT THEY WANT TO. THOSE WHO SEEK SUCCESS DO WHAT THEY HAVE TO.

The difference between being successful and not successful lies in the heart of this statement. Being able to do the things we need to do and not always the things we want to do defines who we are and who we become. Reaching out to others and searching for new solutions to old issues are signs of growth. Allowing ourselves to see new possibilities and choosing to think about things differently is where we begin. When we decide not to be alone in our quest for self-actualization our journey to be all that we can be begins in earnest.

In this part of our journey we look at how to deal with the urges to respond to what is happening in and around us. When I speak of urges I am talking about the need we feel, either consciously or subconsciously, to respond, in some fashion, to a stimulus that we experience. The urge acts as a signal which indicates we want to change or alter our mood or our behaviour. Often we experience this desire on a subconscious level first. For example, the next time you are sitting in a room with other people and one person pulls out a package of cigarettes you will likely see several other people light up as well. Although they may not be thinking about smoking, the visual stimulus is enough to "trigger" a subconscious impulse. The same thing happens when we are "triggered" by other things that we experience or witness. Anger can create a fight or flight response in us. Injustice can trigger a feeling of resentment. Watching someone hang glide can help us feel excitement. Smelling fresh bread triggers a desire for food. There are many, many more. So what are urges? Where do they come from? How do we deal with them?

What are urges?

Urges in and of themselves are not bad things. How we choose to respond to them is the question we need to consider. There are good urges, those that trigger hunger signalling it is time to eat or restlessness which may signal it is time to exercise or become more active. There are urges that may trigger feelings that, if acted upon, may be destructive or damaging to us or our significant others.

There are many theories about how we choose to respond to something we are experiencing. Urges are biochemical responses to a stimulus, whether it is something that we have seen, smelled, touched, tasted, heard, thought or felt. It could be the result of being in a certain place or by seeing someone we know or someone we think we know. It could be generated by a particular object. Urges could come from the feelings associated with being used or taken advantage of in some way. It may be the impulse we feel to meet our needs. The possibilities and combinations are as numerous as the people who experience them.

The stimulus or stimuli affect particular chemical processes in various parts of our brain or nervous system thereby creating a sensation or "urge" to respond to it.

We are likely to respond to the stimulus, and the urge that follows, in a manner that has worked for us in the past (more on that later). An example of this is hunger. When we are hungry, we eat. We eat for nutritional gains but we also eat because it feels good when the hunger goes away. If we could take a pill and satisfy our nutritional needs we would still eat to satisfy the conscious feeling of being hungry.

Where do urges come from?

Urges can come from past learning experiences. Most of us learned, early in our lives, to deal with particular issues in particular ways. When we felt anger, for instance, and acted upon that feeling by breaking something or by hitting something or someone, we may have felt better afterward. We responded in a way, perhaps the only way we knew, that would provide some relief from what was troubling us or what we were experiencing. We all struggle and strive to find ways that seem to serve our needs in the best way possible. These coping skills may not always work out to be in our best interest but they provide some relief, if only temporary, from whatever it is that concerns us. What has worked before will likely work again. If we chose a method or response that provided us with some satisfaction or relief, we are likely to respond in a similar fashion again. We will try to achieve the results of past experiences or situations by duplicating how we responded to them initially. We expect that similar outcomes will follow. However, the method we choose may not always be in our own best interest.

Recently, a client told me that, during a visit to his physician's office, he was told to cut down on the amount of high cholesterol food he was ingesting. The doctor explained that the arteries to his heart were not in the best shape and he was concerned about his overeating. The physician prescribed a new diet and suggested another appointment for the following month. Home he went, feeling down, nervous and lonely. Then a friend called to say that a mutual friend was having a dinner party and he was welcome to attend. Without hesitation he agreed to attend, knowing that there would be many others there that he could talk to or laugh with, thereby dealing with his loneliness.

However, it's a dinner party and he had just been told to knock off high cholesterol food. This client loves to eat and had no idea how he could attend the party yet not indulge in all the rich foods that were sure to be offered. For my client, the benefits of not being lonely outweighed the danger to his health. He acted on the urge to not be lonely without considering the down side of overeating.

I have heard numerous excuses outlining the reasons clients do what they do. If there is one thing that we are good at it's rationalizing our behaviours: "What's the difference if I do it just one more time" or "At this point whether I start today or tomorrow won't really matter" and on and on. The point, though, is that it does matter. If we don't start to respond differently today opportunities to continue growing and changing can't happen tomorrow. In other words, we stay stuck doing what we always did.

How do we satisfy the urges we experience?

The frequency, duration and intensity of urges can be affected by diet, the amount of exercise we get (review the section on stress, page 46), the pace of our life or our other commitments, our thoughts and beliefs concerning our past successes when dealing with particular situations or circumstances, and boredom.

Unchallenged minds become playgrounds for fools.

We deal with our urges in many different ways. In our everyday lives some have to have a cup of coffee in the morning to get their day started. Proper exercise and diet would do the same thing but which is easier: caffeine or the more involved regimen of diet and exercise? Once again when dealing with urges to respond, we will usually go back to what has worked in the past. The expectation is matched with the outcome--at least in the beginning. How do we deal with being embarrassed? Usually we want to find a way to embarrass the other person as well. No one likes to be laughed at. The urge is to get even. How do we react to an act of violence? Our first impulse could well be retaliation in kind. How might we deal with rejection by a spouse? Some of us may go out and find somebody who would see us as attractive or appealing. The urge may be to rebuild our self-esteem or repair our damaged ego by getting involved with someone else as quickly as possible.

If we are lonely, sad or depressed we may begin to overeat or to use sexual conquests as a remedy for our negative emotional states.

One of our most powerful emotions is anger. If we are afraid of being angry we may use alcohol or drugs to excess in order to make the anger go away. Boredom is another issue in many people's lives and we each deal with it differently. Some may gamble and others may get involved in a high-risk activity of some kind. We learn that by smoking cannabis we can relax, or by engaging in bulimic behaviour we can control what goes in and out of our bodies, thereby providing an element of control that may not otherwise be experienced. Some say there is a "rush" during the act of purging that satisfies them. **Our attempts and subsequent successes at meeting our needs become our learned coping mechanisms.**

When we recognize that what we are doing may not be in our best interest we open ourselves to the possibility of learning to meet our needs in ways that will provide us with a more positive, esteem-building approach. It is all up to us. It always has been. Change happens the moment we make the internal decision to do so: that is self-management.

When we continue to respond to things in ways that are not in our best interest we continue to fertilize negative emotional growth. We perpetuate the killer of our positive self-image and our spiritual health. It is difficult to feel good about ourselves when we continue to make the same mistakes.

> **The difference between perseverance and obstinacy is that one comes from a strong will and the other comes from a strong won't.**
> **--Henry Ward Beecher.**

Unfortunately, many people get stuck at this point. They understand they need to make some changes, and they are willing to look at doing things differently, but they don't know **how** to change or where to look for that information. They are not sure what to do now.

If we can learn it we can unlearn it

Anytime we risk self-evaluation and decide that we are not working in our best interests we move closer to taking a psychological leap of faith. That is, we understand that we have to change some of what we do and how we do it. We may be willing to look at some of our current coping strategies with the idea of changing them but we may be unsure of what to do next. It means that we may have to give up doing things the old way not knowing any new ways. For many that is a scary proposition, one that stops them from going any further in the process. We feel it is better to remain in control of our situations (even though our methods may not be as successful as we would like) than to be uncertain and take a risk of looking or sounding foolish or unrespected. We're stuck in a "mental limbo" because we don't want to risk our sense of security.

Many of us feel like a fish out of water when we consider trying to do things differently especially if we have managed ourselves, responded to our urges, in a particular way most of our lives. Accepting the way we currently manage our urges to respond because we know of no other ways is, however, not particularly useful. It suggests that we are willing to accept old habits as being the best we can do and that we have to live with them.

For example: If we are feeling a sense of injustice and usually respond by a show of force or by lashing out verbally we may want to continue using this method of dealing with our feelings because we know that we can get people's attention. We believe that we satisfy our need to be heard. People may pay attention to our outbursts but that doesn't mean that they hear us. How do we say what we need to say and feel that we have been heard? If we are going to put our energy into accepting our old ways, wouldn't it be better to put that same energy into developing new methods of dealing with the urges, developing new belief systems, and using new techniques or strategies so that we can get more of what we need? That way we are not hanging on to old behaviours. How do we <u>not</u> fight back verbally or physically when we are challenged or confronted? How can we work through anger, loneliness, rejection, sadness or resentment? How can we salve our egos and our self-esteem **within** our relationships instead of looking for the answers outside them?

Three things have to happen to begin the process of unlearning the old coping strategies and learning the new:

1. Recognize that what we are doing may not be getting us closer to our **REAL** goal(s) and thus make a decision to look at other approaches to dealing with our roadblocks to happiness. Do we decide to deal with the loneliness we feel in our guts or do we put two more cream-filled donuts in there instead?

2. Understand that we can not process and experience two emotions at once. We can't experience happiness and sadness simultaneously. We need to challenge and clear out some old beliefs **before** we can put any new ones in their place. If we want to experience more inner peace, we must recognize that our loneliness, for instance, may stand in the way. If we are sitting at home feeling lonely and sorry for ourselves we will have to get up off the couch and get outside.

Join a club. Do whatever it takes to put ourselves around other people. It's not a cure but it's a start.

3. Remember that this is not a race. Progress is the goal, not a quick fix. As we remain open to new information, attempt new methods, and evaluate their effectiveness we begin to develop new coping mechanisms that are more in tune with our best interests. We can then decide to give up our old methods that actually work against us.

When we are able to undertake a genuine exploration of our motives and then become willing to accept the idea that other approaches or solutions **may** be better, we begin to shift our thinking. This shift in thinking allows us to reframe our experiences (the outcomes of our activities), our responses, and, as a result, develop new ways of seeing our issues.

For example: It is just as easy to envision the glass being half full as half empty. It depends on how we choose to see it. If you're a pessimist you'll likely see it half empty. If you're an optimist you'll likely see it as half full. It's our choice as to how we see it. Although this is a simple concept we gain a great deal of internal power for ourselves when we adopt this new attitude. In another case, if we practice honesty we learn we don't have to protect a lie. Honesty is less stressful, it takes less emotional energy because we don't have to remember who we lied to and what we said, and it develops trust.

When we begin thinking about the **POSITIVES** of **not** engaging in a destructive activity or an impulsive response as opposed to reverting to the old way of doing things we take a giant step toward building a more positive sense of who we are as a person.

I believe the ultimate goal of most people is to feel that we have worth as a human being and that we are and can be valued as a person. When we begin thinking and acting in ways that promote that sense within us we will begin to "fly with the eagles." We cannot soar when we engage in activities that hurt us and damage our spirits.

We will not be successful at everything we try. However, this process of changing our thinking--what is known as a paradigm shift--begins by recognizing that changes need to be made and by putting forth the effort to make them. It takes courage and persistence. **If we continue to try, we will succeed.**

Successful people don't quit, they regroup.

People are recognized more for the number of times they "get up off the canvas" than by what they have or possess. So what if we don't always succeed and what someone else does to work through their issues may or may not work for us. But we need to continue to try, to find **our** own way.

Our successes are often dictated by the circumstances in which we find ourselves. It is more important that we develop a way of thinking that will help us work through ALL our struggles, regardless of what they are, **a way of thinking and doing that helps us approach our concerns from a position which allows for the greatest control over the outcomes**. An example of this approach might be to "never make an emotional decision while in an emotional state of mind."

How do we get to where we want to be?

Urges to respond to how we feel about something are often uncomfortable so we try to drive them away as quickly as we can in any way that we can.

> For example: Sadness is a major issue for most people. We don't like to be sad. Couple that with loneliness. How do we respond?
>
> Some would light up a "joint" (cannabis) so that they can become pre-occupied with another feeling that doesn't translate into sadness. They listen to some music and get lost in the rhythms or the lyrics. Smoke enough and they marvel at how much a shadow on the wall looks like a wild animal or a mountain scene. We can choose to medicate ourselves so we can deal with the sadness and loneliness. Or we could get up off our backsides and join a team or a club of some kind, take in a movie or go dancing with a friend

thereby enjoying the benefit of interacting with other people. One takes more effort than the other.

If we're shy, we might have a couple of extra "shots" just to get into the mood before we go to a party or so that we can dance better or be more open and talkative. Most of us can relate to the nervous feeling we get when we first arrive somewhere where there are people we don't know. Drink enough and you really don't have to worry about who is watching you--you won't care. Or we could choose to take some dancing lessons with our partner so when we go to the party we will have a great deal more confidence in front of others.

We could take some public speaking courses to overcome our shyness or nervousness. It's also something that we can do with our partners.

Using alcohol to excess usually becomes a very solitary activity regardless of whether you are with friends, your partner, or by yourself. After enough alcohol is consumed your senses and your awareness of others and their needs becomes clouded. You become more centered on yourself which excludes others. If sadness or loneliness or boredom are issues that you are experiencing the excessive use of alcohol or any other mind altering substance or activity will only distance yourself from the very thing that you want. It works against your best interests.

We can either do something that will make the uncomfortable feeling go away or we can do something that will create a more positive feeling about who we are so that the urge doesn't materialize. The choice is always ours. We can stay lost or we can ask for directions for how to do things differently. We can begin to look for alternatives and we can explore new ways of seeing things.

If I were to stand in the middle of a circle of people and hold up a globe what would each person see? The people behind me would see one side of the world and the people in front of me would see the other side of the world. The people on either side of me would see different areas as well. They would all be looking at the same globe but because of their perspective they would see different places on the sphere. The same analogy holds true when we are looking at any situation or problem we face. There is always more than one way of looking at something. When we are able to understand this concept we become more open minded. Besides, we can always slide back to doing things the way we used to if we aren't comfortable with the new methods we investigate.

The ways and means

It is difficult to develop our potential as human beings until we are able to see ourselves as competent at something, to have a sense of self-worth or self-esteem. The first part of our journey, therefore, had to do with recognizing our strengths and assets. We are far more capable and competent than we realize. Our perception of ourselves is the single most important tool that we possess. It is ours and no one can take it from us. No one can develop it for us either. We can, however, give it away, and often do, when we allow other people to make our decisions or determine what is good for **us**.

Self-belief is the key

Once we see we possess strengths and resources that we can call upon, we begin to feel we can deal with those roadblocks that stand in the way of our happiness without the use of coping behaviours that may create outcomes which are not in our best interests.

With most of our urges, the important part of dealing with them will be to resist the impulse for an immediate response. We can ask ourselves, "What is the worst thing that could happen to me if I don't respond to the urges I am feeling right now?" We begin to recognize we do not have to act on the urge we experience in order for it to go away--that we can and will survive it.

We begin to see ourselves as increasingly successful in responding to our impulses--our urges. We begin to BELIEVE that we can be successful. "I can and I will" are statements to use instead of "I will try" or "I think I can." The use of positive affirmations and positive self-talk help us to develop self-belief. I know it sounds corny, but it works. As our belief in ourselves develops and we experience some successes we become ready to consider new and alternate ways of dealing with what comes our way. We feel more confident and competent. We develop an upward growth spiral. Success builds upon success.

We cannot control events that happen around us but we can control how we respond to them.

A cognitive-behavioural approach

Using a cognitive-behavioural approach to help people work toward their self-declared goals makes more sense to me than using any of the other approaches available. It supports the premise that what is learned can be unlearned. This is not to say that other methods don't work or aren't helpful. In the end the person who presents the issue to be worked through will find his or her own way of resolving it anyway. My job as a clinician is to help clear away some of the "chaff" so that the people who have sought my assistance will have a clearer picture of what it is they need to deal with and how they might attempt to do that.

Our cognitions are formed by our perceptions, our beliefs because of what we hear or see and our beliefs based on what we think or know to be true. They are influenced by our past experiences. If, for instance, we have learned to deal with negative feelings by overeating, being sexually indiscriminate or drinking excessively, and those methods worked to make those negative feelings go away it is likely that we will continue the same practices. We will continue to use those same methods until we decide that the activity is not in our best interests, and/or we learn a more effective technique to make them go away.

There are two parts to this approach. The **cognitive** part deals with how we think and how our thoughts affect our perceptions about ourselves and what goes on around us. It is the basis of our individual belief systems--how we live our lives, what we value, and why. It is the basis upon which our decisions are made. It influences what we do. The **behavioural** part deals with how we implement our decisions--how we go about getting our needs met based on what we consider to be valuable and important to us. It is also connected to our belief system. How we think and what we do are the engines that drive our feelings.

To make changes, to improve our techniques, or to expand our knowledge base, we must recognize these two requirements:

1. Know what to do:
    a. Work to build the skills we need to deal with our issues or roadblocks. If we don't have or believe we have the particular skill we need to deal with the issue we can learn it. It won't help us right now but it will the next time. If we have difficulty dealing with stress, for instance, we might take a course on meditation or progressive muscle relaxation. Let's look at utilizing the personal strengths we possess so we can learn or develop new methods of coping more effectively.

    b. We must be able to use our experiences in conjunction with our thoughts. This is the basis for learning. When we recognize that screaming intimidates people instead of gaining their cooperation and their trust we can stop yelling and start asking what other approach might work? Has there been a time when we were successful at gaining cooperation in the past? What did we do differently? Could we do that again? We should evaluate the outcomes of our experiences and determine what works and what doesn't, and then do more of what worked and less of what didn't.

2. Be motivated to do it:

    Nothing succeeds like success. When we employ new strategies and experience some success (that is, we are reasonably pleased with the outcome of our effort), we are likely to try the same method again. The catch is we have to be prepared to risk a negative outcome first. There has to be some prior motivation for us to attempt a change in how we would normally respond to the impulses or urges we feel. Those could come from our families or friends. They could come from the judicial system or they could come from within us when we reach a point where we say, "I'm not getting what I want or need by doing this. There has to be another way." Our efforts may not be successful, but we need to be willing to try another way. If we're not, it will be very difficult to make any positive changes in how we respond to the urges that drive our actions or behaviours. **We satisfy the urge by creating a positive outcome. This satisfaction is called positive reinforcement.**

In the past, if we used alcohol to try to calm down or control our anger, we could throw $5 or $10 in a jar every time we were able to delay the impulse to respond instead, or talk to a friend, go to a movie, or go work out at the gym. Experiment. The goal is to try different ways of working through the anger without using alcohol and to do whatever it takes to delay the impulse to respond to the anger. At the end of the month the money we have put aside can be used to buy something that we always wanted--some new CD's or a new CD player. Can you remember a time that you were able to think or work your way through a situation that angered you? What did you do? How did you do it? There are many different techniques that you could use. List some others on a piece of paper. Keep a list of them close by so that you can refer to them with little effort. Rewarding ourselves is the positive reinforcement--the benefit of doing "it" differently.

Change needs an impetus, a reason why we choose to alter or change the way we do our business. Fear is a poor motivator for change. Its effects only last for a short period of time. When people are threatened with failing health, for instance, they only stop overeating or abusing substances briefly before engaging in the activity again.

To help us change our thinking, we can:

a. Understand that we do not have to act on the urges--that we can and will work through them. We will not go crazy because of them. What's the worst thing that will happen to us if we don't act on the urges we feel?

b. Understand that we are not responsible for the urges as they present themselves but we are responsible for dealing with them in an appropriate manner. We also need to know that even though we wish the urges would not return, they will come again. This does not indicate that we are weak or that we are doing something wrong.

c. Consider the benefits of not acting on the urge we are experiencing. Often we think only about the positives of satisfying the urge and we don't think through the whole activity to its conclusion. We may act, for example, on the urge to use alcohol to cope with a nervous feeling but we must recognize how that will affect our ability to drive safely or to enjoy an evening with friends or family. Does acting on the urge outweigh the benefits of joining with family and friends?

d. Engage in a some distracting activity if the urge is really intense, such as counting by threes to 500 or counting backwards by fours from 1000, anything that demands some concentration in another area. We cannot process two emotions or thoughts at one time. If we are thinking about numbers we are not thinking about urges. We have to concentrate on the other function, the number function, for this to work.

e. Use a "coping card," a laminated card about the size of a credit card that has the positives for working through the urge written on one side and perhaps some phone numbers of supportive people or organizations on the other. We could put a picture of our children or our girlfriend or boyfriend, husband or wife, parents, anybody or anything that will help us to stop and think about the losses we will incur if we engage in an activity that supports the urge.

f. Write in a journal describing in detail what we are experiencing and how we plan to work through the situation. Then write about how it feels to have successfully worked through the urge. This creates a history of our successes that we can refer to the next time we find ourselves in a similar situation. We read the journal entry and we know that we can be successful again. As the number of our successes increases so does our confidence and our self-esteem. We continue to develop the positive sense of self that is vital to our spiritual growth. It's part of our journey.

g. Think about the different things we can do ahead of time to work through potential high-risk situations. It could be a family reunion. It could be a backyard barbeque or a friend's wedding reception. It may be an interview with the boss or a confrontation with a neighbour. It may be having to spend time around someone that we don't care for, making a presentation during a board meeting at work, or discussing a problem that continues to come up with our children or spouse. Plan ahead so that if/when the time occurs we will be ready with a plan of action. No surprises.

h. Evaluate the outcomes of our efforts and think about how we could be more successful or do things differently the next time. What else could we do?

i. Recognize that putting ourselves in situations that have been difficult for us in the past just to "test" ourselves is not a responsible way of learning to deal with our urges. Putting ourselves in lower-risk situations with a plan in mind and then evaluating how we did is preferable. The key is to have a plan. Success comes from continued effort. **Thinking--evaluating--thinking again--doing.**

We don't plan to fail, we fail to plan.

To change our behaviour, we can:

a. Develop a strong support network of people to call on when we need to. This is probably one of the most important things we can do.

b. Share our feelings, thoughts and emotions with others whom we trust. Being able to talk about what is going on around us with a good friend is the next most important thing that we can do. We don't ask for answers; we just ask them to listen. We are capable of coming up with our own answers. It is very important to take what is building inside us and put it outside us so to gain a different perspective on it.

c. Keep a daily journal. The act of writing things down helps us put our thoughts and feelings out in front of us. It becomes easier to recognize them for what they are and for what they mean to us. It also makes room for new thoughts inside. If we are really able to let go we will feel our hand glide, almost unaided, across the paper. Something magical happens when we are able to do this. It's as if we drain ourselves out through the pen in our hand. Think about a time when you missed a good friend so you sent him or her a letter. How good did you feel after you did that? It is the same when we write to ourselves about ourselves.

d. Practice the plans we have created for any potential high-risk situations in circumstances that may be of less risk to our emotional and mental safety. The key here is to put ourselves in situations that we have control over so that we can gain confidence in our ability to deal with the subsequent urge(s) that may present themselves. As with all things, though, this is a process. It takes time to develop the skills and techniques so that they become an automatic response.

   We will be more successful if we expect steady but not immediate results in our efforts at self-management. We may need to practice with a friend or part of a support network so that our efforts and successes can be assessed immediately. This immediate feedback is important because it represents the opposite of the immediate gratification that we seek when we succumb to our urges. This provides us with beneficial reinforcement. It feels good to ride the wave of success.

e. Pay attention to how we respond to particular situations: during which times? in what places? who was there? Engage in the regular practice of learning and monitoring how our emotions dictate our responses. We seldom enjoy the emotional decisions that we make while we are in emotional states. Recognize what it feels like to sense the onset of anger, frustration, loneliness, sadness, hunger, etc. **BEFORE** the urges to respond to them develop. The sooner we intervene in the development of our urges the easier it will be to deal with them, if they continue to develop at all. A journal can be useful now. When we sense sadness or loneliness, for instance, we can write down what we are thinking about at the time, what we are doing, and what we feel we are experiencing.

We become familiar with the symptoms so we can take steps to deal with them as soon as we recognize them for what they are. We may also see that particular times of the day or specific people provoke to our urges. This can be powerful information.

f. Act as if we are not bothered by the loneliness or resentment we are experiencing. We can ask ourselves how we would like to be seen instead of looking lonely or angry. How would we like to be feeling instead? What would we be doing if we were not bothered by these urges? It is important that we continue to share what is going on inside us. This effort does not encourage a non-acceptance of the urge but rather helps us experience what we will feel like when it doesn't bother us anymore. It also helps those around us recognize what we will be like when we are not bothered by negative emotions or struggling with urges of some kind. We will receive valuable feedback from those we trust.

We spend too much time concerned about the things we can't do and not enough time doing the things we can.

When we are working through urges, here are some questions to ask ourselves:

1. What am I feeling right now? Identify the feeling by name.

2. What does this feeling usually mean to me?

3. What am I thinking about when I am feeling like this? What is going through my head?

4. Why do I believe that acting immediately on this urge is the only way to deal with it?

5. How do I explain this fact (from #4)?

6. What are the advantages and disadvantages of pursuing my immediate course of action--what I am thinking of doing?

7. What is the goal I am seeking by doing what I am doing? Am I doing what I want to do or what I need to do? Am I acting in my best interests?

8. Did what I thought would happen actually happen the last time I responded this way or was the outcome different from what I thought it would be? (This is an important questions to ask.)

Our responses to these questions provide clues to new techniques. If we expected we would feel better by pursuing a particular activity or by responding in a certain way but didn't, we may want to consider another approach. If we feel temporarily satisfied but now feel guilty, what have we gained? Why engage in an activity or behaviour if we aren't getting what we need or want from the effort, especially if it isn't moving us closer to what we really want? Learning is about asking questions and seeking answers: "What do I learn from the questions asked and what will I do with the information I gain?"

Life is not a problem to solve. It is a daily experience that presents us with an opportunity to develop as human beings. It provides us with a chance to connect our emotional, mental, physical, and spiritual parts. When one of our parts indicates that it is not functioning as well as it could we can either look at the situation as a problem or we can see it as an opportunity to change and to grow. How we see it is our choice based upon what we want and what we are willing to do to get it--not on old excuses.

It is important to understand that we do not have to act on the urges we experience; that we don't have to continue to do the things we have always done just because we know no other way; that, in and of themselves, urges are uncomfortable and stressful and harmless. We could wait them out and survive quite nicely. They will come and they will go. We can learn to make them go more quickly.

It is true that the more committed we are to the coping strategies we developed to help us deal with our feelings, emotions, or high-risk situations, the more difficult it will be to let them go. If we have experienced success on some level, why give them up? The question you need to ask yourself is this: "What does success mean to me?"

If we recognize that the strategies we use lead to positive outcomes there will be no need to give them up. But if we evaluate the outcomes of our efforts and find that we are not pleased we need to ask ourselves, "Did we do what we wanted to do, according to past experiences or did we do what we **needed** to do?" Did the outcomes benefit us in a positive way? If not then we will need to learn new strategies no matter the level of commitment. If what we are doing is not acting in our best interests we need to begin doing something else. This is especially true of the coping strategies we developed when we were young for they are the road map for how we continue to get our needs met.

The more successful we are in working through our urges to respond, the more confident we become that we can deal with a wider range of situations, and the more often we will use what has provided us with positive outcomes. We become more confident and we feel more competent. Our self-esteem increases. The key question is this: **"Am I acting in my own best interests?"**

Draw a horizontal line and mark on it a scale of 1-10. On the left end mark a one which represents "needs work." On the right end mark a ten which represents "as good as it could be." Consider the question, "How effective are my coping strategies when managing my urges?" Where on the scale do you need to be in order to feel good about your ability to manage the urges effectively? Place a mark on the scale and write the date as well. Where on this scale do you see yourself at this time? Place a mark and write the date. What do you have to do or what can you do to move 1 notch closer to your goal? What skills can you develop to make that happen? Revisit the scale in a month's time to check your progress. If you haven't moved your mark consider some other strategies. If you have--great. Keep doing what you are doing and continue to consider new ideas. Look for other situations where you could use your new strategies.

It is easier to stay lost than ask for directions

1___2___3___4___5___6___7___8___9___10___

Here are some other questions to consider: (Write the answers in your journal or in the back of this book)

1. Can you recall a time when you didn't act impulsively on an urge to respond to a feeling or an emotion? What did you do? How did you do that? Could you do that again?

2. What will you be doing differently when you are able to successfully work through your urges?

3. How will your life be different when you do not act on the urges you experience?

4. What will other people recognize about you when you are able to deal successfully with the urges you experience?

5. What is different about the times when you don't experience any urges? What were you doing? Who were you with? Where were you?

6. When you are able to develop the coping strategies you need how will that impact on your life? How will that affect the quality of your life?

7. How will you know when you have dealt successfully with your urges?

When all we think about is the cost of our experiences we're not understanding the wisdom that we have purchased.

Our ultimate goal should be to manage our responses and not try to manage the event. Once we are able to work our way through the initial urge to respond, the number of opportunities to make decisions we consider to be in our own best interest increases dramatically.

We do not have to act on the urge to respond. We can learn to work our way through it. We can use our past experiences as learning tools. What did we do? How did that turn out? How could we do it differently? Our self-esteem and our belief in ourselves will grow stronger as we continue to make appropriate and successful decisions that reflect what we consider to be our own best interests. The key to our inner peace is directly related to the confidence we feel in our ability to manage ourselves and the issues we face.

When we can problem solve, reduce our stress levels, communicate our needs more clearly and effectively to others, and learn how to think before we act, we will continue to fill our spiritual "life-wells."

Don't be afraid to fail

You've failed many times, although you may not remember. You fell down the first time you tried to walk.
You almost drowned the first time you tried to swim, didn't you?
Did you hit the ball the first time you swung a bat?
Heavy hitters, the ones who hit the most home runs, also strike out a lot.
R.H. Macy failed seven times before his store in New York caught on.
English novelist John Creasey got 753 rejection slips before he published 564 books.
Babe Ruth stuck out 1,330 times, but also hit 714 home runs.
Don't worry about failure.
Worry about the chances you missed when you don't *even try*.

Published in *The Wall Street Journal*, United Technologies Corporation

This chapter is called "It is easier to stay lost than ask for directions." It is often easier to continue doing what we always have done than to ask for help in seeking new ways to deal with our roadblocks to happiness and peace. Sometimes we just get tired and give up. Sometimes the task seems impossible. We have to be ready and willing to find other ways of responding to our feelings and our emotions if what we are doing now hurts us in some way. Easier ways are not always better ways. One thing is for sure. If we don't continue to try we will never get to where we want to be.

6.

REFUSING TO LOOK AT THE MAP

THE OUTCOMES FROM IMMEDIATE DISPLAYS OF ANGER ARE RARELY PRETTY AND SELDOM USEFUL.

Our emotions are not to be seen as good or bad. They are a part of our spiritual being that help us learn about who we are as people. They help us appreciate what is or can be good in our lives. When we feel love or patriotism or passion we are moved to defend our rights and freedoms. When we experience jealousy or envy we can choose to work harder to improve ourselves and make some changes in how we approach our day-to-day living. Negative emotions can motivate us in positive ways. If we are disgusted by injustice we can work to develop new laws that are more equitable or fair.

When we don't allow ourselves the opportunity to experience our emotions we deny ourselves the chance to grow from the insights they can provide. We stifle our burgeoning sense of self. Without having experienced jealousy we would not know security. Without having felt sadness we would not know joy. The knowledge we gain about ourselves from our feelings and emotions is at the heart of our evolutionary journey.

Anger, friend or foe?

Anger is, in my mind, the most powerful and potentially destructive of all of our emotions. The results of our demonstrations of anger can destroy a lifetime in an instant. We can be so blinded by our anger that we can lose complete control of our actions. Have you ever heard the phrase "white rage?" It means that it is possible for us to go from mild upset to searing destructive rage in a heartbeat and back again and not be aware of what happened to us. Call it a white-out if you like. We can use anger like a rapier to slash at people verbally. Verbal and emotional abuse can be just as damaging (many would argue more damaging) as any physical abuse. Anger can also be the most powerful and potentially beneficial and useful of all our emotions. It really does depend on what we do with it--how we respond to the situation that stirs anger within us. We must realize that we can and do have the choice as to how we will respond. Our response depends upon our ability to manage ourselves and not let our emotions manage us.

What anger is

Anger has been defined in so many ways and means many different things to different people. It is difficult to put a universal definition to it but some understanding of what it is needs to be put forth here:

> "Anger is a physical state of being that indicates we are ready to put all of our physical resources--our power--into an action or response that we believe warrants our attention."

When we consider what anger is, however, we need to understand that there is a vast difference between what we are physically (or psychologically) experiencing in our state of anger and how we choose to express the anger. Anger and its expression are not the same thing. As well, many people mistakenly identify aggression as anger. They are not the same thing either. It is certainly possible for someone to be aggressive without being angry. Aggression is more about attitude and learned behaviour than it is about physical arousal.

Is anger a bad thing? No, it is not. Do we need to get angry sometimes? Yes, we do. Is it OK to get angry? It sure is. Anger helps to mobilize us--to spur us on to bettering ourselves--and to protect ourselves or others who, for whatever reasons, may not be able to look after themselves. **Anger is not the issue. Our expression of it is. Learn to use it as a strength.**

Anger is as natural a response as breathing or blinking. It is not something to fear. It helps us to know when something is wrong and that we need to be prepared to deal with whatever it is.

If we trust that our angry responses or feelings are simply indicators of other issues, and not an opportunity to lash out, our feelings of anger can help us identify what the underlying issues are when we consider the source of our anger. If we are angry because we were over-looked again for a promotion at work, anger can prompt us to look at whether or not we are really qualified for the position. We may decide to take a night course on labour relations or management styles so that when a promotion opportunity comes up again we will be considered more seriously. Getting angry and feeling that someone doesn't like us or is prejudiced against us will only defeat our purpose. We will deprive ourselves of any chance of advancement.

There are other benefits of anger

Feeling angry toward someone or something can motivate us to assert our wants and needs. It can help us clarify how someone's behaviour affects us when that person may not be aware of it. Anger can be a positive force in our development of self-esteem. It can help us establish boundaries for what is acceptable and what is not. Expressing anger appropriately can be of enormous benefit to our health. Instead of spending an inordinate amount of energy trying to suppress our anger--causing us to be stressed, fatigued, miserable, edgy, nervous, irritable or confused--we can learn to express it and let it go. When expressed appropriately it can actually help to solidify our relationships instead of destroying them. Those around us will know that they have nothing to fear from us when we use self-management skills and don't let our anger manage us. They can trust that we will not hurt them somehow when we are angry.

What it isn't

Anger is not an opportunity to blame other people for how we feel or for what has happened to us. If we abdicate our responsibility to look after ourselves or to make our own decisions, we must accept the outcomes of that choice. We have to be careful we don't use our anger as a chance to "mask" our disapproval or disregard for someone else by being sarcastic or rude (passive-aggressive behaviour). We can always deny that a particular comment was meant as a put-down if we are called on it or we can let the slight stand if we are not. So we aren't really at risk ourselves when we do this. It's sort of fighting from the tall grass, at night, with night vision goggles on. There is no risk for us, but this behaviour is not fair for them. It is not an excuse to hurt other living things, human or otherwise. When we haven't learned how to use our anger to our advantage it can grow inside us until we become blinded by the sheer volatility we experience. The result is that we often hurt other people. It is not an emotion for us to use to take advantage of others who may not be as strong as we are. We must not use it for revenge against other people or attack their vulnerabilities. Punishing others and "teaching them to never do that again" is not a useful way to spend our time. It keeps us from growing. It keeps us stuck in a negative state of mind. Our anger is not for manipulating or controlling other people so that we can get what we want. Using our anger to vent our negative feelings on other people is not only unhealthy but can be dangerous for all concerned. Very often those people are the ones closest to us and the ones we love the most.

If anger is the warning that something is wrong, then its purpose is to "right the wrong," not to win.--Author unknown

When is anger bad?

Anger that is expressed inappropriately is like an infection that penetrates our protective skins--our boundaries--and spreads in the bodies and the minds of those exposed to it. Sexual, physical, spiritual, emotional, verbal and mental abuse all penetrate the skin of our friends and neighbours, our children and our partners. We violate the trust they bestow upon us when we yell at them and call them names; when we intimidate them either verbally or physically; when we label them as stupid or useless; when we don't listen to them when they are hurting and don't validate their feelings, their thoughts and their dreams. We become unsafe to be around. We begin to crack their "protective shell," which is the skin of their humanity and of who they are. It disconnects us from all the good that is there to help us. It prevents us from getting close or staying close to others. It prevents others from wanting to get too close to us. Anger is often about our past, our fears, or injustice.

Where does anger come from?

Perhaps bad anger originates from how we were treated or mistreated as children--how we were parented. Maybe it is about the breaks that we didn't get and felt we should have had. It can come from a thousand different places. But if we don't say good-bye to what is behind us we can never move forward. We stay stuck. I'm not suggesting for a moment that we need to forget what happened but we need to acknowledge that it happened--past tense--and decide not to allow the past any more power over our present and our future. If we are going to get angry let's get angry about how we have let our resentments steal time from us. Let's use our anger as a positive motivator so that we give no more power to the past. As we hold on to old resentments and anger we give them continued control over us and instead of hoping they will eventually fade away they continue to be strong. We continue to be victimized. We continue to fuel the fires.

When we examine anger more closely we can see that it is often a response to some other emotion previously experienced. Think of a time when you were embarrassed in front of your friends. What did you feel? Maybe you got cheated at the garage and realized that the mechanic had just overbilled you. How did you feel? Something usually happens to us first; then we get angry. Anger can be a sign that we have not dealt with an issue which presented itself earlier.

How often have we gotten mad at an inanimate object like a hammer that "wouldn't hammer properly" and we ended up throwing it across the room? What about the zipper that wouldn't zip so we ended up ripping it apart "just to show it who was the boss?" Where is the logic in being angry at someone or something for being what it is? Yet we do it all the time.

I see us as being giant glass jars with an open top. Every time something upsetting happens to us and we don't deal with it, a marble gets thrown into our jar. Over a period of time our jar begins to fill up. It fills up because we have been told that we should not let people see us angry. "Don't let them see that they got to you" is a common refrain. And the jar fills up. Perhaps we were never encouraged or taught to express our anger appropriately. Now we may find ourselves with few or no skills to deal with what displeases us. And the jar fills up a little more. Or maybe we were discouraged from showing our anger openly because it was seen as defiance, so we learned to pack it away inside us hoping that it would just go away. Perhaps we were punished for daring to disagree. We were told it was not polite to argue or to show any outward signs of being upset. And the jar fills up even more. Maybe we are afraid of becoming angry because when we do we get out of control and that scares us.

This is one of the reasons why people self-medicate. They fear becoming angry so they have a few drinks to calm down. And now the jar is full. It won't hold another marble. The next thing that irritates us is likely to make us explode because there is no more room for any more marbles. The marbles begin to spill out on the floor. We erupt like a volcano at the most inappropriate times over the smallest of reasons. The cat meows too loudly so it gets a kick. The paperboy misses the front porch so we chase him down the street to teach him a lesson so that he doesn't dare miss again. Maybe the baby cries too long and gets beaten to make him be quiet. We lash out because we don't have the skills to deal with our anger, we have not identified the source of our anger, and we have not learned how to deal with our emotions appropriately.

Anger is often about injustice. It's about us not getting our due. It's about something that happens that should not have happened. It may not even be about us directly. It could be about a friend who is mistreated in some way but we take it on as our own problem. We feel that the world is out to get us, that everywhere we go everything that happens happens directly to us and it probably happens just to keep us down.

I know that I feel a sense of injustice when I read about someone who has murdered a child or a senior citizen just for the pleasure of it, yet there seems to be no adequate response on behalf of the people who feel they are becoming prisoners in their own homes. There is fear in the streets for our safety and the safety of our children and not just at night but in the middle of the day as well. Taxes go up just because we got a raise at work. It seems we will never get ahead. So injustice abounds. If we don't deal with that sense of injustice, it will eat us alive. It festers inside of us until we explode.

Those around us wonder what the hell is going on with us. This is very powerful stuff.

Anger has many disguises

As with stress, the issues around our anger may seem complicated. We may not always recognize anger for what it is, for it may have a different face. We may see hostility and aggression, for example, as being the same as anger. They are not. Hostility is an *attitude* that can certainly contribute to demonstrations of anger and violations of other's rights. Aggression is a *behaviour* that demonstrates anger and usually culminates in the loss of someone else's rights. As they are different from anger they are different from each other.

We need to be able to recognize our anger for what it is so we can deal with it right away. We need to ask, "What situation has promoted what I am feeling?" Once we have identified the source of the anger we can deal with it as soon as we are ready rather than let it develop into full-blown resentment or a bubbling angry rage.

Please use the following list of words as a way of identifying your disguised anger sources. Circle five words that you recognize as being ones that create an angry response in you more quickly than any of the others. List them on a separate piece of paper in five distinct columns. Go back over the original list of words and write down, under each of the five columns, any words that you can associate with the key word at the top of that column.

As an example, at the top of one of the columns I might put the key word Sad. Under sad I might list the following words: fearful, cheated, isolated, helpless, rejected, scared, grief-stricken, etc.

THE 'MASKS' OF ANGER

abandoned	blamed	cheated	crushed
ambivalent	bored	condemned	cynical
anxious	burdened	confused	deflated
betrayed	challenged	conspicuous	despairing

diminished	discontented	distracted	distraught
dominated	empty	envious	exhausted
fearful	flustered	foolish	frantic
frustrated	frightened	grief-stricken	guilty
helpless	hurt	sarcastic	ignored
imposed upon	inadequate	intimidated	isolated
jealous	left out	miserable	nervous
overwhelmed	persecuted	pressured	put down
rejected	sad	scared	tense
threatened	misunderstood	bugged	depressed
annoyed	irritated	bothered	agitated
pissed-off	enraged	furious	maligned

If you can think of other words that are not on this list, please add them and carry on.

Once you have made your lists in each column, write down what the opposite of each would be: for example, Dominated---independent or nervous---comfortable. To understand what the opposites are gives us an idea of what we need to work toward--a goal. When we work to be more of something (feeling independent) we automatically move away from something else (feeling dominated).

Own it--it's yours

One of the things that I have witnessed in my work is the ease with which some are able to blame others for their behaviour. I often hear the statements "You make me so mad" and "If you didn't do *this* I wouldn't do *that.*" Somehow making other people responsible for our anger seems to justify what we do. We can do whatever we want because we are not responsible. It's always somebody else's fault. One of the KEY concepts of self-management and the skills involved is to recognize that there is no cause and effect to our response. Undeniably there are and will be events that happen to us that will certainly elicit an aggressive response. But the event and our reaction to it are independent of each other. How we respond is our CHOICE and has more to do with our belief systems than anything else. If you learned early on to punch out anyone who gives you grief because you can't let anybody disrespect you, this will become your response to situations in which you think you are not being respected. Remember: What we learn we can unlearn. We can learn anew and choose to respond differently.

The flip side to this perspective is this: If we are going to make other people responsible for our behaviour and the outcomes that occur from the displays of our anger, by extension we also grant them the responsibility for our happiness. In essence we put them in charge of our emotions. We become powerless to act in our own best interests when we allow others to have that kind of power over us. Let's begin by saying, "I get angry when certain things happen to me" and not, "You make me angry." **We must decide that our anger is ours and ours alone. We are responsible for it when it comes, how long it stays, and under what circumstances it goes. We are responsible for how we choose to respond to it. In this way we take back control of our lives instead of allowing the anger to control us. When we are able to accept this responsibility, we become masters of our anger. We can then use our anger to our advantage--as a strength. This is one of the KEYS to successful self-management.**

We will not have any kind of internal peace until we make this decision. Blaming someone else for our anger doesn't do anything for us. That just keeps us in a reactionary mode always dealing with what has happened instead of what can happen.

> **If we believe that something outside of us is the problem, we will always look outside of ourselves for the answers. If we do this, we become someone else.**

What's the anger about?

If we want to continue on our spiritual journey, anger is the next stop on that journey. It is the emotion that forces us to face ourselves whether we want to or not.

If, for example, we react aggressively to embarrassment, does that indicate a far deeper feeling of insecurity? Our self-esteem takes a direct hit when we are insulted or humiliated, especially in front of our friends or families, and the urge to strike back is powerful for many of us. However, the more confident we feel about ourselves the easier it will be for us to deal with the anger-promoting situations we will encounter. The intensity of the anger we feel will be in inverse proportion to the level of our self-esteem. If we are feeling high self-esteem we will feel less threatened and therefore less angry. If we go back to the first stop on our journey we can now see the importance of working to raise our self-esteem. The work we have done on our journey so far is designed to help us develop a growing confidence in our abilities to deal with our roadblocks to peace, prosperity, and happiness. There is nothing that can hurt us if we bring it out into the open and deal with it appropriately. But left in our inner darkness and hidden away, our anger issues will only grow in strength until they destroy all that we want and all that we see is good.

When we go to that place deep within ourselves and come face to face with the issues that haunt us and when we acknowledge their presence, we have completed the hardest part of this journey. The rest is about learning new skills.

But for many of us this can be a frightful place. It may mean that, once there, we may have to re-define our ideas about who we are or who we want to be. That might be a frightening task because it could mean changing an identity that we have worked for years to create, one that has served us well or at least one that has protected us from hurt and pain. If we have always been a tough guy, one who had to fight others and be aggressive in order to keep people away so they would not see our vulnerabilities, we may need to risk being vulnerable.

It will mean that we have to re-evaluate our coping strategies to assess their true value. Does how we react or respond serve us in the long run as well as it does in the short run? Being a tough guy might mean safety but it may not move us closer to getting our other needs met? Using our intellect to coerce or influence other people so that we can feel superior to them may satisfy our need to belong somewhere but most people will get tired of being used and move on, leaving us behind and alone.

Some of us wear masks

Have you ever been to a masquerade party? Why do people wear masks when they attend? It's to conceal their identity. They don't want people to know who they really are.

Some people continue to wear the same masks that they've worn for years because they are afraid to let people see them for who they really are. They create the personae necessary for the time with hopes of being accepted by their peer group, by the people they work with, or perhaps a group of people whom they would like to associate with.

The masks I am referring to are behaviours, attitudes and characteristics that people adopt that allow them to be anything or anyone they feel they need to be so they can fit in. They seldom represent what is felt deep inside. They usually represent the opposite of what people need or want.

People can wear a "happiness" mask, meaning they always appear to be happy and content, whether they feel like that or not. They believe that if people saw them that way they would be accepted or liked. Inside they could be sad or jealous or angry. They could wear a "party animal" mask thinking that everyone likes to be around someone who is fun to be with. Inside they may want to go to a movie with someone special or enjoy a quiet walk on the beach. They could wear a "cool" mask appearing not to let anything get to them while in fact they are feeling frightened or anxious. They could wear a "tolerant" mask allowing other people to take advantage of them instead of saying, "Excuse me but I didn't appreciate being treated that way. Please don't do that again." They could wear the mask of anger to keep people away so that they will not know how much they hurt inside or how disappointed they are with their lives.

I often hear people say, "If they knew who I really am they would not like me." It's risky business allowing other people, especially those close to us, to see us for who we really are. Wearing masks to appear to be someone or something other than who we are is very damaging to our self-esteem.

It says, "We are not good enough the way we are. We need to be someone else."

When we see what we want for ourselves in others we are reminded that we have work to do. There is something we need to address or change in ourselves but may not know how to make those changes. I remember a fellow at school who seemed so peaceful and content with himself. He was easygoing, smart, athletic, and consequently popular. Many of us put him down and criticized his attitude. In retrospect it is easy to see that we were jealous of him because he was what we wanted to be. Maybe when we try to be ourselves but are not accepted as we would like we get angry at ourselves for being stuck and angry at others for having what we want. Our inadequacies are reflected back to us as in a mirror.

Change becomes possible when we recognize and accept the person we are and that we can't be someone we aren't. Trying to be what we are not is the same as attempting spiritual suicide.

I recognize now that I don't want to be someone else; I want to be me. There will be those around me who will accept me as I am. There will be those who don't. If I walk into a room of 100 people and 99 of them comment favourably on my new suit and one person doesn't I used to focus on that one person and feel uncomfortable because he or she didn't like it. Now I understand that I am not responsible for someone else's taste in clothes. Not everyone will like me, but now I know that I don't have to wear the masks anymore in an effort to please everyone. I don't have to be all things to all people. When you are able to get to this place you will enjoy a sense of spiritual freedom unlike anything you have experienced before. Your anger and stress levels will decrease dramatically. Your attitude will say, "I'm OK and I hope you are too."

Anger is about us--it is never about them.

"Attitude" is not a bad thing

The other key element in our continuing journey toward effective self-management is our ATTITUDE. It helps us see things differently. It helps us do things differently too. If we are not open to change, change will not happen. If we are not willing to look at how we could do things differently, we will never learn by our efforts. So attitude plays a huge role in our human evolution. Anger directly affects our attitude. When we are hanging onto our resentments our focus for the day is different. We may be looking for revenge instead of solutions. We have a negative attitude instead of a positive one. While we are plotting our revenge or our response to what we perceive as an injustice we miss opportunities for growth. We miss chances that may have been presented to us but we were not able to see them for what they were because our positive vision for the day was blurred by anger and get-even thinking. We can not experience both positive and negative thinking at the same time.

If we spend all of our time trying to get even we'll *never* get ahead.

To live a positive life and to feel that for the most part you are doing well spiritually, emotionally, physically and mentally you need to have a positive attitude. It will be difficult to achieve a sense of inner harmony without a positive attitude. Attitude is one of the things that is solely ours. No one can give us one and no one can take it from us. We can have a positive attitude whenever we decide to have it and it will last as long as we want it to. Developing a positive attitude depends on how we choose to interpret what's going on around us and the quality of what we experience, as this story illustrates.

A young man spent a few lovely days in the Foothills. He climbed a hill or two, and there, while he rested and enjoyed the view, came a young couple into view. The girl appeared to be in a foul mood, complaining they should have never tried to climb that steep slope on such a hot day. The man she was with was taking the brunt of her emotional outpouring. It was his fault she was having such a bad time and he should have known better, and on and on. At that she decided to reverse course and go back down the hill. She slipped and slid, cursing all the way. Shortly thereafter an elderly man and his wife, both taking their time and apparently enjoying their adventure, slowly made their way toward the first young man. They paused often to take in the view and to catch their breath, chatting pleasantly all the while. As they passed by she commented what a wonderful time she was having and what a marvellous idea it was to be hiking. Both couples faced the same steep hill with the same difficulties and the same weather. One party was mad and the other glad. What was the difference? Attitude. They considered the experience from two different perspectives, thereby creating an entirely different experience.

As soon as we decide to take responsibility for who we are and how we feel we are well on our way to "having it all." We become truly empowered. Taking responsibility for our anger is a giant part of that process. It's our choice. It's up to us. It always has been. Assuming responsibility for our actions is the essence of self-management.

Anger is not bad

Anger is not an enemy to fear or to get rid of. Anger does not dictate our behaviour in any given situation. We do that by choosing a particular response. The anger we feel is as natural as any other emotion we experience. It has just made us aware of the need to be prepared to react to a stimuli of some kind. It is one emotion of many that we may experience in any day or week.

Understanding our anger and being able to use it to our advantage is an important part of managing ourselves. We can use anger to motivate ourselves and others. It can be a powerful ally for us to use to further ourselves. We can use it to further a common cause, for instance. Look at some of the great social movements of our time.

Greenpeace does tremendous work in helping to protect the environment, making us aware of the wrongs that are being perpetrated against nature, and in many cases the wrongs against us without our knowledge. The organization has amassed a large contingent of like-minded people who have agreed to work together for the common good and not the good of a few. They feel that if we don't treat this earth with the respect it deserves our children and certainly their children will not enjoy a life as we now know it. We are not allowing Mother Nature the opportunity to cleanse herself or to regenerate. These angry people have joined together to create a formidable force and have channelled their anger into a powerful cause. Good for them and good for us.

Mothers Against Drunk Drivers is another organization of angry people who have joined together for a common cause and who are making a difference. The World Wildlife Federation is another. In 1979 Lee Iacocca, then Chairman of the Board of the Chrysler Corporation was told by the Wall Street Journal to "let it go," to let the company die with some dignity. But rather than do that, he got angry. And he got his colleagues angry. And they got their employees angry. They got angry enough to set aside their differences and work together to cut their costs, double their productivity, rebuild their factories and thus secure thousands of jobs that would have otherwise been lost. Chrysler is now profitable because people got angry together for a common cause instead of angry at one another to the detriment of everyone. Amazing changes can be made to happen when people pool their energy and resources because of their common anger.

In order for us to stay healthy we must be able to learn how to express our anger in healthy, appropriate ways. Expressing anger appropriately is a skill that we can learn just like any other skill that we have learned. It takes hard work, persistence, time, and practice to develop new ways of dealing with our anger but, just as we used our anger to hurt ourselves and others, we will become comfortable using it to our advantage. If we consider how trapped electricity can eventually burn out a circuit, trapped anger that is not discharged appropriately can turn into resentment and eventually burn us out or escape in ways that we had not intended.

The goal is not to get rid of it; the goal is to learn how to use it to our advantage. That is effective self-management.

Truths and falsehoods about anger

The truths

- ❐ Anger is something that can build up in you. If you don't deal with it as soon as you identify it for what it is, and at a time when you are prepared to deal with it, it will continue to build until you explode verbally or become physically violent.

- ❐ When someone punches something or someone yells and screams, throws things or smashes things, that person is out of control. Talking or looking for solutions for the issue that presented itself is, at this point, probably out of the question.

- ❐ We may have conflicting views or disagreements with others but that does not mean that we must get angry to resolve them. Rarely does anger play a role in the satisfactory resolution of our problems. We are more likely to realize a level of satisfaction through negotiation or by stating our position assertively.

- ❐ Men and women are both prone to anger and violent outbursts.

- ❐ Anger can result from the way a person sees or perceives an event or situation.

- ❐ A person who batters or beats up someone chooses to do so. **No one else is responsible, especially not the victim**.

- ❐ Angry people have thoughts, ideas and feelings that can be recognized and altered or changed before they act out.

The falsehoods

- ❐ Anger is an unhealthy emotion that we should try to hide.

- ❐ Every time there is a conflict between people there will be violence.

- ❒ You have to be angry before you can act violently.
- ❒ Whenever there is anger, violence is sure to follow.
- ❒ If your parents were aggressive and angry, you will be too. There is nothing that you can do about it.
- ❒ Certain races of people are more prone to anger than others.
- ❒ Anger is caused by the other person.
- ❒ Your anger will stay with you until you hit something or someone.
- ❒ You are not responsible for your actions when you're intoxicated.
- ❒ The more severe the problem, the more angry and violent people become.

For the most part, these truths and falsehoods hold true except where there is a psychiatric diagnosis or some other extenuating medical circumstance. People need to be accountable for their actions. We need to understand that we alone have the responsibility and the power to deal with our anger appropriately.

Other ways we use anger

Anger can be used to set boundaries for people. I have witnessed this behaviour many times in the work I do. Clients come to the agency where I work and immediately begin to complain about everything they see. Nothing is good enough. Every expectation that we have for appropriate behaviour is challenged. Sometimes they use inappropriate language or they become loud or boisterous with an edge to their voice that says, "Stay away from me" or "Leave me alone--I'll be fine." Others give them a wide berth, sensing the anger that appears to be close to the surface. Usually they are scared, shy, fearful or running from someone or something. They use the anger to create a boundary so that others will not glimpse their insecurity or their fear and will be more likely to leave them alone. We often use anger to keep people away from us. Anger is the one emotion that people seem to respond to more quickly than any of the other emotions we present.

We also use anger to justify our actions and our activities. When we experience some negativity or injustice we strive to get even. We take out our anger on others. This is sometimes done in a passive manner, as was done in the example:

> John's boss came down on him for someone else's mistake but wouldn't listen to an explanation of what happened. Instead of trying to find a way of helping the boss see that he was not responsible for the mistake, he just took the criticism and went about his business for the day. At the end of the day, however, as he was walking through the parking lot to go home, John took out his car keys and proceeded to scratch the boss' car from fender to fender. He felt better because, in his mind, he saw justice being done. Payback.

Watch how children respond to anger-promoting situations. We see them acting in aggressive, passive-aggressive or violent ways because we haven't helped them develop the skills necessary to express their anger any other way. We are their teachers. What do they learn from us when we tell them to go to their rooms until they feel better or we slap them, yell at them, or otherwise mistreat them because they have dared to defy us or have acted out in some way that has embarrassed us as their parent. Maybe we should let them tell us why they are angry and deal with that instead. They have their issues too. They look to us for guidance. What kind of guidance do we show them when we punish them for experiencing a basic human emotion? When we are the recipients of their attempts to express their anger we consider them to be direct assaults on our authority as parents. Their attempts at expressing their anger turns into a power struggle. How often do we say these kinds of comments: "Don't you talk to me that way!" or "If you ever do that again, I'll smack you so hard they'll pick you up in Baltimore for speeding." Parents are destined to lose this struggle every time.

You can beat them or force them to comply but you can't beat the anger out of them. They just become more passive and sometimes more aggressive when they express it. They also become justified in their response to us.

There are shopkeepers who get short-changed by a supplier and then short-change their customers. Workers who don't feel that there is equity in the workplace slow down or sabotage a piece of machinery. And so on. People need to be able to feel that they have been heard, that they have been taken seriously and that they matter. Unfortunately, there is a circle to the anger or violence that we put out. We become angry or violent toward others and now they feel that their rights have been violated. They feel that they have been done an injustice, so they plan to "get even" anyway they can, and around and around we go.

When we choose our response we must also accept the natural outcomes of that choice.

Some of the myths about anger:

MYTH: That anger, unless it is justified, should not be expressed.
MY RESPONSE: Because anger, regardless of the source, is not expressed we find ourselves in difficulty. If we identify that we are upset about something we need to deal with that as soon as we determine what our appropriate response will be and then do it.

MYTH: In a family it is important to keep the peace at all costs.
MY RESPONSE: We should all endeavour to do what we can to help ensure that our family homes function safely, democratically and consistently. They need to remain a healthy place for all to experience. But the question is this: At what cost to **us**? If our natural human rights are not respected and we don't do what we need to to gain or protect those rights because it will upset the house, tough. Upset the house. The house does not remain a safe and healthy place to be unless all the people living there are given the opportunity to express how they feel in a manner that is not detrimental to anyone else, is not

judgemental of someone else, and does not take away someone else's right to the same self-expression. This means that we respect one another and we don't use our anger to hurt anyone, including ourselves.

MYTH: A woman who expresses anger is a "bitch" or a "nag."
MY RESPONSE: Where is it written that we should include or exclude what is responsible behaviour based on gender? Anger does not discriminate between the sexes, nor should we.

MYTH: Children should be seen and not heard.
MY RESPONSE: This one is very close to my heart. I could never understand why we would tell our children that they have nothing useful, constructive or substantive to say that anyone would find interesting or important. Isn't that what we are saying when we tell them that they should be seen and not heard? If a child is hurt would we not attend to him or her? Experiencing anger, especially to a child, can be as painful and as frightful as any physical hurt. Why wouldn't we attend to that as well? We need to encourage our children to speak whenever they feel the need to do so. We also need to teach them to wait their turn and be respectful of other's rights as well. If we do our job properly WE can help our children learn what they need to know instead of a stranger in a classroom or someone on the street who may not hold our same values. Besides, how else will we measure the growth of our children and begin to understand what's going on in their world if we don't let them speak? They'll tell us if we listen.

MYTH: Children who talk back to their parents are not respectful.
MY RESPONSE: Children who talk back to their parents are trying to find out where the boundaries are and how far they can go. They may well be asking us to behave properly so they can learn from us. Respect is a two-way street. We need

to respect them as much as we want them to respect us. I am not suggesting that we allow our children to abuse us in any way but they need to understand what is appropriate and what is not. It is up to us to help them understand that talking back is not acceptable but that asking for answers to questions is. We also need to help them understand what is acceptable so they can do that instead. We are their teachers. That is how it should be.

MYTH: Males are naturally more aggressive. When a man is being aggressive he is really being assertive.

MY RESPONSE: Males may be more aggressive because of the testosterone that is present in our systems. That, however, does not allow us the right to be any more aggressive than anyone else. If anything, we should be aware of our naturally occurring aggression and work to be sure that we use it to our advantage at appropriate times and places. Maybe that's at the arena, on the field, at the gym or any other physically demanding venue. We don't have the right to take it into our homes and our place of work to intimidate other people. Being a male is not an excuse to act in an unacceptable manner. Being aggressive is not being assertive. Being assertive means that we stand up for our rights as human beings while not impeding someone else's right to do the same.

MYTH: When you are hurt by someone you should turn the other cheek.

MY RESPONSE: When you are hurt by someone you help them understand it is unacceptable for them to do that to you and not to do it again. You have the right to be angry at anyone who hurts you. You also have an obligation to try to deal with that hurt in a way that won't hurt you or someone else in return. How do you respond to the situation so that the outcome will be in your own best interest? Never turn your cheek so that you can be abused again.

Anger is not the problem. It is our response to the anger we feel that can be the problem. We need to develop methods to control our **impulse** to respond to the situation or action that has presented itself. If we can stop the *immediate* response to anger we are likely to make better decisions about what we can or will do. True power comes to us when we can work with our emotions for our own benefit.

The greatest remedy for anger is delay.--Seneca

All about Mary

Recently a colleague shared a story about a client I'll call Mary. Mary was surrounded by a cloud of rage. This client let the intensity of her anger keep everyone at a distance, yet she craved an intimate, loving relationship with her family and friends. She stated that her entire family, parents and siblings alike, was fuelled by rage.

One afternoon Mary became involved in a discussion about anger and assertiveness. She said that she was confused about how they were different from one another. Mary explained that, for her, acting in a passive manner meant she was responding to low-level anger (the issue was not a big deal), behaving assertively suggested she was experiencing middle-level anger (she was uncomfortable with what was going on), and raging behaviour meant that she was feeling very aggressive (she did not consider other people's needs but would explode until her own were met). She thought out loud: "That's why I am aggressive--because I am full of rage."

She remembered being six years old and observing her passive, accommodating mother being dominated by her loud and physically abusive father. Mary wanted to be powerful so of course she had no choice, she believed, but to be what she had witnessed--loud and aggressive. She learned that that was how you got your needs met.

The group helped Mary recognize that she did indeed have a choice, but today as an adult choosing to be powerful did not mean choosing to be aggressive. Behaving assertively would get her needs met (power for Mary) while respecting the needs and rights of others. If she chose to act this way she would encourage the possibility of developing closer relationships with her family.

Mary went quiet. After a few seconds of reflection, she softened her posture, raised her head, looked the group straight in the eye and smiled.

It might appear insignificant, but a recognition of personal choice has great potential for bringing about change. Mary recognized that she didn't have to rage to get her needs met and she could choose to make that change anytime she wanted.

What do I do when I want to blow?

The solutions to our problems are often not as complicated as the problems themselves. We tend to make them complicated because we feel that something simple wouldn't work. We need to "keep it simple." Use the skills that were discussed earlier in this book. They are basic and they work. Go over the section on assertiveness. That may help you say what you need to say so that you can address the issue without losing control. Look at the section on problem solving and use the matrix or the step goal sheet. All of the strategies and techniques we need to work toward possible solutions are right here within us. If we search our own experiences and past responses we can come up with a host of possible solutions. What has worked before? What hasn't worked before? Even if we haven't been as successful as we might have wished, we now know what doesn't work so we can try something else. Perhaps learning a new skill is what is needed. So do that. There are many excellent programs and workshops available through the YM/YWCA, public libraries, local community colleges and other social agencies in your area.

There are several different ways of dealing effectively with anger and the impulse to respond to it. Some basic methods are discussed in the coming pages. But before anything else happens we need to make the internal decision to deal with our anger differently, to make the change. We need to see the value of dealing with our emotions in a different way. If we don't do that we will find it more difficult to initiate or maintain any long-lasting change. In other words, we need to decide for ourselves, based on what is or will be in our own best interests, that change is necessary, that we have a desire to make a change, that we will be open to new ideas and information, and that we are prepared to make the effort necessary to begin to change. Once the internal decision is made, effective self-management will follow.

What we know so far

1. We need to see and feel that the changes we make (in this case regarding how we deal with our anger) will be beneficial to us somehow, and that they have value. The changes that we consider making need to represent what we want to do and not something that we feel we have to do. **We have to see a benefit to making a change.**

   If we base our decision to change on some outside motivators, such as the legal system, threats of retaliation of some kind from family or friends, or any other source the pressure to change may come from, we will be more likely to feel resentment because the change won't be of our own volition.

   Fear is an effective short-term motivator but a poor long-term motivator for maintaining change. I know of many people who have been told that if they don't stop smoking or drinking excessively they will dramatically increase the chances of dying prematurely. Most stop for short periods of time and then slowly slide back to their old patterns of use. They may try to hide it from others at first because of the criticism they are likely to receive but the threat or fear of death fades for the majority.

2. The changes we consider can be made by **doing** something within our realm of possibility, such as using counselling, taking a course of some kind, reading some self-help books, and watching how others deal appropriately with their anger. Whatever we do has to be doable for us and something by which we can attain a level of competence fairly quickly.

3. We need to believe that we can maintain the changes we make over a period of time by continuing to do what works best for us, and that we will meet our needs by maintaining those changes we make.

4. Most of us want to live our lives with as much harmony and pleasure as possible. We need to continue to evaluate our actions and decide whether what we are doing is still working for us or if we need to make further changes. We have to see that the quality of our lives and the lives of those important to us have been positively affected by the changes that we make. Constant evaluation equals constant growth.

5. It is necessary for us to set a particular time-frame for starting to make the changes we feel are important otherwise we may never actually get started. Once started, we need to decide to do things differently over a specific period of time (a week, a month, six months) and then evaluate how things have changed. It is important we give ourselves enough time to get reasonably comfortable with the changes we have made and then ask those around us, those who we trust, for some positive feedback on what they noticed about us and how the changes we have made affected them.

6. Taking the time to write things down slows down our impulse to respond. It may sound hokey but it works. If anger is an emotion that is damaging our chances for happiness, we need to look at other ways of dealing with it. The following is a useful exercise that we can use:
   (a) Describe the issue that has presented itself and then ask yourself, "How much time and energy do I want to put into dealing with this?"

   (b) Is this issue worth my continued attention? If the answer is yes, go on to the next question. If the answer is no, move on to more productive and beneficial pursuits.

   (c) Now ask yourself, "How does this issue affect me directly and am I justified in my response to it?" If the answer is yes, move on to the next question. If the answer is no, move on to more productive or beneficial pursuits.

(d) Once here, ask yourself, "Do I have an effective response that will address the issue, one that will enable me to act in my own best interests but would allow for a win/win solution?" This may not always be possible but we should try for it anyway. If the answer is yes, proceed. If the answer is no, reconsider questions (b) and (c) again. If the answer is yes to each one of those, rethink your options until you feel good about what you plan to do and go back to question (d).

Create two or three different options so that if one response doesn't work or does not seem appropriate at the time, you have another in mind.

Winners and losers

I was listening to two people discussing their views on anger and the reasons we should and should not respond to it in a violent or vengeful way. They were discussing who wins and who loses when revenge is plotted or carried out.

Each point of view seemed logical. One person was saying that the old eye-for-an-eye idea had merit and that revenge felt good. Satisfaction is experienced and boundaries are preserved. The message is sent: "Don't mess with me." And haven't we been told that it's good to release our anger? I must admit that his logic appealed to me at first. Then the other person suggested that the one who invests his time and energy into getting even is the real loser. Whoever remains a victim does not move ahead. That person has not thought about what needs to be done to get past the situation that promoted the anger response and so has stayed stuck. He or she will continue to be stuck for as long as it takes to plan or plot the revenge. The "wound" stays open. It would be better to decide on a more appropriate response, carry through with it, and move on to activities that would be more productive and beneficial. Violence begets revenge so where does the circle stop? How much time is too much time when we are investing our energy in get-even schemes? In one of Clint Eastwoods' movies, his character said to a bounty hunter who had come looking for him that "dying ain't much of a living." The same thought holds true in this case. Wasting time getting even "ain't much of a living either."

Anger is not always about revenge. It is not always about something that someone has done to us or said to us. It can be fostered by our own disappointments over decisions that we made or expectations that were not realized. We could be angry at ourselves for allowing opportunities to slide by. We could be angry because we are not becoming all we want to be or thought we could be. Fear and anger are emotions that can be very intensely interwoven. We may find ourselves fearful of being hopeful again and of considering possibilities. We choose to live with the disappointment and we do not try again rather than experience what we see as failure in not attaining something that was built on hope and promise. That fear creates anger in us because we want to move ahead in order to have more of what we feel is important.

Consider the man in his late forties who still doesn't have a home purchased or a newer car or a cottage at the lake or a job that is rewarding and fulfilling or a retirement portfolio of some kind. We want all of those things that we believe should come with hard work. That's what we were told we could have if we worked hard, wasn't it? These days most of us are lucky to have a job, let alone all the other things that we feel are our right.

Consider the woman who has worked hard all of her life to provide a safe and comfortable environment for her family, who has worked full time or part time, as well, to help pay the bills and who now wants to go back to school or pursue a career. She has dedicated a good part of her life so that others may be successful in theirs and now can't pursue her dreams because of money or poor health or a partner who is so angry because he couldn't have his dreams. Now neither will she.

Anger is all around us. More often than not, it is created by us. Just as often, we hang onto it longer than is healthy for us when we could have let it go. It is our inability to deal with it appropriately that keeps us in the circle of anger. Effective anger management depends on the degree to which we effectively manage ourselves.

Get past "then" so that "now" doesn't ruin "when"

Anger is very much a "NOW" emotion. It is happening to us now. It is very much influenced now by what happened "THEN." What is it we feel we can do NOW about THEN? Probably not much since we cannot reverse or alter what has happened in the past. By doing nothing about the anger we feel NOW we allow it to influence what will happen to us in the future which is our "WHEN." The decision to be proactive or reactive plays a huge role in our happiness. We need to understand that our happiness is our responsibility and it can be ours whenever we decide to have it. What role does our anger play in our happiness? Do we let it stand in our way of making the decisions we need to make NOW so that the remainder of our lives, our WHEN, will be as we had always hoped or imagined it would be? Are we afraid of being hopeful about the possibilities? Do we stop ourselves from being excited about something for fear of being disappointed yet again? When we stop reaching for our goals and become angry at the results do we misplace our anger onto those we love the most? And don't we get angry at ourselves for not taking the chance--once again? And around and around it goes. We begin to think it is better to just go with the flow. Don't get excited about anything and you can't be disappointed either. This is a very reactionary perspective that yields only more disappointment and anger.

FEAR=REACTION=ANGER=NO GROWTH=FEAR=ANGER=?????

None of us ever wants to feel disappointment or rejection or that we are not good enough. We try to avoid disappointment and yet it is the natural outcome of not being proactive in our daily lives. We are encouraging exactly what we fear and then we get angry about it. Perpetuated anger will hurt us, not necessarily in a physical sense, but more in a spiritual sense. It will eat away at our self-esteem. It will keep us focused in a negative way.

In all the situations where anger is the primary feeling, the important consideration is our response to it. We need to own the anger because it is ours. We are more likely to generate an appropriate response, one that will reflect what is in our best interests, if we can work through the impulse to react.

We are taking responsibility for our actions and dealing with our anger **proactively** when we ask ourselves:

1. *What am I feeling?* Go back over the list in this section of the masks of anger words. Circle or write down the words that best describe what you are feeling at this time. This will help to indicate any situation, interaction, or circumstance that may have contributed to our feelings.

2. *Why am I feeling this way?* Think about which of our needs are not being met or are being denied us. This helps us to begin to formulate a response to whatever is going on for us.

3. *What can I do about it?* This is the part that slows us down. Remember the statement that started this section. We seldom like the outcomes from emotional decisions that we make while we are feeling emotional. By going through this exercise we feel like we are doing something positive in order to respond. It is important to feel as though we have stood up for our rights and that we have or will be dealing with any perceived injustice whether it is self-inflicted or perpetrated by someone else. By not reacting immediately we can assess our role in what happened and ask ourselves, "What can I do to change the outcome of this?"

4. *What am I going to do about it?"* This question helps us make a decision on a plan of action that will enable us to deal with the situation. When we stop-think-and-decide we are being proactive in taking care of our needs. At the same time we are acting in a way that is less likely to hurt ourselves or someone else in the process. We could decide NOT to decide on a plan right now because we may not have all the information we feel we need. Deciding not to decide is still deciding to do something.

When considering solutions remember to focus on the issue and not on any particular person.

How much of our anger comes from being misunderstood? How many times have we tried to say what we wanted to say yet we have come away feeling more angry than when we began? The art of communicating is the secret ingredient to everything that we try to accomplish. If we cannot communicate in some way what we feel and what we need from those around us we will feel angry, disappointed, and frustrated more often than we are peaceful, satisfied, and calm. In our attempts to say what we need to say we start out with a goal in mind and a desire to not get into an argument this time. Yet, despite our best efforts, the outcomes are generally the same. **Learn how to communicate effectively. It is the key to happiness.** There are some great books available on communicating effectively: for example, Dr. Deborah Tannen's book *You Just Don't Understand,* Dr. John Gray's book *Men are from Mars, Women are from Venus* and any of *The Keys to Loving Relationships* series by Gary Smalley.

Go back to the fourth stop of our journey and use the D.E.S.C. model (page 124). You have the tools now. Use them. They work. One of the hardest things to do when we are in a heated discussion is to keep to the point. We have a tendency to drift off toward other unresolved issues and bring them into our present conversations. Soon we are arguing about something that has nothing to do with what it was we first wanted to address. This is called kitchen sink communication. We throw everything (unresolved issues) into the argument but the kitchen sink. It's never useful or productive. It is usually frustrating and anger provoking. **Stick to the issue(s) at hand. Deal with the NOW issues.**

Always keep in mind that just because we begin to use our new skills doesn't mean that those around us will change how they respond to us. This is about us--not about them. It is about us doing what we need to do so that we get closer to **our** goals not about trying to manipulate others so that we get our way. **We** need to use our strengths (go back pages 14-18) to find and develop new ways of dealing with the issues that confront us. If those around us respond differently because of what we do, that's a choice that they make and that's a bonus to us.

Anger expressed appropriately is called passion.--Author unknown

It's up to us to see it differently

Part of learning any new skill is being able to look objectively at the role we have played in the solutions or outcomes of the issues that presented themselves. If we didn't like what happened we need to ask ourselves this: "What could I have done differently so that the outcome would have been more to my liking?" If we look at things from a different perspective we will see other solutions. For example, if I were standing between two groups of people with one group on my left and the other on my right and I held up a pocket watch and asked what each group saw I would get two different answers. They each saw the same watch but saw it differently. Obviously the one side saw the face and the other side saw the back. If I were to turn it around each group would see what the other had just seen. They were each seeing the same watch but from two different perspectives. Not until they were presented with the other side of the watch did they know what the other side looked like. There is always more than one way to see the same thing. You have to **want** to see the other side before it will present itself. Once you can see the other side you can then consider the alternatives because you have more information to work with. As soon as we decide to see the anger we feel in a different way, we re-gain our power over it instead of it having power over us. "I get angry when certain things happen to me" replaces "You make me angry when you do that to me."

The following is a worksheet to help you develop some new perspectives and skills when dealing with your anger-provoking situations. It is an excellent way of tracking how, or if, you deal with anger and how it may affect you.

Using the following outline, take the time to write down, when (date), what time of day you experienced anger (morning, noon, night), where you were at the time (at home, work, traffic jam, at the pub, etc.), who was with you or around you (friends, strangers, workmates etc), what you were feeling (list of anger words, pages 164 and 165), how intense the experience was (1 being mild upset, 10 being in a rage), what you did (throw something, yell at someone, hit someone or something, etc.). Do this for a week, being sure to write in this log each time you felt anger.

Date and Time	Place/setting	Who is there	Anger experience (feeling)	Anger intensity Scale 1-10	What you did (actions)

This worksheet will help you track any patterns that exist with respect to how you become angry. Are you more angry in the morning? Is that because you work shifts? Maybe there are particular times of the week, month or year that are more stressful for you. The coming of winter is like that for me. I love the heat of the summer months. When fall approaches I get more stressed because I know that, not far behind, winter is coming with the dreaded snow and ice. This is useful information for those who are close to me as well.

How can you interact differently now that you have this insight into yourself and your behaviour? Do certain people or places trigger anger feelings that may be demonstrated inappropriately later? What is it that you feel when you find yourself in certain situations or with certain people? What is it about them that bothers you and what can you do knowing that? How intense was the feeling? Were you in a rage? Were you mildly upset? How did you behave? What did you do? And most important, what were the outcomes of your actions? What happened?

Once we have this information we can begin to take action that will help us change the pattern of how we experience anger and possibly the outcomes.

We can avoid certain people, places and things that seem to trigger our anger. By using the log we can see the patterns that occur over a period of time. If, for instance, we see that there is a particular time of the day or week when we are more angry more often we can create strategies to deal with those times as they approach.

We can also see how different approaches or attempts to deal with certain situations may be more successful than others. Once we see which approaches work and which ones don't we can then choose do the things that were more helpful for us and stop doing the things that weren't. It sounds simple enough but for many this is difficult to do. We need to question the "benefits" we get from being angry. For example, anger can energize us, focus us on a singular train of thought, relieve us of being responsible for outcomes, or it can help us channel our energy into a collective effort which feels good. We all appraise these benefits differently based on our value systems and our principles. Psychologists call this "cognitive appraisal." But the one common point we can all consider is this: If we don't see that there is a **need** to change our approach to dealing with our anger, any attempts we make to change will be short-lived. We have to accept the motivating factors as being important to us--that they have value and will move us closer to what we really want.

Men and women tend to experience anger differently. Men tend to deal with anger when its intensity gets to about a five or six on the ten-point scale. Men tend to slough off the little things with the result that they grow into bigger things that can cause more stress. More stress equals more anger. This means that men especially need to be more vigilant with regard to their feelings and decide to deal with minor irritations as they happen. Women, on the other hand, tend to deal with anger as it happens, when it is at the lower levels of the scale, so that it doesn't build into something harmful or energy consuming. Women seem to be able to identify their triggers more readily than men and deal with them before they become more stressful.

Keep it simple

❐ Admit that you are angry and that you are responsible for your anger.

- ❒ Step back from the situation as soon as you recognize it for what it is.

- ❒ Identify the source of your anger and deal with it as soon as you feel you can. That may mean tomorrow or the next day. It doesn't mean immediately. **Stop--think--act when you are ready--evaluate.**

- ❒ Listen to the feedback that others are giving you without interrupting them. They may have some useful information for you. Feedback is just another perspective and doesn't serve as suggestion or criticism.

- ❒ Instead of blaming yourself for setbacks learn from the experience so that the next time you are presented with a similar issue you can approach it differently.

- ❒ Get active. When you feel anger welling up inside get yourself involved in some strenuous physical exercise (unless there is a medical reason not to).

- ❒ Learn to meditate, NOT medicate.

- ❒ Learn to laugh at yourself. When you are able to look objectively at what you do, some of it can be pretty funny stuff. The problem is few of us see the humour and many of us feel the embarrassment. So many of us are more concerned about how others see us--the external forces which can control our responses--and few of us understand that we will be much happier and healthier when we accept ourselves for the decent human beings we are. We don't have to prove anything to anyone except ourselves. Once that happens we can become more **internally** focused.

- ❒ Talk to someone you trust. Otherwise, the issues and feelings that you are experiencing will eat you up inside.

- ❒ You can always seek professional help. There is nothing weak about seeking the assistance of an unbiased third party. If you were hurting physically you would see a physician. It makes sense to see a trained professional if you are hurting emotionally, mentally or spiritually.

- ❐ Understand that anger usually follows, or results from, another emotion. Be aware of how you are feeling and what you are feeling so that you can deal with the primary feeling before it develops into anger. Where does the anger really come from?

- ❐ Accept that your feelings are yours and make no other person responsible for them. They belong to you.

- ❐ Understand that using anger is one way some people get what they want. They manipulate others by intimidating them. The outcome from this approach usually sees the intimidator getting control but never getting co-operation or respect. Those intimidated will usually find a way to protect themselves.

- ❐ Ask yourself what role YOU played in the situation that has promoted your anger and if you escalated the situation to serve a purpose.

In the past many of us dealt with our anger in ways that got us what we wanted with little or no concern about how that affected those around us. We learned that certain methods produced certain outcomes. Those same methods also damaged our relationships and friendships either directly or indirectly. We can unlearn those skills and replace them with new learned skills that are more appropriate and still get us what we want today all without hurting someone else in the process or negating their personal rights. When we are able to do this we gain the inner peace that we seek.

One of the responsibilities we have as parents is to help our children learn how to deal with their anger in appropriate ways. This is, perhaps, the single most important skill we can teach them. Children who have been encouraged and taught to express their anger appropriately tend to be less violent when they grow up, tend to get into less trouble with the law, and tend to stay in school longer than others. If we are trying to figure out what is going on with the younger generation we need look no further than our own homes.

I'm not saying that we are not doing our job as parents or that some parenting goes on under some very difficult and trying circumstances. I'm saying that we need to go further. First of all, we need to look at how WE manage our own business. That is how our children learn--by watching us and then imitating what they see. If they see violence or disrespect they will likely be violent and disrespectful. If they hear anger and inappropriate language they will probably talk the same way. The responsibility to teach our children appropriate learning and coping skills is not up to anyone else but us. Not our schools and not our legal system. US. We need to teach by example. We need to learn and demonstrate that we are in control of ourselves and that we can self-manage our lives.

Some key points

- ❒ It's OK to be angry. It is a human emotion that is necessary for our protection and survival. It is NOT OK to hurt ourselves or someone else out of anger.

- ❒ We do not inherit behaviours; we develop them. We learn them and we can unlearn them as well.

- ❒ How we respond is our choice. We have **RESPONSE-ABILITY.**

- ❒ Our own behaviour is the only behaviour we can change. It is not our responsibility to change someone else's to fit our needs.

- ❒ For as many people that live on this planet, there will be that many ways of dealing with anger. We have to decide for ourselves how we will respond in ways that are in our own best interests.

- ❒ When we are talking to someone we should avoid name-calling and labelling. Words like "stupid," "idiot," "lazy" and "useless" only serve to anger the person we are trying to communicate with. The anger between both people will feed on itself and serve no one.

- ❒ If we want to discuss how someone else's actions affects us let's begin by saying something positive to the person we are trying to communicate with and, if possible, try to end on a positive note. This is not always possible but we need to try. "I have always seen you as someone who cared for other people's feelings so I thought that I could talk to you about . . . " is a good start. When we open any conversation with a complaint or a criticism of some kind we are likely to be seen or heard as blaming them for what is happening. People feel less offended or embarrassed when they are not being made the scapegoat for whatever is going on around them. They are more likely to hear what it is we want to say. It is important to help others feel that they are, or can be, part of the solution instead of part of the problem.

The short of it all

Admit
Neutralize
Get away
Examine your anger
Return

A Admit to yourself that you are angry. Become aware of the signs and feelings that go along with what defines anger for you.

N Neutralize yourself. It is just as easy to get calm as it is to get angry. It's just a different point of view. You have to do different things to experience the anger, that's all. Understand that you need to work through the impulse to respond immediately. Breathe deeply. Keep your hands in your pockets. They will be safe there. Don't argue. Once you have uttered the words you either have to take them back, which can be difficult to do, or you have to let them stand, which may stop any kind of solution from forming. Work to divert your attention from the situation until your blood pressure drops and the adrenaline level is reduced.

G Get away. Get out. Do whatever you need to do to take time out to clear your head and to regain your control regarding any actions you are considering. Evaluate your response before you give it. Is it appropriate?

Will it get you what you want? Will it hurt yourself or someone else? Go for a walk or a run. Talk to someone you trust. If no one is around talk out loud to yourself (in a private, quiet place). Although I am not an advocate of violence, if your anger level is rising go work out on a heavy bag or shadow box.

E Examine your anger. Who are you really angry at? Does this person you are angry at deserve your anger? Does this have anything to do with someone else? Are there other unresolved issues that are connected to what is happening right now? Always take a good look at what is REALLY going on before going any farther.

R Return when you are ready to deal with what is really going on. Returning is good but only if you have fully considered what it is you are going to do and say. Are you sure that it will be appropriate? Be sure to stick with the facts and don't bring any outside issues into this discussion. Resolve the issue at hand.

The people who have given up--the ones who have quit trying to find their peace and their serenity--are those who become violent. They are the ones who take from others just because they can, but they have a false sense of power. True power is measured in people by their continuing struggle to find their way at no one else's expense. To do otherwise is to quit or to lose. Those who quit trying and revert to violence to find their way have taken the easy way out. They are not strong at all. The very thing that they seek is the thing that continues to elude them: power and control.

Draw a horizontal line and mark on it a scale of 1-10. On the left end mark a one which represents "needs work." On the right end a 10 which represents "as good as it could be." Consider this question: "How satisfied am I with my ability to manage my anger? Where on the scale do you need to be in order to feel good about your ability to manage the anger you may experience? Place an X and mark the date. Where on this scale do you see yourself at this time? Place an X and mark the date. What do you have to do or what can you do to move 1 number closer to your goal? What skills can you develop to make that happen? Go back to the scale in a month's time and consider the same question. Check to see what progress you have made. Evaluate your progress and consider what else you can do to continue moving up the scale toward your goal.

Consider the questions below. Your answers will provide information that can help you decide what you will need to do next in order to manage your anger more effectively.

1. Can you remember a time in your life when the triggers (things, situations, people, etc.) that anger you now didn't bother you? What was happening for you at that time? How was that time different? What were you doing differently? How were you thinking differently?

2. When you learn some new skills to deal with your anger how will that make your life different? How will that have an impact on you?

3. Who is likely to give you the most honest feedback regarding any changes you decide to make? What would you like them to see if you decide to deal with your anger differently? How would you like them to see you? What would you like them to say about you?

4. What will have to happen for you to decide to make some changes regarding how you deal with your anger? Will you be acting in your own best interests to let it get that far?

5. How will changing the way you deal with your anger have an impact on the people around you? How will that affect the quality of your relationships?

6. Is there a connection between your stress levels and your anger levels?

7. When you are able to recognize anger for what it really is how will that skill benefit you?

8. Can you remember a time when you successfully dealt with an anger situation without hurting yourself or someone else in the process? What did you do? Could you do that again in a similar situation?

9. What can you do to recognize anger earlier? What will you do then?

10. What are some of the things that you have done recently that have worked with regard to dealing with your anger?

What we know for sure

Intimacy and unresolved anger can not exist in the same place at the same time.

All of the signs are there for us to see. We each know how our anger affects us and we have a pretty good idea, deep within us, why that happens to us. When we disregard the "road signs" we are well on our way to the "big crash." **If we refuse to look at the map we will get lost for sure.** If we are not prepared to look for new directions we stop evolving as human beings. We will not attain the level of inner peace that we all seek and dream of having. When we refuse to re-evaluate what we do and why we do it we deny ourselves the opportunity to grow.

When we experience growth, change and learning, we experience the essence of being human. We feel self-reliant. We are able to manage ourselves effectively when others are having difficulty. To deny ourselves the opportunity to do that, in itself, creates anger within us and thus the circle continues.

Anger can act like a cancer enveloping our spirit. If we don't learn to own it, work with it and learn to use it to our advantage our spiritual selves will succumb to it. Those who don't do this work become defined by their anger.

It is our **decisions** that govern our successes, not our emotions. We can use our ability to think first and then act in our own best interests. The greatest power that we can discover within ourselves is the power to work with our emotions and use them to our advantage. That is what self-management is all about.

I truly believe what most of us ultimately want is to have a relationship with ourselves, friends, partners and our families that is solid and fulfilling. We want one that adds to our sense of purpose and belonging, one that makes us feel good inside, one that is sort of warm and fuzzy just as when we think about going home.

Subject to Revision

The world is always changing, and we need to change with it. As time passes, our knowledge increases, our experience broadens, and we gain more understanding. Everything is subject to revision--our perceptions, our opinions, our self image, our image of others, our desires, our relationships, our friendships, our goals, and even our past. We may learn something about our past that changes the way we feel about our present state, which in turn affects our future. It soothes me to know in my heart that things don't have to stay the same. In fact, it is my saving grace. It encourages me to try to improve myself. It keeps my mind open to other possibilities. It's a constant check on my humility. It helps me to remain teachable. I'm comforted by the fact that everything is subject to revision.

L.F., New York

7.

GOING HOME

RELATIONSHIPS ARE NOT THE ANSWERS TO PROBLEMS. THEY ARE THE REWARDS FOR GETTING YOUR LIFE IN ORDER.
—HORST S., quoted in *Believing in Myself*

Being in a relationship is a wonderful experience when it is going right. There is no feeling like it in the world. You are on top. Nothing seems to matter except when you will see each other again. Some of us experience that nervous excitement that steals even our appetites away. Then it grows into something more comfortable and the novelty begins to wear off. Oh, we still look forward to seeing each other but we begin to feel the need to do other things. And so it goes.

Relationships with others help us to grow. We are able to see ourselves through the eyes of someone else by way of supportive and compassionate feedback that will help us evaluate our interactive skills. Ideally, we provide the same opportunity for the partner we choose.

But when they go wrong they are the most painful, frustrating and debilitating experiences. Relationships that have gone sour have been the ruination of many people. Some never recover from the experience. Some remain angry and bitter for the remainder of their lives. Others form new relationships but never quite get past the old one. They transfer some of their animosity and resentment to the people currently in their lives. Some feel that if they let the other person get too close they will get hurt like the last time. They become determined to make sure that won't happen to them again so they hold back a part of themselves to maintain a safe distance emotionally, which often leads to resentment and frustration and sadness in their current relationship. When the current relationship falters it reinforces the decision to hold something back so that the hurt won't be as devastating. A circle of behaviour is created and is difficult to break.

In my work three out of four clients that I see report they have returned to the use of destructive substances because of relationships that have ended.

It's the loneliness, sadness, emptiness, resentment, anger, abandonment and/or rejection that they can't deal with so alcohol, drugs, food, sex or gambling create a diversion and kill the pain. Those who don't use substances often revert to old behaviours or patterns of thinking. Many get the "poor me's" and stay stuck in victimhood, forever feeling sorry for themselves.

Relationships have the power to make us or break us if we let them. They are such an immensely important part of our lives because they help to provide the feeling that we belong somewhere and that we have purpose. Much of our self-esteem is derived from the success of our relationships.

Yet many of us don't do the things we need to do in order to keep them healthy. We don't recognize that the success of our relationships depends more on our "people skills" than on our feelings. Obviously we have to feel love for the person we chose to be with, but beyond these feelings we need to be able to communicate appropriately, and problem solve, and manage ourselves effectively so that anger and stress don't pollute the emotional and spiritual environment that we are trying to create. We must participate equally in the relationship for it to be fulfilling. Many loving relationships falter because of poor skill development and not because of a lack of feelings.

Some pay more attention to making money and keeping their portfolios healthy than they do their relationships. Sure, making money is important but it doesn't cost us anything to do what needs to be done each day and to say what needs to be said each day so that the relationship stays strong and healthy. When we don't make the time to do and say these things we wonder what went wrong. We hear ourselves saying,"I worked hard to provide *this* and *that* and this is the thanks I get." Often we blame someone else for what happened. I encourage my clients to look at the role THEY played in the whole business. We need to ask ourselves, "What is or was my role in what is happening or has happened? How did I contribute to the outcome?" If the relationship is over with no hope of re-building it we must ask ourselves, **"What can I learn from this? How can I do it better the next time?"**

For many of us, it is difficult to admit our role in what happened. It is much easier to stay angry or resentful, and to blame others. There is some comfort in our anger. It keeps us focused on something other than our pain.

Some people believe that all they have to do is get someone interested in them and the rest will work itself out. Yet once those people are involved in a relationship with someone they try to change their partner into someone they would like them to be so that they are more comfortable with them. WRONG. A more potent recipe for disaster has never been conceived.

Successful relationships are determined by what we bring into them from our past learning opportunities. This is the baggage we carry with us. Some of it is good baggage--what we have learned that will help to make any new relationship better and some of it is not so good--the changes we need to make but refuse to make.

Before we get involved with someone again we need to ask ourselves if we have any outstanding issues that need to be dealt with. Is our anger or our negativity still a factor in our lives? Are we hoping that someone else will be able to take away our negative feelings or keep us from engaging in self destructive behaviour? Have we travelled some of the other roads previously discussed in this book so that we have more to give and better skills with more knowledge to draw on? Have we done our work so that this relationship will be all we hoped it would be when we first fell in love with each another?

Many great books have been written on this subject. Many great researchers and clinicians have documented their findings. I'll not claim any credit for what they have done.

I will, however, outline what I believe are the most important considerations when we are beginning a new relationship, trying to hang on to the one we've got, or making the one we are in even better than it is. If you are interested in some of the books that are available anything done by Gary Smalley, Dr. John Gray or Dr. Deborah Tannen would be a great place to start. You'll find many others in any library or your local book store. In all cases you have to decide for yourself which information is useful to you.

Where do we start?

Any time we are trying to do something we will be more successful if we start with a goal, with the end in mind. Where do we want to be? What do we want to be doing? Where do we want to be doing it? Who do we want to be doing it with? And so on. If we don't know what we want and where we want to be, how will we know if we are travelling in the right direction and doing the things that we need to do? How will we know if we are there yet?

So it is with relationships. We need to determine what the goals are for any relationship we begin. If you are already in one, what are your goals for it now? What has to happen for it to be better than it is? How can you make that happen? What are you willing to do and what are you willing to put into it?

There are three generic goals to consider. This short list, which is in no particular order, may not have some of yours on it so substitute where you want or need to. Think long and hard before you write anything down. What do you want? How are you going to get there? Who do you want with you on your journey?

> Our goal may be to feel as though we belong somewhere and with someone. We all need to feel that we have a place, that someone wants to have us in their space because they trust us and can rely on us. This is one of the five basic human needs we all strive to attain. If we look at the development of street gangs, we recognize this a need to belong to a "family unit." The members feel protected, trusted and needed. There is a very strong sense of loyalty and trust that is offered for membership. The gang members have a place that fulfils a need to belong to something somewhere. They have a relationship with each other, a bond.
>
> Why is it so hard for society to break them up? Because we have nothing better to offer them in return for their non-participation in the gang. We cannot compete with the sense of belonging and acceptance that they experience. Isn't this what we all want? Until we can come up

with something better, gang memberships and gang violence will increase. Violence is the common thread that binds them all together. We don't see too many happy gang members. They all have axes to grind. If we were to pull back the emotional scabs we would find anger, hate and resentment boiling at the top. Gang environments are the only logical places for them to go. The members get to fulfil two needs: the need to belong and the opportunity to act on their feelings of resentment, anger and frustration. If some people have not had the opportunity to develop appropriate methods of dealing with these feelings what do you think is likely to happen?

This is not to suggest that relationships are like gang memberships but rather illustrates the strong need that we have to belong to someone or something, somewhere.

Another goal is to have somebody share our dreams and our fantasies, someone to be with who will not laugh at or judge our thoughts and feelings. To be able to share our innermost being with someone takes a great deal of courage and trust. Being able to trust another human being that much can be meaningful yet frightening at the same time. Those dreams may include having a family and raising children to be resourceful, respectful and resolute so that they can go on to be solid citizens of the world. They may include wanting to become a professional athlete or a top-notch criminal lawyer. The dreams come first. They need to be understood and nurtured and accepted as ours. Just being able to share our dreams is important.

Being able to tell someone how a picture or a story makes us feel doubles the pleasure of the insight. Have you ever watched the most beautiful sunset you have ever seen and wished that you had someone to share it with? Good relationships help us to feel as though we are not alone in the world, that we have a travelling companion who is trustworthy.

Still another goal is to be with someone who will help us become all we can be; someone who will provide us with positive feedback and constructive criticism; someone who will support us and encourage us without trying to live our lives for us or trying to live his or her own life through us.

We still need to do our own work. No one can do it for us. But it would be nice to have someone with us on our journey who is as excited as we are about the growing opportunities that present themselves. Just as important for us, and our spiritual and mental growth, is the chance to provide the same kind of encouragement, support, and opportunity for someone that we care about as well. Relationships are about "us" and not just "me."

The quality of my journey is largely defined by the quality of my companions.--Earnie Larsen

What are relationships?

What do we mean by the word "relationship"? If you were to explain it or describe it to someone what would you say? Describing the word is like trying to describe what a cherry tastes like or what love is. The word means something different to each of us. One thing is for sure. We can determine who we have relationships with and we can describe how those relationships will affect us. Those relationships include those we have with our children, partner, parents, friends, work mates, social connections, clubs, groups, the guy at the garage, the doctor and so forth. With everyone we come into contact we establish some sort of relationship. For the purposes of this journey we will concern ourselves, most often with those relationships with our families, partners and children.

I'm the most important person I know

The most important relationship we have is the relationship with ourselves. That's not narcissism but rather realism. There is no other more important. The relationship we have with ourselves helps us understand and communicate what it is we have to give to someone and what it is we need from them, why we need it, what we are prepared to do or give to get it, why that need or those needs are important to us, and what that will mean to us if we do or don't get our needs met. Our relationship with ourselves keeps us healthy and safe so that we can give to others who are important to us. If I'm not OK I can't be OK to or for someone else. If I'm to be strong for others I first need to be strong.

Why we need to know our needs?

It is important for us to know what our wants and needs are so that we can communicate those to any prospective partner or friend. It is important for us to know and understand our strengths and to have worked through some of the issues that stood in the way of our peace, prosperity, and happiness. Now we are in a position to respond honestly to those we are in relationships with should they ask us if we can meet the needs they feel are important in them. As with any relationship, **honesty** is the basic building block. We have to be honest with ourselves so that we can be honest with others. We need to know ourselves before we can share ourselves. This is the part that many don't get right when they are considering developing a relationship. Seldom do people discuss what their needs are and why they are important.

During a recent counselling session a client suggested that she now realized how she had only chosen to see her prospective mates in two dimensions. I was intrigued by this and asked her to continue. She said that she only saw what she wanted to see: the physical or sexual aspects and the monetary or economic aspects. She had always thought that if you could find these two things in someone, the rest of the relationship would sort itself out. You could learn to love somebody based on what they had or what they could give you. Part of what had contributed to her extended use of substances were her feelings of loneliness, sadness, rejection, resentment and anger concerning the failed relationships she had experienced. She believed that there was something wrong with her because she could never find happiness. The men she chose to be with always turned out to be "bums" and "takers." What she now understands is that there is a third dimension that she needs to look for and that is whether or not this person is capable of understanding her needs. Did he want to understand them, and would he try? She closed by saying that sex would now not be something she would use to entice someone to be with her but rather something to enjoy after he had proven himself. She realized she may not have as many dates in the future but also could see that she would not be as sad and angry because she felt "used." I could not have said it better myself. I closed the session by suggesting that there was a fourth dimension and that was the decision we make to choose an appropriate partner based on the first three dimensions.

Somehow we believe that by becoming involved in a relationship with someone all our problems will work themselves out. By some miracle the other person will know, intuitively, what we want or need without us having to mention them. The single most common reason why relationships fail is that one or both of the partners stops getting their needs met. They begin to look elsewhere for what they consider to be important to them--satisfaction of the needs that they can't or don't get met at home. Those needs are often honesty, trust, commitment, communication, sex, respect or a sense of belonging.

There are many other needs and wants that play integral parts in any successful relationship, but first we need to take a closer look at who we have relationships with.

Who are our partners?

How do we choose our partners anyhow? We **do** choose each other. This is not some random selection we make on a whim. And yet, how often do we actually think about who they are? How do we choose our partners? What do we look for? What do we want? What do they want? Can we give them what they are looking for? Do we have anything in common? Do we have some similar likes and dislikes? Do we like the same music? Read the same books? Enjoy spending our down time in the same fashion? Will they allow us the room we need in order for us to grow and become all that we can be? Will we be able to nurture and support them so they can become all they can be? What do we really know about them?

These questions highlight why it so important to have a good relationship with ourselves, for we are more informed about what we want and what we don't want. We are more clear about what we will and will not accept. The red flags go up quickly when we hear or see certain signs. If the new person in our lives wants to control how we spend our personal time and always wants to make the decisions about what we do when we are together, a red flag should go up. If he or she is always criticizing us or negating us in some way, we should see this a warning sign that all is not what it may appear to be. We can then decide to move on, before any emotional connection is made, if we are in touch with our wants and needs. We don't settle for less than what we want or feel is important for our personal growth.

Conversely, we can indicate that we are interested in getting to know the other person better when we see and hear things that appeal to our own sense of what is good for us.

Choosing a partner or a mate should not be about feelings and emotions alone. It should be about knowledge of ourselves and of the other person. We need to decide whether or not this other person will respect what we consider to be important to us--our own best interests. We also need to decide whether or not we can accept what the other person considers to be important to his or her personal growth. This will be one of the most important decisions we will ever make. Choose wisely. If the other person is thinking the same way about us, the chemistry can be magical. Enjoy it.

It takes work to have fun!

Many of us have been captured by the TV notion that love will conquer all--that if we love each other the relationship and all the problems we are carrying with us will work out. Love conquers all. We have seen too many love stories or read too many overly romantic novels. The only way that relationships stay alive and flourish is by working at them every day. Knowing what to do or not do and when to do it or not do it. Working to understand what our partners need and giving it to them unconditionally. Later we'll look at building up a surplus fund of love credits so that the relationship will have something to draw on when times get tough.

One mistake is to do nice things only when we want nice things. This does not build any trust or honesty into the relationship. We need to be doing nice things every day just because it feels good. Breakfast in bed, for instance, doesn't taste as good when there is an expectation of some payback in return for our good deed.

Working at the relationship can mean that we choose to put someone else's needs ahead of our own because we understand how important that would be to our partner. We don't have to negate our own needs in the process. Relationships should be about giving and receiving without expectation. The greatest source of grief in any relationship occurs when expectations are not met and resentments begin to ferment. If you really want to cause harm to the relationship disregard your significant other's wants and needs.

When you give more you get more, and when you get more you give more.

Working at the relationship also means putting out the effort to keep things interesting. Boredom can spell disaster to any solid relationship. For example, I tend to become very wrapped up in my work at times and from time to time my partner points out to me that she feels as though I don't care for her. When I thought about this I actually became offended. However, I began to practise what I preach and asked her to elaborate on what she meant. What she was trying to tell me was that every once in a while she wanted me to surprise her with an activity that she didn't have to plan for us. She wanted me to plan something too. Well, I'm not very creative when it comes to doing different things but what I heard was "I'm bored with this routine." Having me plan something different and spontaneous was what she was asking for. She was trying to tell me to pay more attention to that because that is important to her. She is not asking for much. It doesn't have to be a big splashy event but I have to put as much effort into our entertainment as she does. That's fair enough.

Boredom not only affects a relationship by not doing interesting things as a couple, but also by being boring, as a person, in the relationship. We have to work every day at not sliding into the realm of complacency. There is a real danger in being complacent. It means that we stop doing the things that attracted our partners to us in the first place. **If we are bored we will be seen as boring by those around us.** We each need to have outside interests that we can come home and talk about as opposed to the usual "how was your day?" Don't get me wrong. I think it is valuable to ask about each other's day because we can gain some valuable insight into how our partners are doing. But that can't be all the conversation that takes place.

Relationships need our time, not our things

Living things need to be cared for and tended to. They need to be fed and nurtured. Our relationships are similar in several ways. Just as a garden needs to be weeded so that the plants can grow strong and healthy, so does our relationship need the same attention to be sure we are not ignoring it or taking it for granted. Our garden will need clean air, water, sunlight and rich soil if it is to flourish. Our relationship will need acceptance and understanding, encouragement, patience and support if it is to flourish. We need to spend time learning about each other so that we can provide that care and nourishment to each other on a daily basis.

We often give to our partners what WE would need in a particular situation instead of thinking about what THEY need in that same situation. If, for example, a situation arises that calls for discussion and compromise but I withdraw, thinking that is what I would need so I'll do the same for her. I'll give her space and time. My partner, however, may need to sit down, right now, and talk it out so that she can feel better. I think that by withdrawing I am giving her what she needs when it is really what I need to do. This is often the source of resentment and even anger. When people don't get their expectations met they can become disappointed, resentful and angry. What our partners really need from us is our time, interest and understanding, not the things that we can provide.

Having a good relationship means putting an effort into understanding and comforting our partner when all we want to do is sit down and relax after a tough day's work. It means helping with the work necessary to keep a home neat and clean. It means being an equal partner in the parenting issues that constantly come up in any family home and working together to support each other even if we don't agree with the other's position. Talk about the issue afterward when the children aren't around instead of in front of them. It also means taking the time to be a good listener. It means hearing what our partners are telling us without our feeling the need to comment or put our two cents' worth in. If they want our advice they will ask for it. It means learning to interpret what our partners or our children really mean when they say they are sad, bored, feeling ignored or unhappy? It means learning how to communicate clearly and appropriately so that we are constantly aware of the emotional and physical boundaries that must be respected 100% of the time.

If we are not willing to put forth our best effort EVERY DAY we are not likely to have the meaningful relationship that we all desire. No one gets into a relationship to be unhappy, at least no one I know.

Earlier this year I had a client in my office who had just gone through a very difficult time in his marriage as a result of his use of alcohol. Things had deteriorated so badly that his wife had left him. She helped him understand that, although she still loved him, she was not interested in putting any more time or effort into the relationship. She, however, would support him in his efforts to stay sober. At our first meeting he told me he could stay sober if he thought they would get back together again. This is not the way to win back your sweetheart. What she needed to see was that he was prepared to stay sober regardless of what happened to their relationship. It took me some time to help him see that it was important for him to stay sober no matter what happened to the relationship.

Eventually he understood. After three months he called me for another appointment at which time he suggested he wanted to try to resurrect his relationship with his wife. I suggested that he may be wiser to build a new relationship with her if that was what he wanted to do. I asked him to go home and think about how he could do that. The next week he came back with a wide grin and stated that he was planning to "court" his wife just as he had when he was trying to convince her that he was the best thing that was ever going to happen to her. He loved her and he was going to do all the things that he had done before to help her understand how he felt about her. So he set about sending her flowers because he knew she loved flowers. Then it was a poem he had written. Then he asked her if she would meet him in a coffee shop for some conversation followed by a walk on the beach. This guy pulled out all the stops.

In the end they got back together again and are currently living in a very happy home. I asked him what was different this time around. He said that this time he hasn't taken the relationship for granted. Before, he would go for a day or two without having a shower. He would walk around with a day-old growth of grey hair on his face. He never thought about wearing a clean pair of jeans when he was seen in public with her. He took things, and her, for granted. He knows now that he can't stop behaving this way just because she has taken him back as a lover and a friend. He understands that he has to show her EVERY DAY that he loves her and cherishes their relationship, even on the days when he doesn't feel like it. "Funny," he says, "but it seems the more I put into the relationship the more I get back from her. I get what I give." How true it is.

We-ness

A sense of we-ness needs to be established for any relationship to be solid. This means that we are in this together. We commit ourselves to be open and honest in all that we do. We believe that, regardless of what happens, we will work our way through it and come out the other side as a stronger couple. It means discussing, understanding and accepting some common values so that each person feels he or she is an equal and valued partner in the relationship. It also means agreeing to work toward some common goals. This is one of the most important developments that needs to occur in any relationship. We have to work at reinforcing this feeling in our partners all of the time and vice-versa. This is a two-way street. We need to know that our partners are not going to bolt when a better deal comes along.

It can be too easy to let our partners deal alone with the everyday issues that present themselves and to let our personal concerns get in the way of doing what we need to do to keep our relationship solid. When we maintain a sense of "we-ness" we feel more secure in the relationship. Without security, we are simply two travellers heading down the road in the same direction never destined to meet at any one place. We are single people travelling together knowing that, at any time, the other person may take off in the another direction when the going gets too tough.

In any relationship, we must not assume anything. Let's not assume that we know how the other person is feeling or what the other person is thinking. Always check it out so that we know for sure. Our partners will appreciate the effort because it says that we care enough to ask. This is really important to any successful relationship. An old saying states this: "Never assume--it can make an ASS out of U and ME." Generally, if we are left to assume anything, we will usually assume incorrectly.

Relationship Bank Accounts (RBA's)

A Relationship Bank Account is a metaphor for the collection and storage of positive things or incidents that happen in a relationship. When we do something thoughtful for each other, when we are able to work through an issue to a positive conclusion or a WIN/WIN solution, or when we reach a common goal, the relationship becomes stronger. As we experience positives together we "bank" the good feelings they provide. Our relationship now has more reserves to draw on during those times when things aren't going as well as we would like. We make deposits into the RBA when we do the little things that matter in our day-to-day living; when we are thoughtful, kind and caring; when we are able to be open and honest; when we are able to give our partner what he or she needs instead of walking away or turning our back and saying, "Hey, that's your issue to deal with, not mine"; or when we remember an anniversary or special occasion.

Every relationship goes through hard times. During those hard times we make withdrawals from our RBA that, in turn, help us get through the tough times and back on track. If the RBA is empty, the relationship is likely to go bankrupt because there is nothing to draw on, no positive memories or experiences to focus on. It is important to make as many deposits as often as possible so that the account always has something there if we need it. It will sustain us in our time of need. It is the little things that happen regularly that count, not just the one big deposit. In other words one deposit is still one deposit no matter the size.

Kids are people too!

The other major relationship to consider is, of course, the one that we have with our children. I don't believe that there is one parent who sets out to make his or her child or children unhappy. I do believe that we all strive to do the best we can with our children and that our ultimate goal is to have a happy, healthy and safe home. **Our primary job as a parent is to help our children understand that home will always be a safe and secure place to be.**

Children need to be treated with the same dignity, respect and concern for human rights as any other living person on the planet. They are not our property or our slaves. If we don't treat them with fairness and respect, we fail them as teachers and caregivers and we should abdicate the privilege of parenting. I feel very strongly that this is an issue where we, as adults and parents, need to re-evaluate our thinking. We need to look at our values, ideals, old attitudes and perspectives. Some parenting practices that made sense thirty, forty or fifty years ago may no longer apply. This is not the same world as the world our parents raised their children in. Old parenting attitudes don't always apply now so to try to enforce them today will only make enemies of our children.

I'm not advocating a lack of structure or responsibility. I'm suggesting that our **approach** to parenting needs to reflect the changing world we live in. Any of us can learn how to parent differently but we have to be open to the possibilities of change. We can maintain the old values, such as honesty, trust, and mutual respect, for they will never be outdated. We need to teach them and provide models for them in new contexts.

Here are some concepts to consider:

1. The job we assume as parents is to take care of and to provide for our children. It is not the job of our children, when they are young, to take care of and provide for their parents. Let's allow our children to be children. They will grow up soon enough.

2. The messages and boundaries for what is acceptable and what is not

need to be clearly stated. They can be questioned at any time without fear of punishment or retaliation. If we are going to ask our children to act and respond in certain ways we had better be prepared to act likewise. Otherwise there is confusion and guessing about what was meant and why. We need to stay away from "do as I say and not as I do."

3. Even though a child's behaviour may be unacceptable we continue to show that child that we love him or her and that we are able to separate "the deed from the doer." Shame and guilt are not useful tools for shaping a child's life. They are weapons of destruction. No child ever learns a valuable lesson by being shamed. Experiences are to be used as learning guides.

   If we were attempting to train a dog to obey by beating it, all we would get would be a dog who was compliant, fearful and broken-spirited. What makes us think that our children would respond any differently?

What has to be maintained by force is doomed.–Henry Miller

4. The boundaries concerning physical, emotional, mental and spiritual health and safety need to be clearly defined and respected without exception for each member of the family. They are **NEVER** violated.

5. Feelings are allowed to be expressed in an open and appropriate fashion. They are never used to hurt any adult or child. They are discussed openly so that children learn that it is OK to state how they feel as long as that is done with respect for others. This is a learned skill taught and demonstrated by parents.

   Ninety percent of my clients report that either they were never encouraged to express their emotions openly or they were never taught how to express them appropriately. There were times when they felt they had to suppress their feelings in order to gain favour with their parents or to be seen favourably by others. At other times they were fearful of being reprimanded either by physical discipline or verbal threats of violence.

6. As parents, we need to act as teachers and guides so our children learn their values and lessons in our homes. Otherwise our children will learn their skills anywhere they can. That place usually turns out to be in the schoolyard or on the street.

7. There needs to be some established rules for living in the home. The rules for living should be fair and not rigid. They need to outline what is and is not acceptable behaviour. There needs to be clearly stated expectations and clearly stated natural outcomes for ignoring the rules that have been agreed upon. If the children are old enough they should be allowed to participate in how the rules are established. They should also participate in determining what the natural outcomes will be for any unacceptable activities. By allowing the children to participate in the process we teach them how to negotiate for what they see are their rights. They now have a stake in the outcome of any agreement that is made. Any natural outcomes that are experienced, pleasant or otherwise, will be their responsibility. This process takes the parents out of the role of being the "rules police." Remember, the natural outcomes were agreed to by all before the rules for living went into effect.

   A daughter might, for example turn the legal age to drive the car. She gets her licence and then comes to her parents to ask for the use of the car. They sit down and discuss how the car will be used, how often, under what circumstances, and what the expectations are of her as a driver. It is agreed that, should she get any speeding tickets, she will not have the use of the car for a specific period of time. She also agrees that she will pay for her own gas. If the gas tank is empty when she comes home, she forfeits the use of the car. This way mom or dad doesn't have to worry about not having enough gas in the car to go to work the next day. Mom and dad can agree to cover the insurance until she is working, at which time she will be expected to contribute to the premium. If she doesn't or can't save up enough to cover the premium, she does not drive the car until she is able to pay her share. Now she knows what the natural outcomes will be if she does not live up to her end of the deal.

She can't be disappointed or surprised by the consequences. She becomes responsible for her actions.

8. Our children are not expected to do more than their age would suggest is reasonable. In some families the children are asked or expected to perform duties and to accept responsibilities that are not appropriate for their age. This forces them to grow up faster than they should. These expectations can cause them a great deal of stress, as well. I have never accepted the idea, for instance, that a 10-year-old child be solely responsible for younger brothers or sisters. I understand the need for childcare because both parents are working to make ends meet, but putting that kind of responsibility on a child is not a good idea. The child can barely be expected to care for himself or herself let alone be responsible for the life of a two-or three-year-old. "Babies taking care of babies" doesn't work for me.

9. We need to constantly affirm and encourage our children. Instead of picking out the things that they don't do well we should focus on the things that they are good at. Children will learn from their successes faster than they will from their mistakes. Most children will work overtime to please their parents in order to get recognition and positive feedback. They need to feel that they are loved and that we think they are good at something. If we focus just on the things they don't do well our children will become discouraged and soon will stop trying to please us. To them it may seem that no matter what they do we always find something wrong. I'd stop trying too. As parents we should focus on encouraging our children as opposed to expecting perfection from them. They will do the rest.

10. We need to develop a sense that, as a family, we are organized and able to plan for or respond to a crisis should that happen. It provides a sense of stability and safety for our children. We can teach our children by how we handle any crisis of our own. They watch us and evaluate us all the time. We are their source of strength and knowledge. If we have difficulty working through our problems they may well see us as being in crisis all or most of the time. Our children may believe that going from one crisis to another, with little or no resolution, may be normal.

They can become used to living with "crisis tension." Often children who come from this kind of system grow up creating their own crisis situations so that they can feel normal. I certainly see that scenario a great deal with some of my clients.

Children Learn What They Live

If children live with criticism, they learn to condemn.
If children live with hostility, they learn to fight.
If children live with fear, they learn to be apprehensive.
If children live with pity, they learn to feel sorry for themselves.
If children live with ridicule, they learn to be shy.
If children live with jealousy, they learn what envy is.
If children live with shame, they learn to feel guilty.
If children live with tolerance, they learn to be patient.
If children live with encouragement, they learn to be confident.
If children live with praise, they learn to appreciate.
If children live with approval, they learn to like themselves.
If children live with acceptance, they learn to find love in the world.
If children live with recognition, they learn to have a goal.
If children live with sharing, they learn to be generous.
If children live with honesty and fairness, they learn what truth and justice are.
If children live with security, they learn to have faith in themselves and in those around them.
If children live with friendliness, they learn that the world is a nice place in which to live.
If children live with serenity, they learn to have peace of mind.
With what are your children living?

--Dorothy L. Nolte

Our children did not ask to be born. But they are here and they are ours. We need to provide them with as much security and love as we can. They need to feel valued and wanted. We can do that by being sure their physical and emotional needs are understood, and that we do all we can to meet those needs.

****

We build'em from the ground up

Relationships are built using the same principles as we would use when building a house.

First we have to have a solid foundation upon which to build the structure. Without it we have something that may stand on its own for a while but eventually it will crumble. TRUST is that foundation in our relationships. We cannot build any kind of lasting relationship without it.

Next, we need to build four walls that are strong enough to support all the stressors that will be placed upon them. In our relationships our ability to COMMUNICATE provides the support we need. The clearer we are about what we need, what we want, and why that is important to us, the stronger our structure will be. We also need to develop the capacity to listen. Being able to listen is an integral part of any communication. It is important to hear what our partners need or want from us so that we can provide the same support for them. Communication provides support and strength.

Every house needs to have a roof to protect it from the elements. Not every roof is the same, however. There are different pitches and different sizes. There are different colours and different building materials used. But no matter what shape or colour or size, it is still a roof doing the job it is supposed to do. So it is with people. We come in different sizes and shapes with different views on what is right or wrong. We see the world from different perspectives and we see how we function in it very subjectively. We may disagree on how things should be but that doesn't make any one of us more or less right than the other. It just makes us different from one another. Just like the roof. We need to understand that, as people, we may have our differences but we are still people. We need to ACCEPT OUR DIFFERENCES and work with them instead of trying to change other people into who we think they should be.

We should celebrate our differences--not try to destroy them. Wouldn't the world be a strange and boring place if the only colour car we ever saw was green; that every house was yellow; and that every human being was white. It is the differences in our individual characteristics and qualities that make us strong and resilient as a species. Our relationships, not just with our partners and children, but with our neighbours, friends, and work mates improve dramatically when we accept our individual differences. There is less stress among us and certainly more freedom.

Once the structure is built and protected by our roof we get to decorate the interior. We get to design and develop our living space to suit our needs. Once the work is done to build our relationship then we enjoy the SEX AND INTIMACY that naturally follows. We cannot have intimacy without trust and communication. Intimacy develops when we are accepted for who we are as people. I don't believe that a mutually satisfying sexual relationship can be experienced without developing intimacy first. So sex and intimacy are the rewards for doing the hard work first. They are the finishing touches that keep our home beautiful. They help provide the comfort and warmth that we are looking for. Without them relationships can be cold and lonely.

The Animal School: a fable

The Administration of the School Curriculum with References to Individual Differences

Once upon a time, the animals decided they must do something heroic to meet the problems of a "new world." So they organized a school.

They adopted an activity curriculum consisting of running, climbing, swimming and flying. To make it easier to administer the curriculum, all the animals took all the subjects. The duck was excellent in swimming--in fact better than his instructor--but he made only passing grades in flying and was very poor in running. Since he was slow in running, he had to stay after school and also drop swimming in order to practice running. This was kept up until his web feet were badly worn and he was only average in swimming. But average was acceptable in this school, so nobody worried about that except the duck.

The rabbit started at the top of the class in running but had a nervous breakdown because of so much make-up work in swimming.

The squirrel was excellent in climbing until he developed frustration in the flying class where his teacher made him start from the ground up instead of from the tree top down. He also developed a "charlie horse" from over-exertion and then got a C in climbing and a D in running.

The eagle was a problem child and was disciplined severely. In the climbing class he beat all the others to the top of the tree, but insisted on using his own way to get there.

At the end of the year, an abnormal eel that could swim exceedingly well, and also run, climb and fly a little, had the highest average and was valedictorian.

The prairie dogs stayed out of school and fought the tax levy because the administration would not add digging and burrowing to the curriculum. They apprenticed their children to a badger and later joined the groundhogs and gophers to start a successful private school.

Dr. George H. Reavis, Assistant Superintendent, Cincinnati Public Schools, 1939-1948

Does this fable have a moral? Yes.

Perhaps we should allow people to utilize the natural strengths they have to the best of their ability. It would be better for us to encourage them instead of discourage them to become who and what they want to be. Everyone is good at something and no one has the right to make someone else into something or someone they are not. When that happens we encounter resistance which usually ends up with someone running away. We must learn to celebrate our differences instead of denying them or trying to change them. If we can do that it is likely someone will celebrate ours as well.

The four building blocks relationships are built on

1. Trust
2. Communication
3. Accepting and celebrating our differences
4. Sex and intimacy

TRUST

Trust can bind people together; lack of trust can tear them apart in an instant. It is a quality that is sought by us all in our relationships. We have an ongoing responsibility to earn trust every day from the other significant people in our lives. It is difficult to gain, yet easy to lose.

The importance of trust in any relationship cannot be overstated. Without it we have no foundation from which to grow as a couple. It is **the** spiritual necessity of any stable relationship. Just ask anyone who has had a trust betrayed how it feels. Ask how easily that person will give it the next time. We will bestow it upon those people we want to be closer to, those who we feel deserve it because it is just as important for us to give it as it is to receive it. Such is the power of wanting and needing to feel connected to another human being. We will risk and continue to risk trusting others knowing the pain that awaits us if we guess wrong. Therein lies the conundrum of our existence: "Do I, or don't I, and when?"

Being in a true relationship with another person is the second most important relationship we will experience. Knowing and accepting ourselves for who we are and feeling comfortable with that information is the most important relationship we will ever experience. Trusting ourselves and **then** trusting others.

> **The glory of friendship is not the outstretched hand, nor the kindly smile nor the joy of companionship; it is the spiritual inspiration that comes to one when he discovers that someone else believes in him and is willing to trust him.**
>
> **--Ralph Waldo Emerson**

The basis for trust

First, trust has to be based on a **mutual respect** for one another as people and a deep understanding and respect for the others' rules for living--how they have chosen to live their lives based on what they feel is important for them. If their rules for living are discordant with ours, we have to make a decision as to whether we want to continue in the relationship and to what extent. We have no right to coerce, persuade or alter in any way the other people's decisions about how they have decided to live their life. We can challenge their beliefs, for I believe that's healthy, but that's it. When we go any further we begin to run the risk of abusing the trust that they have invested in us.

Next, trust has to based on understanding and offering **equality** as a basis for being involved with another person. This means, in a sexual sense (if sex is part of the relationship), that we are as equal in giving pleasure as we are in receiving pleasure and that boundaries for involvement are observed. It also means that we observe the rights of the other no matter what gender, to pursue or to participate in any and all activities that he or she feels are necessary to become all that person can be. We give support and expect support equally. To do anything else is to foster resentment and eventually trouble.

We base the development of trust on mutual respect and equality but the **elements** of trust-building depend upon these:

1. **Honesty.** We must be true to ourself and be true to what we believe are the principles by which we live our life. We owe it to ourselves and to our partners and children to be true to our beliefs. When we compromise our principles and values we damage our self-esteem. Our

partners and our children begin to see someone who they cannot believe in because they hear us saying one thing and see us doing another. What to believe? We must say what we mean, mean what we say and never make a promise we are not prepared to keep. Trust demands honesty. Honesty helps build security.

It also means that we will not distort, misrepresent or lie about our intentions or our actions. Honesty suggests that we will say what we believe and not what we think others want to hear from us. But we need to do this with compassion. If honesty is not tempered with compassion it can become harsh and destructive. We help our partners and our children understand that we are giving honesty and we expect it in return.

2. **Openness.** We must demonstrate a willingness to hear other points of view without condemning or judging them. If we are going to encourage others to be open with us we have to be careful not to argue or debate the validity of their feedback to us. Rather, we have to hear it for what it is. If we are trying to build a sense of trust in our relationships we'll need to hear other's comments as simply their view on how they see and feel about things and not as a judgement of us or what we do. If we are able to do this we encourage dialogue between us. If we don't, others will become closed to us. Most people will not risk being negated more than once or twice.

   Openness also means being open to correction and positive feedback from those we profess to love and care for. This is a tough one, especially for men who have been taught that there is no room for error, and compromise is a word that suggests weakness or giving in. There are many who must be seen as right all of the time, even when they are not. Question a man's decision-making ability and he is likely to consider his manhood challenged and on the line. Of course this is nonsense men have to get past. It is very stressful being right all of the time--especially when we're not.

   If you want to openly or directly challenge a woman, challenge her ability to nurture and to care for someone. Some would say that these traits are innate. We could argue the nature vs. nurture question here and miss the point. The point is that it is important to understand what really challenges a person and then DON'T do it.

3. **Respect.** We must, not only respect other people's right to decide for themselves what is in their best interests, but also to respect them as human beings. We need to respect their boundaries without trying to change them to suit our needs. If we are willing to give respect we have the right to expect it in return. If we do not get respect, we hope that our partner is open to hearing what that is like for us. If things continue, without change, we have to ask ourself whether this is a relationship that can be fulfilling for us based on our needs.

   Being respectful also suggests that we demonstrate our respect by valuing and honouring our partners, especially in public places. We need to behave in a manner that says, "You are important to me as my partner and as a person."Mutual respect is a cornerstone of any relationship. Holding hands and opening doors for each other is a simple way of doing this. Gawking at other people while you're with your partner would NOT demonstrate a sense of respect.

4. **Security.** This element means developing a sense of "we-ness," a sense that we are in this together. We will work through the issues and problems that present themselves together. When we consider our relationship we feel that we are not alone and that each is committed to love and respect the other without any conditions attached.

   This should not be a licence for one to abuse the other but rather a statement that says, " I will love you, blemishes and all." It also means that we each try to do the best we can to provide as much financial and emotional security as possible. If we are spending money that we don't have or are not discussing how money is spent in the home we are not developing a very secure feeling about our commitment to the survival of the relationship.

   Security also means that we build a sense of **safety** into the home. "Safety" here has an emotional, spiritual, mental and physical sense.

We protect our loved ones' safety by **NOT** labelling them as stupid or useless or any other derogatory term. It means that we don't yell and scream at them and embarrass them in front of others. We don't intimidate or threaten them in any way. And we don't play mindgames with them either. The people living in the home have to be able to express themselves in an appropriate manner without the fear of being judged or abused. Of all the places in the world, our homes have to be safe to live in. We can't fear being there. That's what security means.

Security is related to fidelity. Fidelity may be an old-fashioned word but it is a mandatory requirement for any successful relationship. We have to believe that for as long as the relationship exists and until it is declared over, each partner will remain faithful to the other. Once we cross this line, trust, honesty and certainly security go right out the window. Being unfaithful damages the spiritual part of the relationship to a degree that sometimes cannot be overcome. Infidelity can also place the very life of our partners and our children at tremendous risk because of sexually transmitted diseases. AIDS and other diseases do not discriminate. They will attack and kill anyone regardless of age, race, religion or gender. Our partners don't deserve that fate since they only dared to trust us.

5. **Consistency.** This element is self-explanatory. We develop trust by being consistent in the other four elements. If we demonstrate security one day but not the next, the relationship becomes unsafe and confusing rather quickly. If we are not honest all of the time it will be difficult for others to trust us at any time especially when we need it the most. Another element of consistency requires us to do what we say we will. If we say we will do something, we should do it. If we are saying one thing and are doing another it will be difficult for our partners or children to trust in what we say. Inconsistency creates doubt and doubt creates insecurity.

The work has to be done first

When we give our trust we give it hoping that other people will receive it and not abuse it. We hope they have done the work they needed to do too so that they will not bring any "old baggage" into this new relationship. There is no way of really knowing whether or not our prospective partner has dealt with his or her issues, although there are certainly signs that become evident if we are willing to look for them. We need to see that third dimension. Those who try to control us, change us, or make our decisions for us, and those who use sex as a reward, or exhibit jealousy in the name of love are indicating that they have some work to do and may not be ready for a relationship. However, when a relationship is new we get starry-eyed. We get excited and don't look for the reasons not to be in the relationship. We rationalize why it is right for us and overlook the signs that may indicate what could be wrong with it.

It is our responsibility to make sure that we are ready for a relationship and that we are prepared to give it all we can. If our partner is ready to do the same it is likely that the relationship will be as rewarding and fulfilling as both of us had hoped.

One situation that I see many times in my work is how people use relationships with others to make them feel good. There is nothing more compelling and emotionally powerful than a new relationship. It has the capacity to make all of our bad feelings go away. What better cure for pain and sadness than to start a new relationship? This is especially true when a relationship has just ended painfully or bitterly, leaving us abandoned or rejected.

We can't just end a relationship one day, start another one the next and hope it will survive for any length of time. We end up compounding our misery and taking out our anger and frustration on the person who deserves it the least. We have to heal and that takes time and effort. It takes hard work and soul-searching because relationships don't fall apart without each partner playing a role in the demise. We need to evaluate ourselves and ask the question, "What role did I play in what happened there?" Until we do that and then work to strengthen our skills we are not ready to get involved with another person or persons. Remember that relationships are not the answers to problems; they are the **rewards** for getting your life in order.

Saying "sorry" is not a bad thing

Regardless of how hard we try not to, we will occasionally mess up. We will say the wrong thing at the wrong time. We will do the wrong thing at the wrong time, and sometimes we will do both. Such is life. What we need to understand is, as a result, we can damage our partner's or our children's spirit. That spirit is that innermost place where self-esteem and self-worth resides. It helps us determine who we are. It is a vulnerable place in us all. When we trust someone we allow them access to that place and it hurts when it is abused.

How do we know when we have injured or unknowingly damaged someone's spirit? There are signs to look for. We would likely see the other person become less open to our touch, less attentive to our needs, or less willing to listen to us or to be around us. The person may be angry with us. If we are paying attention and are sensitive enough we will notice the changes almost immediately. If we notice the changes but do nothing to address them we are likely to damage the spirit further.

It is better to eat crow when it's young and tender than when it's old and stringy.--Anonymous

We inspire trust in our partners and our relationships when we are able to admit when we have messed up. There is no shame in saying we were out of line or that we have said something in haste that we regret. In a trusting and loving relationship the partners know that each other will take responsibility for his or her actions and respond or react accordingly. When we try to deflect our responsibility by excuse-making and justifying our actions, more damage is done. This is when our partners are likely to become angry and become less open to our efforts.

An old saying says, "If you make a mess, you clean the mess." If we make a mistake or find ourselves having damaged our partner's or our children's spirit we need to say, "I'm sorry. I didn't mean to hurt you," or "I didn't realize that my comment or my response embarrassed you." Whatever we did (within reason of course) doesn't matter. What does matter is our willingness to admit that we crossed a line, that we now realize it, and that we are apologizing for it.

How do we mess up?

- ❐ By not acknowledging or admitting that we were wrong--that we "crossed the line."
- ❐ By being rude to them, embarrassing them, and not acknowledging their right to be heard, accepted and understood, especially in front of other people.
- ❐ By not respecting their rights and values or by ridiculing their values, thoughts and ideas especially in front of other people.
- ❐ By labelling and name calling--saying things like you're stupid or dumb or lazy or fat or ugly, even if said in jest, is hurtful and potentially damaging.
- ❐ By being critical of their efforts to do their best.
- ❐ By dismissing their needs or assuming they are less important than ours.
- ❐ By demanding or forcing them to do something that goes against their values--their rules for living.
- ❐ By physically or verbally abusing them or just threatening them in some way.

How do we fix it?

1. Admit that we were wrong or that we were out of line. We need to do this with a quiet, soft and sincere voice. If we mean what we say and we want to be believed we must be sure that our body language and the tone of our voice matches the message we are trying to send.

2. Attempt to touch them. Hold their hand or just sit close to them while you are talking. If they move away don't push it.

3. Validate their feelings. Help them understand that WE understand, as best we can, how they are feeling. Don't make the mistake of saying, "I know how you feel." No one knows how the other person feels because their pain or their joy is theirs alone. We can, however, understand that something was uncomfortable or painful or sad. We can share in their joy and be happy for them but we'll never know what those feelings feel like to them.

4. If we have offended them or hurt them in some way we need to listen to them while they are trying to tell us what that experience was like. There is no need to defend ourselves. The issue is not about us; it is about them and how THEY feel. This is no time for a lecture on how we have been misunderstood or that he or she may have over-reacted to what was said or done.

5. Don't be afraid to ask for forgiveness. The worst thing that can happen is they will not give it to us right away. Maybe they need time to process what we have said. Maybe they need some time to calm down and to evaluate how they will respond or what they will say. That's OK. Leave them alone but don't ignore them. Perhaps ask them to talk about this again later in the day.

One of the questions that I am often asked is how to get the trust back. The truth is you don't get it back until you EARN it back by doing the things that are covered in this chapter. We need to demonstrate sincerity, consistency and fidelity; provide or build security; be open and honest; and respect others for who they are and want to be. That is how you earn it. There is no magic here.

✎ Ask your partner to mark on the line below where you are, as a couple, with respect to the level of trust he or she feels in the relationship. Then you do the same. Don't be alarmed or surprised if you have very different ideas about where the mark should go. Becoming aware of this information is more important than where the marks happen to end up. We rarely see things or evaluate things the same way. The information can be invaluable in helping to understand what is good in the relationship and what we can do that would make it better. Most important, it provides an opportunity to talk about the relationship in a way that is non-judgemental. The marks simply indicate where each of you feel you are and is not an indication of what the other person is not doing. **A word of caution: If you are not prepared to hear the answers, don't ask the questions.**

This can also provide a guide for the future. In a month's time, or whatever time-frame is appropriate, go back to the scale and see what has changed. If there has been some change talk about what has been different and what that is like for each you. Then continue on with what you are doing or decide what else each is prepared to do now. If there has not been any change re-evaluate what happened and consider other approaches. Keep trying. Change doesn't happen overnight. It is a process. Any change, growth or move toward a greater sense of self-management has three elements: a need to change, a desire to change and a willingness to be open to other perspectives or possibilities. We could add a fourth element here--persistence.

(Needs work) 1___2___3___4___5___6___7___8___9___10 (Best)

After you have completed this exercise and you have put your mark on the scale discuss some or all of these questions with your partner:

1. What can I do to help move your mark up a notch? Your partner should want to ask the same question of you.

2. What will that mean to you when you go up the scale, even one notch?

3. What will I see that is different in our relationship that will indicate that you are feeling more trusting? How will I know?

4. What do you need from me? What has to happen in order for you to feel more trusting?

Be the change you want to see in the world.--Mohandes Gandhi

COMMUNICATION

When we think about communicating an idea or expressing a thought, observation or feeling with someone, do we ever consider how complicated this interchange is? Do we understand that what we say to others may not be heard or understood in the way we meant for them to hear it? Did we stop to think about what we wanted to say and why we wanted to say it? Were we clear about what we wanted to say? Do we know that men and women interpret information differently? Do we consider that our body language and the tone of voice say as much as the words that we are speaking? Do we understand that our gender values influence how we interpret what we hear or see? There is so much that we take for granted when we try to say what's on our minds to other people. It isn't as easy as saying what you need to say and that's that. Without being able to communicate clearly, we have little hope of developing a meaningful relationship with others.

The main goal of any attempt to communicate is to be **heard** and **understood**. Think of the times when we tried to say what was really important to us but were unable to make ourselves understood. How long did it take before we began to feel frustrated and eventually angry? Good communication skills are like the walls of our house. They provide the structure upon which our roof is placed. By developing good communication techniques we become more successful at helping our partners understand what we want and need from them and we help them understand how we see our differences.

Say it how it is

One of the cardinal rules for effective communication is to talk about how we feel and not how someone or something makes us feel. In other words, say what we need to say from our own experience. If you are bored, for example, say, "I'm feeling really restless and need to get out for a while" instead of this: "I'm really bored sitting around here. Why can't you take me out somewhere."

Our feelings belong to us alone. We need to take ownership of them and not blame or credit other people for how we feel. Other people are not responsible for how we feel--we are. Besides, they are not responsible for being our entertainment committee. We don't communicate effectively when we are blaming others for what is going on with us.

To state the obvious, men and women are different physically and emotionally, and we process information differently. When we are trying to say what it is we feel, seldom does our partner hear that message in the way we meant it.

Here are some examples:

1. When she says, "No one pays any attention to me," perhaps she is trying to say that she is feeling uncared for or unloved. She may be saying that she needs a hug because she needs to know she is still important to her friends or partner. Women need to experience a sense of family or harmony and will work very hard to make that happen. There are times when she may need to know that her efforts are appreciated and not taken for granted.

2. When he says, "It's not a problem," he may be trying to say that he needs to handle the issue on his own, that he is not interested right now in any feedback or outside comments or information, but that those important to him can trust him to be working toward a solution of some kind. Men want to be seen as good at something, or being able to do something that is unique or special. And there is still that social expectation for men to be strong, intelligent and self-sufficient, especially when it comes to decision-making.

3. When she says, "We don't talk anymore," she may be trying to say that she needs more time and attention, or that she needs to feel more connected to her partner.

4. When he says, "I'll be fine," he is trying to say that he is working through whatever issue has presented itself and that he is capable of doing that on his own. Give him some room.

5. When she says, "I can't seem to keep this house clean anymore," or "The kids are driving me crazy," she may be trying to say that she is feeling overwhelmed or tired or that she needs some time alone. She may want an offer to help clean the place or to help her with some parenting issues so that she can relax.

6. When he says, "I got it. Thanks anyway," he is trying to say that he is taking responsibility for working through the issue or that he can handle the situation and is enjoying doing that. Men need to be seen as competent problem solvers. Somehow he feels that if he can't or doesn't take care of this business he may be seen as less manly or less capable.

The point here is that we need to take the time and make the effort to **hear and understand** what it is our partners are trying to tell us and not assume that we know what they mean. It's as much our responsibility to be sure we know what our partners are trying to say as it is for them to be as clear as they can be about the message they are trying to send.

John Gray, in his book *Men are from Mars, Women are from Venus,* does a wonderful job of explaining this aspect of communication.

There are no absolutes. The ability to communicate is not an exact science that is done correctly every time nor will we be able to predict exactly how the receiver of the message will respond in any given situation or set of circumstances. But we can say with some certainty that gender is an issue. For instance, men and women are likely to process information differently; we are likely to respond differently to the information presented; and we are likely to require different types of support systems around us as we think about how to respond.

He does/she does

Not every man will respond in a predictable manner. Not every woman will respond in a predictable manner. Many women will say, "Hey, I do this too!" Many men will say, "But I've reacted that way as well!" These are probabilities, not absolutes. Understanding how and why people respond as they do can help us understand more about what our partners may need from us in certain situations. They may be useful in helping us respond to them in a way that will allow for calm and reason to prevail before we go any further. We demonstrate respect and caring for our partners and/or our children when we try to communicate in a way that says, "I hear you and will try to understand you." Many arguments can be side-stepped by one or both parties if we know what our partners are trying to say to us, what they need from us and if we work as hard as we can to give that to them.

Women tend to be **overt** with their feelings. That is, they are more likely to entrust a close friend with what is going on in their lives and seek some support or feedback. Men, on the other hand, are more likely to be **covert** with their feelings. That is, they seek solitude so that they can sort out the issues and make some sense of what is going on. They are more likely to keep their feelings to themselves or, at the least, confide in one trusted friend. Even then it is likely that they won't disclose all of their thoughts. John Gray likens it to "going to the cave," figuratively speaking. Men are likely to withdraw to think. Women are likely to seek some input from others.

There are no rights or wrongs here, only differences in communication styles:

1. She may say, "I need to talk about this right now. I don't want to let this drag on." She wants to focus on the issues at hand. She wants some resolution to the problem that is facing them. Women are also better at recognizing potential anger-provoking situations earlier and tend to deal with them more quickly than do men.

   He may say, "I need some time to think about this. Let me be for a bit and then we can talk later." He wants to get off by himself for a while so that he can sort out what is going on. What are the real issues for him and for them? He needs some time to formulate a clear response so that he doesn't say some thing inappropriate. Most arguments happen because one of the people involved feels they are cornered or being pushed.

2. Women communicate more for the purpose of interacting with others and for getting feedback. Women work much more diligently at developing and maintaining a consensus in their lives than men do. My partner, for instance, can be on the phone for an hour and never repeat herself or talk about the same topic. It is part of her social life. It is how she interacts and stays connected with or in contact with those people she does not see very often. She is able to discuss things with trusted others and say things that she feels are important. She cannot always talk to me about her feelings or her issues. I understand that.

   Men communicate with others more for the purpose of determining where they fit in relative to those around them and for gaining information. They want to know who is doing what and why. It's important for them to know who knows what. They see information as power. Those who have more information are seen as being more important and more powerful--even more affluent. Listen to a group of people discussing a topic at the next barbeque or party you attend. Who is doing the talking? How attentive are those around this person? What do people say about that person afterwards? How often do you see a woman taking the lead in any conversation that is either a mixed group or a male-dominated group? Men are not generally as interested in being close to another male as they are in knowing what he knows. A man who is seen as well-spoken is automatically considered to be well-educated, knowledgeable, and probably a professional of some kind making good money.

   Men usually demonstrate an economic use of words. I get on the phone to either deliver or receive information. "Give me the facts," or "Here are the facts," and "I'll see you later." I may make some small talk but rarely does it go beyond that. If there is something important to say I'll mention it when I see that person face to face. There are exceptions to this norm, of course.

3. Women are more likely to discuss an issue openly and immediately so that the issues or the information remains clear. Decisions are more easily come by when the facts are fresh. Women are more likely to make decisions based on how they feel about something or how the outcome

would affect their relationships with others. Their decisions are based more often on their senses and intuition.

Men tend to find discussing the issues openly, before having a chance to think about them, would only make coming to a decision about anything more difficult. Men sometimes need to get off by themselves so that they can think things through. They tend to base their decisions on logic (no snickers, please), facts and statistics. Emotional considerations don't play as big a role in their decision-making processes.

They tend to judge more by "black" or "white" as in "You are either coming with me or you're not," "You either want to go or you don't," "They are either guilty or innocent,"or "They are either on our side or they are not."

4. Women tend to enjoy discussing their feelings and emotions and how they relate to certain issues of the day. They are more open with their thoughts. Women also recognize that they have all the skills necessary to compete in a man's world. They are equally capable of being outstanding engineers, scientists, doctors, accountants, bus drivers, truck drivers or race car drivers. Women are just as capable of making the tough decisions as men.

   Men tend to discuss factual, statistical, logical or philosophical topics as a norm. These are non-committal as far as any discussion concerning their emotions and feelings are concerned. They may become emotional about a topic they are discussing but that is not the same as talking about their innermost feelings. For instance, I can become very angry and resentful when I discuss what I view as the failure of the criminal justice system to advance my rights as a law-abiding citizen as opposed to advancing the rights of the criminals who don't respect social norms. But I seldom discuss the fear that goes with that anger and resentment.

   That said, I believe that an increasing number of men are allowing themselves to be more vulnerable and open with their feelings. This may be a consequence of the steadily increasing number of men who are single parents. Men are granting themselves the opportunity to show that they are just as caring and nurturing as women and that they are every bit as capable of assuming the responsibility and the role of parenthood.

5. Women want to be validated and accepted for how they feel. They would like their partners to communicate that validation. Women want to be seen as nurturers and to be thought of as caring.

   Men want to be validated for who they know, what they know and what they have achieved. They want to talk about how they climbed the corporate ladder. There is importance attached to knowing someone who is popular or who is well thought of by others. It is as if, by some osmotic process, they will become important too just because they know that person. Men need to be seen as successful and competent.

6. Women are more likely to want to talk first and relax and then communicate how they feel about someone by making love to their partners. If there are issues to discuss they will want to talk about them first, thereby gaining some sense of consensus. For a woman, making love is more about what goes on **outside** the bedroom than what goes on inside it.

   Men are more likely to want to make love first and then talk about issues or situations with their partners. Men are more likely to want to make love as a way of determining if their partner is still in love with them or if their partner has forgiven them. For many men it is the one way they can communicate how they feel about their partner because many have difficulty talking about their emotions openly or comfortably. Some men believe that by making love to their partners everything is, or will be, OK. It is a way of patching things up or "fixing" things. It says that things are all right again.

Dr. Deborah Tannen's book *You Just Don't Understand* illustrates very clearly the differences in communication styles between the sexes.

The point to remember is that we need to understand that there are different processes at work here. If a man needs to withdraw to consider his response or his decision, he needs to help his partner know he is not running away from her. He may simply need some time to make sense of what is happening and to sort things out so that he is clear about his position and why. Re-assuring her that he will return to discuss the issues is extremely important. If she needs to discuss her problems or ideas with others, we need to understand and encourage that as well and not get into this idea of "what is said in this house stays in this house."

What happens when the wheels fall off?

Do you ever wonder what really happened when that discussion turned ugly and developed into an argument? "That is not what I had in mind," we say. If there ever was a "love killer" it is engaging in constant arguments. Arguments can be avoided. Of that there is no question. But it takes skill to negotiate through the minefields that our lives can become. Use some of the skills outlined on our journey. They will work. There is beauty in simplicity so keep it simple. "What is the issue? How does it affect us? What role did we play in what is going on? "What do you need from me to sort this out?" and "This is what I need from you" are questions that help us to keep it simple.

Think WIN/WIN. Arguments are less likely to continue either now or in the future if both parties feel that they were heard and understood, that there has been some positive resolution to the issues, and that although both didn't get all they wanted they got some of it.

We have to find some middle ground between expressing our feelings at all costs and not sharing them at all. It takes time and trust to develop a mechanism, a formula if you like, that partners can use so that they each get their needs met in any discussion that takes place. The key here is to keep to the point or issue at hand. Discuss ONLY that issue and work it through to a mutually acceptable resolution. We do that by communicating our thoughts and feelings in a respectful, clear, compassionate and loving manner. The goal is not to win. The goal is to gain a mutual resolution to whatever the issue is. Once you start raising your voice, calling each other names, blaming and finger-pointing, it is all over. You are now well on your way to having the "wheels fall off."

Arguments usually end up with one or both people feeling hurt, sad and lonely. This is why it is so important to understand how each partner works through issues. How do they each deal with what is going on internally? What does he or she need from us right now? Then we need to encourage that process to take place. We have to trust in the system that we have built knowing that we will get back together to discuss what is going on when each is ready to do so. Arguments are usually about differences in our values and principles or differences about style and method. No matter what the issues are, if we trust each other and take the time to listen to each other without judgements or criticisms, we can work through most of what presents itself to us.

When we listen to others first, they will be more open to hearing us when it is our turn. This creates an atmosphere wherein both people feel that they have been heard and understood.

What are your rules for fair fighting?

We all have a natural instinct to survive by doing what we need to do in order to protect ourselves, our integrity, and what we believe is right for us. If we haven't determined or decided how we will air our differences--how we will fight fair so that we can say what needs to be said--we are likely to find ourselves arguing more frequently over issues of decreasing importance. Without a sense of reciprocal trust being been built into our relationship it is likely we will become more concerned about how the other presents himself or herself rather than what he or she is trying to say. So the style becomes very important. Is our current style sarcastic, aggressive, condescending or intimidating? Do we try to bulldoze our way through the issues we face so that we can get our own way? How does this style affect our partners? How does our style affect our ability to work through the issues we face and come to a WIN/WIN solution or outcome?

When we consider how much baggage we bring from previous relationships and then combine that with the unresolved issues we face in this current relationship, (you know, the issues that keep coming up because they were never resolved to the satisfaction of both people) it is little wonder that we have difficulty dealing only with the issue at hand. As partners, we need to agree on a style that is acceptable to each, on what is unacceptable to each, and both need to do this BEFORE any confrontation or discussion occurs. It sounds so clinical, doesn't it? However, this is one of the fundamental underlying problems that face couples today. They have no way of working through the issues that are bound to appear in a way that decreases the likelihood of an argument breaking out. We start off with the best intentions and end up yelling or screaming at each other.

Developing the rules for fair fighting is part of that mechanism I mentioned earlier. They are simple mutual agreements made so that each partner has a way of de-escalating a potentially violent situation. By violent I mean physical violence or verbal violence, such as name-calling, threats or intimidation of some kind.

Perhaps it means deciding on a hand signal of some kind that suggests one partner is getting confused or angry. It could be a simple phrase or sentence that means "I need a time out here." It is part of knowing your partner's needs and wants.

Here are some simple rules for fair fighting you might want to consider. Discuss them with your partner or come up with your own.

1. Consider the quotation on page 240. When we let the other person go first it allows us an opportunity to understand what is really going on so we can formulate a response. We could ask for clarification: "I'm not sure I understand what it is you are trying to say to me" or "What happens to you when . . . happens?" Sometimes just being able to explain how we feel is enough to calm the waters. Be sure to express opinions, thoughts, feelings, desires and concerns clearly and as calmly as possible. Take some time to get yourself together if you need to. Use an "I" perspective and not a "this is what you are doing" perspective. No one will stand by and be criticized or attacked without being self-protective. Now you are fighting instead of discussing.

2. Try to appreciate the other person's point of view and how he or she feels about things before responding even if it, or that person, doesn't make any sense to you. Remember it isn't **your** point of view and those are not **your** feelings. They belong to the other person and may make complete sense to him or her. By trying to discredit or downplay what is happening you are discrediting that person, who will likely respond to you in kind. Now the wheels are beginning to fall off.

3. Timing is everything. Don't try to deal with things just before bedtime, just before going to work, just before going to a party or gathering of some kind, and never in front of the kids.

4. Once you get into name-calling and labelling you begin to assassinate character. **Before you go any further, apologize for doing that.**

5. Stay on topic. Be sure to leave old scores or arguments out of any attempt to settle what is currently happening. Leave out any references to any other people. Don't talk about any relatives, in-laws, out-laws (past in-laws), friends, etc. and don't use any of them as go-betweens. Messages tend to get distorted when they are passed on second or third hand. Keep the discussion focused on how things are for each of you and what each would like to see happen that is different.

6. It is one thing to walk away to re-group or to calm down but it is another thing to withdraw or to give the other person the silent treatment. Once you stop talking and trying to sort out the differences, the possibilities for compromise or solutions to the issues also stop.

7. Trash the trash talk. Leave the cursing, swearing, vulgar, intimidating, threatening and accusatory language behind. It only serves to defocus the conversation and takes both people away from any solutions.

8. Don't try to analyse the situation or the other person. This isn't about psychiatry; it is about solution-making. People become really offended when they are being "studied," especially by someone who has no idea what he or she is doing. It only serves to deflect responsibility for working toward a mutually beneficial solution.

9. Tears can be used as psychic warfare. If you're upset and need to cry that's certainly understandable. If the tears are used as a way of controlling someone else's emotions, that is unfair fighting.

10. Know when it is time to call a truce. Know when it is time to say: "I can't do this anymore. I need to take a break. Can we do this later today or tomorrow?" There will be times when no solution can be found. It is important to know when that time has come and, for the time being, that it is OK to agree to disagree.

11. Watch your word choice. The word "and" suggests that we are looking for solutions. The word "but" can suggest that one person is being held more accountable for what is happening than the other. Try also to avoid using the word "why." When we use "why" the person to whom we are speaking may feel the need to explain or defend himself or herself. If there is tension already this won't help.

The purpose of this exercise is to agree on a process that can be used that will help both people stay on track. The goal is to keep the discussion a discussion instead of having it develop into a free-for-all. Those end up creating hard feelings which can really drain the RBA deposits. It's the process that counts and not so much how you do it, at least as long as what you do works for both of you.

Earlier in the section on trust we discussed how openness is an integral part of building trust. Openness in communication is just as important. We need to be open to hearing the other person's point of view and at the very least acknowledge that it exists. We don't have to accept it or believe it, but for the other person to feel that he or she has been heard we have to acknowledge that that person has a right to feel that way or to think that way. We would expect the same consideration. Discussions don't develop into arguments because one won't accept the other's point of view; they develop into arguments out of frustration at not being heard or by not being given the opportunity to be heard.

When either person sees that the discussion is deteriorating, one needs to back off and say: "Can we take a break for a bit. I need to get refocused here." One or both partners have to take some responsibility for not allowing things to get out of hand. Both need to agree that when they see things are sliding toward an argument they will stop it before it gets started. They might agree, for instance, that they will take a time out if they get to the point where they are losing sight of what they are discussing. This is part of that mechanism called "the rules for fair fighting."

"Drawing on my fine command of the English language, I said nothing."--Robert Benchley.

We need to check our own feelings when we get into discussions that begin to take a turn for the worst. Before we put our mouths into action let's make sure our brains are engaged. There will be times when what we don't say will be just as important as what we do say. What is going on inside us? What do we recognize? What are we feeling? Once we determine how we are feeling we are then able to identify and focus on the real issue(s) that need to be discussed, what psychologists call the "source issue." It is important to do this **before** we begin to say things we wished we hadn't.

If we can do this we may be able nip an unnecessary argument in the bud. We don't need to defend our feelings but we do need to have them validated.

Here are some feelings that may lead men to defend themselves :

❒ feeling criticized

❒ feeling rejected, unaccepted or put down

❒ feeling blamed or responsible for an outcome beyond our control

❒ feeling inadequate for not being able to live up to someone else's expectations

❒ feeling as though he is not to be trusted or are not seen as trustworthy

- ❐ feeling unappreciated, especially when he's done his best and his best is not recognized. It is important for a man to be seen as competent and good at something
- ❐ feeling as though he is not respected
- ❐ feeling embarrassed, especially in front of others

Here are some feelings that may lead women to defend themselves:

- ❐ feeling vulnerable and unsupported when she is trying to share her thoughts and feelings
- ❐ feeling that she is not heard or understood--that what she has to say has no merit or importance
- ❐ feeling judged
- ❐ feeling embarrassed, especially in front of others
- ❐ feeling as though she is not valued or respected as a person
- ❐ feeling unimportant, neglected or ignored
- ❐ feeling put down

There are some common feelings that affect us and there are some different ones as well. We all can be triggered to become defensive by experiencing any of these at any time. In our relationships it is **our** responsibility to self-monitor--to be aware of what is going on with us and then to communicate that awareness to those important to us. How can they know what is going on with us unless we tell them? It is not realistic for us to expect them to magically know what we are feeling. It is up to us to be clear. When we are not clear about what is going on with us we affect not only our own inner harmony but also the harmony of the relationships we share with those around us.

We need to understand and allow for the varying styles, methods and techniques each gender uses in order to present their issues and their concerns to us.

If we truly trust other people, we will know that they are not trying to hurt us by what they are saying but, instead, may be having some difficulty in communicating their feelings or their concerns to us. This requires us to be more accepting and less ready to find fault with them. It also means that each of us needs to be very clear about our individual wants and needs in the relationship. Herein lies the TRUE barrier to a successful relationship. If they don't know what we want or need, they can't give it to us.

Being clear now could save you grief later.

I have referred to our "wants and needs." What is a "want" and what is a "need?"

As human beings, we all have basic needs that have to be present in our lives in some form so that we can survive in a spiritual sense as well as a physical sense:

1. Enough food, shelter, warmth, and clothing

2. Some form of contact with other human beings

3. The ability to communicate in some way

4. Freedom to choose

5. Safety, both physical and emotional

6. To be able to trust and to be trusted

When I was gathering thoughts and information for this part of the journey I found it fascinating that no two people described what a "want" was and what a "need" was the same way. It was something different to each and yet there was a basic underlying principle that was evident. They all agreed that a "need" was something that had to be there in order for the relationship to survive. They didn't mean the people but the relationship. They spoke of a relationship as though it were a living thing which, of course, it is. Just as any living thing needs to be nurtured, so do our relationships. It lives because of the energy (food) we give it or put into it; by the way we communicate (tending and weeding); and by the things that we do to keep it healthy and vibrant (watering and turning the soil). If we stop giving the relationship any of these it will begin to wither and eventually die.

"Needs" then are **core values or spiritual values** that must be present in order for the individuals to feel that their basic beliefs about life, their rules for living, and their beliefs about what is right for them are not going to be compromised. These values shall be respected and accepted without judgement from their partner or friend. They are the basis upon which the relationship is built. My colleagues mentioned things like honesty, trust, fidelity, encouragement, security and freedom. There are many more.

The more needs that are met, the more stable the relationship.

It is extremely important for our partners or friends to be aware of what these "needs" are so they can provide the environment in which these "needs" can be acknowledged and validated. It is our responsibility, as a partner in the relationship, to build or provide an atmosphere in which the other can grow as a human being. We need to talk about how that can happen. And this, of course, needs to be reciprocated in order for both people to get what they need from the relationship. Otherwise someone whose expectations won't be met will become angry, resentful, sad, perhaps lonely, and may even feel abandoned. Our needs have to be communicated clearly and heard just as clearly. If in doubt, ASK.

I may be giving 100% of what I can today but it may only be 50% of what you need. Please accept it as the best I can do right now.

Our "wants" tend to be more about our **physical** and **emotional desires**: things like economic freedom, freedom to evolve as a person, the importance of family and children, support, respect, consistency, boats, cottages, travel, and so on. One person's "wants" may, however, be another person's "needs." None of these is written in stone. There are no hard and fast rules about which can be what. They are subjective and not to be challenged or ridiculed. They are interdependent with the values and principles by which we live our lives.

For the most part our "wants" are the things that **enhance** our lives and our relationships. Our wants are what we would like to have or to experience so that the relationship can become all we dreamed it could or would be. The more "wants" we get, the better it feels to be in the relationship. Our "wants" are as important to us as the degree of importance we place on them. In other words if financial security is a "want," how much money would be enough?

Would it be enough to have a mortgage paid for by the time we are 55? If we had enough to put the kids through university, would that be enough? Where is the comfort zone for each? Perhaps it means that we could travel later in life and get a chance to see the places we only dreamed about as children. Maybe one of our "wants" is to go back to school so that we can continue to actualize as a person. One of our "wants" could be to have a large family because family has always been important to us.

It doesn't matter what our "wants" are. It does matter that our partners know what they are so that they can decide, as early as possible, whether our goals are similar--whether we each can have what we want. This is WIN/WIN. If that can happen, great. If that can't happen, it's better to know now than to assume we will work it out somehow. How much can we let go of to get what we want? For instance, I would like to have a large family--maybe six kids--but my partner would like to be able to travel. Given our financial likelihood, we can't have both. Is there a compromise here? Could we have four kids and still travel? Our "wants" don't necessarily have to be the same but they do have to be flexible to some degree. Words like "compromise" and "negotiate" become more than words. They become concepts.

Our "needs" **must** be there in order for us to continue on in the relationship. Our "wants" are the icing on the cake that provides the extras that make the relationship all it can be.

If we want to be a part of a successful relationship, we simply need to give to our partners what we want from them. If we need honesty, we need to be honest. If we need compassion and understanding, we need to be compassionate and understanding. If fidelity is important to us, we need to be monogamous--we need to cherish and value our partners. If we want to be respected, we respect our partners, and so on. This is not rocket science.

Who goes first?

"It is not important who gives it first so I'll take the lead" should be our credo. Have you ever, openly and together, discussed with a potential partner what your wants and needs are regarding the relationship? This is a discussion that should take place long before any sexual activity has taken place.

Sex can make you go blind?

I'm not anti-sex but I do understand that once people make love to one another an emotional bond of some kind usually develops for one or both people. Now the feeling that "somehow things will work themselves out" begins to take form and we don't have the important conversations that need to take place. We don't see that important third dimension. Physical attraction and early sexual activity help to keep us blind to what the other person may be presenting. We sometimes overlook certain things--types of behaviour, for instance. Do we mistake jealousy as caring and not an attempt to control us? We all have experienced that nervous excitement when love is new. We see only what we want to or just the things we like about the person we are involved with. Some can't think about anything else. Some can't eat. For some, time goes by too slowly between visits or dates. I heard it said somewhere that anxiety is the time between now and then. And it's all so wonderful.

With familiarity things begin to change. We notice that some of the little things that we used to like to do for each other don't get done as much. We begin to see things that we would like to ignore but can't. We find that the important things that we saw or felt--what we need so we stay happy and content--are missing more often. We begin to resent not having what we need. We feel less valued and respected. We begin to feel disappointed and then we feel anger. Sex becomes a way of making up instead of expressing how each feels about the other. Men often want to engage in sex as a way of making amends or checking to see if the relationship is still OK. Women will use sex as a tool or a reward for their partner's good behaviour and as a way of keeping a partner closer to home. Sex should never be used as a weapon or a tool. It is simply another wonderful way of expressing one's feelings for another. It is another way of communicating. Too often though it is a way of developing an attraction and an interest as opposed to a way of enjoying the relationship **once it has been established.**

It is never too late to have the conversations we need to have so that we can determine whether or not this person is someone we can build a fulfilling relationship with based on each person's wants and needs. The longer we go without having it, however, the more difficult it may be for the other person to hear or understand what it is we are trying to say: what is important to us and why.

The one cause of a great deal of stress in any relationship is the feeling that one of the partners is trying to change the other into someone he or she doesn't want to be. If we have not been made aware of anything to the contrary, it is in our nature to be comfortable. We will arrange things or organize things so that we face a minimum of change. If we wait too long to have these conversations, it is possible for one or both to feel they are being manipulated or pressured to change in a way that is uncomfortable to them.

If you want to make an enemy of someone try changing them into people they don't want to be.

When you and your partner have some quiet time try sitting together and, on separate sheets of paper, list all the qualities and characteristics or other wants and needs that each believes necessary in any good relationship. What makes a relationship successful for you? Some examples are listed below. Then compare your sheets. This is not done as a way of pointing a finger and saying, "This is what you are not doing." Rather it is a way of understanding what the other person considers to be important. The lists can provide an opportunity to open dialogue between the partners regarding what they have in common, what each does well, and where they can work to build a stronger, more fulfilling relationship. They don't have to mean the same for each. Just know that it is important and to what degree. You can learn a great deal about one another by doing this. If you realize that your partner considers something to be important, ask why that is. If you are not working as hard as you can to provide that, start. This exercise also provides an opportunity to reveal thoughts and feelings that you may have kept bottled up inside and do it in a way that is non-judgemental and non-confrontational.

The lists may include:

-goals
-interests
-leisure time activities
-values
-intimacy
-meaning of trust
-commitment
-romance

-friendship
-rules for living
-taste in music or books
-fidelity
-hobbies
-family
-humour
-respect

-playfulness
-sharing feelings
-personal space
-rights and freedoms
-communication
-patience
-understanding
-love

If things get more serious you can do the same thing concerning topics like religion, money, children, parenting styles, common goals, and so on. All we are trying to do here is find a non-confrontational/non-judgemental way of saying: "This is what is important for me. These are some of the things that have to be there for me to be happy. If you can do that, great. If you don't think that you can or if that is not what you want or need, please tell me now." This may seem too mechanical but some of the couples that I have worked with wish they had done this before they got to their present situation. Now the issues they are faced with are very different. Many have established homes, are part of a blended family, or have settled into a lifestyle that they don't want to leave, and are finding out they have little in common with their partners beside their domestic lives. Still others are having children and are discovering that their parenting styles and what they believe about raising kids is opposed to that of their partners. Before, either partner could have walked away but that is much more difficult to do now. The couple stays in the relationship despite its differences because they feel trapped or they hope that the other person will change and the problems will disappear. Don't assume that anything will change on its own or that the other person will give in or give up as time passes.

✎ Another way of doing this, that may be fun as well, is to create a "Want Ad" and give it to the other person. If you were going to advertise yourself what would you say?

For someone looking for:

- who you are (a little self-disclosure needed but no more than you are comfortable with)
- what you need from any relationship you may be in
- what you want from the relationship
- what you like and what you don't like
- what you have to give
- what you are looking for

"What's for lunch?"

Meaningful communication is a vital part of any relationship. We have to be able to talk about more than the weather and what's for dinner. We need to be able to talk about our hopes and our dreams openly and without fear of judgement or ridicule. Being able to dream is a necessary part of any person's life. People need to have dreams in order to hope that their lives can be all they want them to be. Our dreams can be the impetus for the decisions we make in our lives. How often have we heard of a young boy or girl who says, "I dreamed that I could be a Major

League hockey player or baseball player or an actress or singer." Some of the dreams are basic such as "I dreamed that I would grow up to be a good mother or father and not abuse my kids like I have been abused" or "I just want to live in a nice house and have a good job with no worries or stress." They dared to dream that they could become that person and then dedicated themselves to pursuing the dream. Our hopes for our futures lie in our dreams. We need to share those dreams with our loved ones and they need to be able to share their dreams with us. This helps to build intimacy into our relationships as well.

Nothing happens unless first a dream.--Carl Sandburg

We also have to focus on the **content** of what is being said and pay less attention to the style or how it is being said. We have seen how men and women present their thoughts and feelings differently and how we process information differently. People communicate in different ways with different goals in mind. Whatever their style, it is the **message** that we need to listen to. If we can do this we will find we are able to hear more and argue less. If we are not sure about what has been said, we should ask for clarification. Don't be afraid to say: "You lost me. I'm not really sure what it is you are trying to say to me." Seeking clarification periodically is a good idea because it keeps us on track so that we continue to discuss the topic we started discussing. If we don't find a way to stay on track we can get into "kitchen sink" discussions very quickly and they can become frustrating. "Kitchen sink" discussions happen when old issues that have not been resolved work their way into the present conversation. Pretty soon the issue we started to talk about gets lost and becomes another "unresolved argument."

"How do I love thee? Let me count the ways."
--Elizabeth Barrett Browning

There are many different ways of communicating our thoughts and feelings. We can draw pictures, we can write poetry or letters describing what we need or how we feel, we can verbalize what we feel is important, we can use sign language, and we can use role plays or demonstrations of some kind to indicate what is important to us. Choose a way that is most comfortable for you and use it. The style by which we communicate is not as important as having the message we are trying to convey as clear as possible. We need to be heard and understood.

(Needs work) 1___2___3___4___5___6___7___8___9___10 (Best)

Have your partner mark on this line how he or she feels about your abilities to communicate with each other. In other words, how satisfied is he or she currently with respect to your being able to communicate effectively as a couple? After you have each put your mark on the line discuss the questions that follow:

(This is a process that involves two people. However, it is our responsibility to evaluate the role we play in what happens in our lives and to make the appropriate changes. What happens next is up to us.)

1. What can I do to help move your mark up a notch?

2. What can we do to make ourselves more clearly understood?

3. What can we do to avoid arguing but still discuss the important issues that need to be resolved?

4. When I am able to present my issues or concerns more clearly, how will that make a difference to the way you see or feel about our relationship?

5. What do you need to see or hear from me that would make a difference where you place your mark the next time we do this?

6. How will your life be different when we can communicate our issues or our feelings in a more loving fashion? What will that mean to you?

7. Does anger play a role in how effectively we communicate? When I am able to manage myself more effectively, and therefore my anger, will we communicate better?

☞ Go back to the scale again in a month's time, or any other length of time that works for both of you, and see what has changed. If there has been some change, great. Keep doing what you are doing. If there has been little or no change, re-evaluate what you tried to do and decide on some other approaches. Be prepared to give this process the time it deserves. It won't happen overnight. The important thing is that you both continue to discuss the outcomes together and try new things.

ACCEPTING AND CELEBRATING OUR DIFFERENCES

We have talked about the differences we are likely to experience, as men and women, when we are interpreting or responding to information that is presented to us. We also have established that men and women communicate differently. Those differences are very real. But there are other differences that add to our uniqueness as human beings. Different personality types have different character traits. These differences also figure into the mix when we are trying to understand our partners.

We need to understand that the differences are innate and not likely to change much. We will be better served when we accept the fact that we are not only different because we are male or female but we are different just because we are human. Let's put our energies into learning how to get our needs met without compromising who we are and who our partners are. First, we need to see people for who they ARE and try to understand that they do what they do, not because they wish to disregard or disrespect us, but rather so that they can grow and get their needs met. Then we can let go of our anger around them not being who we want them to be. It can be done. When we can do this our partners and our relationships will flourish.

If you and your partner always agree then one of you is unnecessary.--Dr. Robert Anthony, from *Think Again*

Trying to coerce our partners to change will get us nothing but grief in the long run. We can choose to see our differences as exciting and challenging instead of obstacles that stand in our way of getting what we need. The differences within us and between us are not something that we have to conquer, just something we need to accept and understand. When we do this it gives us an opportunity to see the world through "eyes other than our own." It provides us with a chance to learn about ourselves as individuals.

What do you think of me now?

Let's consider the more obvious differences between males and females with a desire to understanding our differences:

1. Physiologically, men tend to age faster than women so women tend to live longer than men. (I'm not sure that I agree with the idea that men grow older more gracefully. To me, there is nothing more sexy and appealing than a woman in her middle years who strives to be in good shape, who takes pride in how she presents herself and who carries herself with confidence. All these qualities say she is pleased and proud of who she is. That turns my head every time. The experience is even better if it is your partner.

2. Men tend to have a higher percentage of muscle mass than women. Men have larger bones than women so that they can participate in heavier work for a longer time.

3. Women tend to have better sight and hearing than men. (Do you ever wonder how she can hear you all the way out to the garage?)

4. Men tend to be more challenge- or conquer-oriented. This is not to suggest that women are not competitive or that they are not willing to take up a challenge. Men want to demonstrate their physical competence and prowess which most believe is directly attached to their self-esteem. They want to be seen as good at something, especially when that means being better than another male. Testosterone may play a role here. Women tend to be more interested in relating to those around them and developing social

connections. Women are certainly competitive but don't seem to feel the same need for the same reasons as men.

5. Men tend not to show or discuss their emotions as easily or as openly as women. We stay more non-committal. We stick to the facts, statistics and logical stuff. Women tend to be able to openly discuss how they are feeling and how they relate to what is going on around them.

6. Men tend to see themselves as providers and protectors. He's the one that will "take the bullet" for his family. He is seen as the teacher. Women tend to see themselves as caregivers and nurturers. She's the one that will build a home and keep the fires in it burning. She is seen as the negotiator and the mediator.

7. Men would like women to "think" as they do; Women would like men to "feel" as they do.

8. Men want to feel needed, respected, and to be seen as competent and capable. Women want to feel cherished, valued, cared about, respected and seen as intelligent and caring.

9. Men are more linear or sequential thinkers. Men will consider an issue and construct a whole picture of it one step at a time. *This* relates to *this* and *that* relates to *this* and so on until the whole is built. Do it right and then move on to the next step and do that right and then move on, etc. A man would build a puzzle by finding each piece that fit with the piece before it--each piece relates to another piece. Women tend to be more open and aware in their thinking. They seem to have a sense of how things are or should be. They are more likely to look at the big picture and take it all in and then begin to see the parts that comprise the whole. Women are more interested in how the parts relate to the whole. A woman would build a puzzle with the end result in mind and find the pieces that continued to complete the whole puzzle--each piece relates to the complete puzzle.

10. A man's greatest fear is that he would be seen as incompetent and not measuring up to others' expectations of him, especially his immediate family. A woman's greatest fear is that she would be rejected and not seen as caring or nurturing.

11. When dealing with stress men will retreat into themselves while seeking a solution to the issue. This means that they may well get involved with something that is completely outside the issue to allow themselves time to think about it. Once a solution is found they will announce it to those they care about or who are involved. They may often appear detached or uncaring. Only when they feel they need some information that they do not have will they seek the help of someone else. When dealing with stress women will likely approach someone they trust so that they can talk about what it is that is causing them stress. They are likely to involve others so that they can talk it out and get it out. Once done they will begin to determine what they need to do to deal with the stress and then will go about it.

12. Men and women have different "rules for living"--different values that define their sense of integrity and who they are or how they want to be seen. Men value power, information, skill and the ability to achieve something tangible with it. Men want to be seen as successful by their peers as well as their families. Women value being involved or engaged in a variety of fulfilling relationships and being able to communicate and discuss things that are emotionally meaningful to them. They value beauty and sensitivity and harmony or a state of well-being. Women want to be seen as people who share, care and relate well with those around them.

13. Men want to be trusted, admired for something that they do well and appreciated. Women want validation for their vision and their feelings, they want equality and respect and they want to feel that they are understood and cared about.

There are many more but this is a good list to start with. If you can understand these differences you've got most of what you'll need to have all that you want. The key is in the **ACCEPTANCE** of our differences.

What you see is what you get !

I think there is always a danger in trying to categorize or pigeon-hole people into particular slots so that we can keep our understanding of them as simple as possible. People defy labels. They each want to be seen as unique--as indeed we are.

I attended the circus recently. While watching the different performers, I wondered what makes a person want to be a high wire entertainer or a lion tamer or someone who gets shot out of a cannon. Those performers have unique personalities that enable them to be good at what they do. We are all separated by our individual character strengths--none better or greater than the others, just different. Witness the composer of beautiful music who couldn't draw a stick man or the writer who is tone deaf. We all have a multitude of assets and strengths and talents that we can draw on if we are courageous enough to try. I say courageous only because that's what it takes to overcome the fear of failure. Once we get by that we can do almost anything we want.

We can identify distinct and intrinsic qualities in four particular types of people. Understanding someone's character traits can be extremely beneficial when we are trying to understand why people do the things they do and why they respond as they do. This goes beyond gender differences, although understanding gender differences is very important, as we have just seen.

When we try to see those around us for who they are and not who we think they should be or want them to be, we can begin to **accept** them for the interesting and exciting people they are. Our stress, frustration and anger levels dramatically decrease as well. We can give up the impossible task of trying to change others into our idea of who they should be or how they should act. People will defend themselves against any kind of pressure or coercion. When we accept that people have a right to be who they want to be and to do what they want to do, it allows us to decide whether or not we are compatible as partners or friends. It promotes a sense of freedom, especially for them.

Acceptance of this kind allows people to be real and not have to wear a mask to be accepted by others. People simply do what they do because that's who they are. What they do makes sense to **them**. Do we like what we see? Can we accept their ways of doing things without being offended or uncomfortable? Where are we compatible? Where do we complement each other? What can we live with? What can't we live with? How much of what we see is what we want? How can we work with our differences so that we both get what we need? Just as important, how can we communicate our wants and needs? What does my partner, my child or my friend need from me when he or she is distressed?

Instead of getting involved with describing these four character types in complicated psychological mumbo jumbo let's use some easily identifiable and non-judgemental identities like Eagles, Owls, Butterflies and Geese.

The Eagle

The key characteristic is that Eagles love to soar. They strive and struggle to be free. Eagles need to feel free of boundaries and free to choose and to act, often on the spur of the moment. Just as Eagles are known for their boldness and their endurance so are Eagle-type people.

What else?

❐ thrill seekers; risk takers; impulsive and spontaneous; competitive; living for the moment; impatient with routine and rules.

❐ entrepreneurial; pragmatic--concerned with everyday affairs and not some theoretical idea of how things should be; good entertainers and performers; athletic or at least enjoy the competition of athletics; able to make decisions quickly and skilfully; excellent negotiators.

❒ appreciative of skill and attracted to those activities that require a level of skill, action and performance; and most important, variety.

❒ charming and exciting; generous and sharing; never down for long; good with their hands; great in a crisis; wanting to be seen as resourceful and clever; eager often to the point of impatience.

❒ sensuous and exciting in their relationships.

You will know when Eagle-types are upset or "not themselves" when you see or hear them:

- being rude or defiant
- lying or cheating
- pushing the limits and boundaries or breaking the rules without regard for others.
- dropping out of things or not being competitive
- becoming physically aggressive.

What they need:

- a party, a change of routine, a new toy to play with or to divert their attention, some new challenges to work on, a hike in woods, perhaps a gift certificate to go hang gliding or sky diving.

The Owl

The key characteristic about Owls is their ongoing quest for knowledge and information. Things have to make sense to Owl people. They are intuitive thinkers. They seek answers to "what makes it happen?" Owl-type people are conceptualizers. They are thinkers who often leave the doing to others so that they can move on to the next problem or challenge. They seek competence in themselves and others they associate with.

What else?

❒ constant learners; perfectionists; often ask "why"; get very impatient with those who are incompetent; usually set very high standards for themselves and others they associate with; enjoy stimulating conversation with someone they feel is their equal; become annoyed with those who don't get to the point; use language as a tool.

❒ tend to be very theoretical, analytical, logical; needs to see the sense in things; conceptual; create models for others to follow.

❒ highly regard intelligence, logic, clarity; are progressive thinkers.

❒ seen as skilful and intelligent; wise and knowledgeable; obsessive at times; very competent; arrogant; logical; developers of ideas; abstract thinkers who assume everyone knows what they mean or are thinking; good with words and language(s); believe nature can be overcome; can be terse.

❒ in relationships tend to be or are seen as apart from or detached somewhat; objective; thought of as cold and unfeeling, although this is not true; feel deeply privately.

You will know when "Owl" people are upset or "not themselves" when you see or hear:

- indecisiveness, withdrawal, isolation, silence
- sarcasm and criticism of others and possibly themselves
- lack of cooperation; inability to consider alternate points of view.

What they need:

- new problems to solve or a project to work on--work is play; a new book to read; conversation that will stimulate them to learn something new or that challenges a belief; a chance to teach someone; attend a seminar given by someone they respect.

The Butterfly

The key characteristic about Butterflies is their constant search for self. Their goal is to self-actualize--to be all they can be--to know themselves better than anyone else. They live by a moral code of ethics and rules for living that are not to be compromised. Truth and honesty are of the utmost importance. They are the benchmarks by which they evaluate other people. They need to find what meaning of life is and how they can contribute.

What else?

❒ cause-orientated--Greenpeace, World Wildlife Federation, etc; open; romantic; emotional; idealistic and utopia seeking; dramatic, thoughtful and kind; sensitive to the feelings of others.

❒ perceptive; very persuasive and logical regarding feelings; supportive; loving and expressive; family-oriented; loyal; socially adept; empathic, good listeners, and caregivers.

❒ highly regard ethics; harmony; personal relationships; dedicated to others and seek to know others who are dedicated and passionate about what they do; honest and truthful--no'head'games; cooperative; thoughtful.

❒ seen as authentic; sensitive; kind and giving; loving; emotional; valuing the significance of life--purpose of being; poetic and honest when articulating feelings; people watchers; intellectual; truthful.

❒ in relationships they tend to be or are seen as committed to the truth; loyal.

You will know when "Butterfly" type people are upset or "not themselves" when you see or hear:

- crying, depression, yelling, screaming, withdrawal from people
- attention-seeking activities, emotional withdrawal,
- dishonesty, insensitivity and lack of commitment.

What they need:

- a hug; to know that others care about them and they are appreciated; a romantic candlelight dinner; a walk on the beach holding hands; appreciation of their needs.

The Goose

The key characteristic about Geese is their strong need to belong--to find and to earn their place in society. These people are the hard workers with a dedicated work ethic. Nothing is worthwhile unless it is earned. They are honour bound and are dependable service providers who are pleased only when they are seen as responsible and valued by their peers. They want to be recognized as an important cog in the wheel of production and progress.

What else?

❒ very dependable; responsible; parental; structured; dislike change; are sequential thinkers--dogmatic at times; black and white thinkers; enjoy serving the institution.

❒ organized; consistent; caretakers; dedicated; decision-makers; precise or exact; good at evaluating and developing procedures.

❒ highly regard trust; value family and home; consistent; adhere to plans and procedures; crave meaningful relationships; do what they say they will; like structure and rules; have a keen sense of right and wrong; want justice done.

❒ seen as socializers; conservative; traditional; responsible, dependable, reliable; caring of others and their rights; rule bound; earn their way; need to be appreciated; practical; dislike change; enjoy routine; generous; procedural; service-minded; thorough; security-minded, and family-orientated.

❒ in relationships tend to be or are seen as giving, responsible, dependable, and dedicated.

You will know when "Geese" people are upset or "not themselves" when you see or hear:

- depression, fatigue, complaining, whining, anxiousness
- caustic remarks about others and sometimes themselves
- argumentativeness, judgemental comments, indecisiveness, disorganization.

What they need:

- reassurance, a pat on the back, structure, a job to organize, responsibility, a sense of security, rules, to feel they belong.

Begin to pay more attention to those around you who are significant to you and those you have relationships with. Try to understand them for who they are based on some of the characteristics they present. This is not to label them or box them but rather to identify them and what they need. There is no "preferred type." There are just different types.

So often we give to our partners what we would want if we were stressed or feeling down. That, however, is often what they don't need. If I am an Eagle and I am depressed or stressed out, and you are a Butterfly, a romantic evening may not do it for me. A night out on the town might. Or if this situation were reversed and it were the Butterfly that was stressed, a romantic evening may be exactly what is needed. Although it may not be what we would need, the more important question is this: "What does our partner need from us?"

If we think about our children and their needs we can see that, if we have an Owl-type child and a Goose-type child their needs are going to be quite different. If we try to parent them both in the same way we will have some difficulty. Each child has different needs in order to be happy and challenged and content. When people don't get their needs met they get resentful and angry. Kids are people too. They have needs just as adults do. Although as parents we have to convey a consistent standard of values, (that is, what is acceptable, and what is not), to our children regardless of whether they are Owls or Eagles or any other type, we will need to teach those values and their importance in ways consistent with **their** value systems. It is **their** learning experience. It is up to **us** to find a way to teach them, not for them to change who they are to suit us. Do you ever wonder why we hear families say things like "I just don't understand why the other two are so good yet this one is so rotten?"

How to tell our children

Geese value rules and structure. They understand and appreciate the need for clear boundaries to adhere to. Structure and consistency help create a sense of safety for them.

Owls value logic and intelligence. They will understand the need for certain rules if their logic is explained. The rules have to make sense, so explain the "why."

Butterflies value harmony and relationships. They will understand and accept what is necessary if they are spoken to with compassion and in a way that builds a sense of harmony. Yelling and screaming at a Butterfly will only serve to alienate them.

Eagles value freedom and directness. They will understand and accept rules and boundaries if they can negotiate them with you. They require direct answers to questions.

They **ALL** do better when they are encouraged in the things that they do right instead of constantly being chastised and lectured to for what they do wrong. Everyone does better when they are acknowledged and given a pat on the back.

When we learn to accept our differences and learn to appreciate them for their uniqueness we will find the quality of our own lives has increased dramatically.

It all seems so overwhelming, doesn't it? Why can't it be simple? I like you. You like me. Let's get together. In a perfect world--maybe. The fact is that we are different people in so many ways and that's the way it is. We can't change people so we need to find a way to love them for who they are. This is why I said earlier that relationships--the good, fulfilling, happy relationships--take work. Hard work. Every day. When I look around I see many relationships that are happy and long-lasting. I see people who do what they need to do because they have learned **what** to do.

It has now become second nature to them. They do the things they do because it feels good to do them. They see and feel the rewards. When they treat their children or their partners with dignity and respect they get that back from them. When they are compassionate or supportive they get that back as well. They get what they give so they give it back.

We have to consider the physiological and emotional differences between men and women. We have to consider our varying communication styles. There are the basic "human" differences in our character types to remember. All of this information can leave you exhausted or energized. We can become overwhelmed by all that we have to know and remember or we can be excited by the intimacy that develops with each new bit of information, knowledge, and understanding of the other person. I like the last suggestion myself. The more we learn about others, the more we learn about ourselves.

Have your partner mark on the line where he or she feels you are, as a couple, with regard to how much you understand about each other and your differences. Next, you put your mark on the line. Then, as a couple, consider the following questions.

(Needs Work) 1___2___3___4___5___6___7___8___9___10 (Best)

1. Has there ever been a time when you felt more comfortable about who we were as a couple ? What was going on then? How is it different now?

2. What other information do you need to know from or about your partner?

3. When you get that information, how will that improve our understanding of each other? How will that information improve our relationship?

4. What else has to happen for you to move your mark up a notch?

5. What do you need to do or what do you need from your me in order for you to feel more understood?

6. How will you know--what would you see or hear that would indicate that your partner is feeling more understood? If you don't know--ASK.

☞ Go back to the scale in a month's time, or any other time period you both agree to, and see what has changed. If there has been some change, keep doing what you are doing. If there hasn't been any change, re-evaluate what was tried and try something else. Sometimes people try too hard because they are afraid that the relationship will fail. Be your natural self. Make the changes that feel right, not the ones that are forced and unrealistic.

SEX AND INTIMACY

This is the part of building the structure that is the most fun. Now that we are doing our work the play can happen. We are working hard to build and maintain trust in our relationship. We have learned that communication is important and necessary for us to have a good relationship. We know that we are different in so many ways. We are working to accept those differences as we learn more about ourselves and our partners and our children.

All along the way, as we have struggled and learned, we have been building intimacy in our relationships. It is a by-product of our work. It is the natural outcome of our activities. It is also a vital part of any successful relationship. Without intimacy in a relationship there would be no relationship. Our relationships can survive without sex in them. This would be difficult at times, granted, because for some this is their primary way to express how they feel about their partner or what they need for themselves. But if we consider the case where one partner becomes physically or emotionally incapable of enjoying sexual relations, does the relationship end? The chances are less likely if the couple had worked at developing intimacy in their day-to-day interactions. I don't believe a relationship can survive or at least be happy and fulfilling without enjoying a state of intimacy. It is one of our basic needs. One would hope that the relationship is built on more than physical attraction or interaction. If it is not, there is likely going to be some difficulty down the road.

Are sex and intimacy the same?

No, they are not. You can have an intimate relationship with your best friend but that doesn't mean that you have sex with him or her. It is possible to have sex with someone but not reach any level of meaningful intimacy with that person. Sex can be an enjoyable way of sharing mutual pleasure with no strings attached.

It is one of the most risky activities that we can engage in because it renders us the most vulnerable. That is true in a physical sense, obviously, but more so in a spiritual sense.

Meaningful sex, as opposed to merely physical sex (which has no stated emotional connections or expectations), doesn't happen unless there is a intimate feeling connected with it. Intimacy means that we have reached a place in our relationship with another person whereby we are granted the privilege of experiencing his or her innermost thoughts and feelings. We get a chance to more deeply understand that person's spirituality. Obviously, there is a progression here that takes time to develop but all along the way our partners grant us an opportunity to get to know them on a level not accorded others. They grant us this opportunity because we have earned it. We have shown them over a period of time that we are trustworthy, that we would not do anything that would compromise their emotional, physical or mental safety.

Being intimate with another human being feels safe and familiar, warm and special. It transcends just being together. It feels right. Enjoying a feeling of being intimate with someone is gained and maintained by being consistently aware of the need and importance of our partner's right to freedom and space, of being free to choose a personal path with our support, not our condemnation. When we take the time to understand what is important and meaningful to our partner we develop more intimacy in the relationship. It also comes from being gentle, kind, honest, compassionate, safe and secure, and by being faithful. Intimacy is a **state** that exists between two people that says: "You are special to me and I feel special when I am with you. We connect in ways that are special to us alone." When we reach a state of intimacy with our partner we feel complete inside. Our house is now fully decorated. It's warm and cozy, peaceful and safe.

A thoughtful touch says a thousand words

We don't always make the time to say the things that we feel. If we are on our way to work we can't take an hour to have an intimate conversation. But we can walk over to our partner and give a hug or a touch in a way that says, "I'll miss you today" or "I'll be thinking about you today." It takes seconds to do this but it says all the words we need to say. Meaningful touching is an integral part of any relationship. We need more non-sexual touching in our lives than sexual touching. Without it the relationship will begin to wane.

Walking along the street holding hands says "I love you" or "You are important to me." Sitting at the beach watching the sun go down while you are embracing says "There is no one I would rather have in my life than you." The gentle touch as you go through a doorway says "I honour you." This is not a gender issue either. I love to see a woman hold the door open for her partner. Honouring needs to work both ways. It provides constant reassurance of how we feel or what we are thinking about. Non-sexual touching says that we appreciate each other outside the bedroom as well. A strong case can be made for the idea that good sex inside the bedroom begins long before the door is closed. It starts with honesty, trust, security, consistency--intimacy. There are other times when it is important to touch each other besides the times when we are engaged in some kind of foreplay. It helps us say that we are committed to each other in our relationship. It sends a message to others that we are in love and that we enjoy each other's company. Non-sexual touching also develops or maintains our feelings of being intimate with our partners.

Numerous clinical studies have shown that couples who touch each other throughout the day enjoy less stress, lower blood pressure and longer lives. Go ahead, hug your honey. A hug is good for both of you.

Sometimes when it's too good, it's not !

There are those times when, regardless of how good things are going, we need to take a break to evaluate and re-evaluate. We can get so caught up in the relationship and what we are doing together that we begin to lose sight of who we are as individuals. We forget that we have separate needs to fulfil. When we get involved in different activities or develop some separate interests we bring new energy and excitement about what we are doing or what we have learned into the relationship. This helps to keep things fresh and interesting. We both need to be able to do this from time to time. Trouble can arise when we don't help our partners understand what we are doing and why that is important to us. I'm not suggesting that we deliberately stay away from our partners--not at all. Only that we need to have our own time as well and that if we want to get engaged in some other activities for a while, that's OK.

Step back--step ahead

A man will generally appear to be stepping back from the relationship when he gets involved in activities outside of the home because of a hobby, a sport or time with friends. He may feel the need to ensure that his independence is still intact and that he has not lost himself in the relationship. Understandably, his partner is likely to see this as an indication that he may have lost interest in their relationship. That misunderstanding is why communication is so vital to a healthy relationship. What he needs is time to himself so that he can re-energize. He needs to help his partner understand why that is important to him.

A woman, on the other hand, will step back or distance herself from the relationship when she feels as though she has been used, taken advantage of, hurt in some way or misunderstood. She will also step back when she feels that she is not respected or validated in a way she needs to be. Or she may exercise her right to have her own space or time to do the things that interest and excite her. This is not just the prerogative of a male. She too needs time to develop her own identity and to feel she is becoming all she can be.

In cases where one or both partners have distanced themselves for whatever reasons men and women will utilize different styles to re-engage with one another. Men are able to re-engage in the relationship easily and usually with renewed energy. They may want to make love as a way of saying "I'm back."A woman will be cautious. She will take her time trusting her mate again and wait to see what has changed, if anything. She will be more guarded, fearing being hurt or misunderstood again. She will be more engaging over time, though.

The differences and circumstances regarding how men step back from a relationship is often the source of the myth that men are insensitive and don't care. Not true. Men don't respond the same way as women do but that does not make them insensitive. It just says that they are different with different ways of getting their needs met or of taking care of their business.

It's as though a man comes to the fountain (his mate's intimate being) and drinks as much as he can. At the fountain he gets respect, acceptance, trust and encouragement. When he feels full, he'll return to doing the other things that he considers important to his maintaining his identity as the man he knows or wants to become. This could be athletic competition of some kind or a hobby that is challenging and one in which he can distinguish himself somehow. Feeling independent is everything to a man.

Once he has assured himself that he is still capable and independent he comes back to the fountain again so that he can get his needs for intimacy satisfied. The cycle continues.

What men need to understand is that their mates also have the same needs to drink from a fountain (his intimate being). Women need to be able to do whatever else they need or want to do and come back to a loving, validating, understanding, reassuring partner who is her intimacy source. Men need to understand that if they want this cycle to continue, they have to do everything required to replenish her fountain which is his source of intimacy. He has to make sure that she gets what she needs so that she can continue to supply his needs. Now we have his energy feeding her and her energy feeding him. They feed each other so the energy is not lost but passed back and forth.

That's the cycle we all want to keep going. If it becomes one-sided the relationship soon falters and begins to deteriorate because one person gets to feeling angry and resentful, uncared for and unappreciated.

What we both have to learn to do is accept that when we sense our partners beginning to retreat a bit or becoming distant, that's OK. Check with them to be sure everything is all right so we can let them go do what they have to do. It's at these times we do the opposite because we fear our partners are losing interest. We feel insecure in the relationship so we pull harder to keep them near us. Once this happens they can feel confined or hemmed in, even claustrophobic. The natural response is to push back to create more distance and to get some breathing room. Now we have a different kind of struggle happening. What started out as one or both of us needing a bit of time and space to ourselves ends up as "Well, if you don't want to be around me, maybe we should look at why we are together in the first place." This is a cycle that you DON'T want to continue. Again we see the importance of communication--being able to sit down and clearly say what we see is happening, state our needs, and ask our partners to do the same. If you don't do this, the intimacy that has been developed gets put aside for a while and our personal feelings--usually fear, anger, hurt, resentment, abandonment and rejection--come to the fore. This is how arguments begin.

When we're out of 'sync'

As with all things in this life, there are patterns and cycles. Day becomes night and night becomes day again. We have cloudy days; we have clear days; we see happiness and sadness that comes to happiness again. So it is with human beings. We have our times when we are happy and sad and when we are up and when we are down. Few things ever remain constant, including our relationships.

Individually, we will be subjected to a wide range of expectations from those around us because we will be included in activities that may not be to our liking, in natural outcomes from occurrences that are beyond our control, and in other people's issues. There is no telling how that will affect us from day to day. We may not always be constant in our relationships with our loved ones. Our partners are affected in the same way. Outside issues can distract us from what we need or want to do. It is important for us to understand that our partners may not always be feeling good about themselves or be excited to see us. They may not always be there for us when we need them to be. They have their own "stuff" to deal with and in doing so may not have any time for us. They may close us out for a while. The way they feel won't always be a direct result of something that we have done or have not done. One of the greatest loving gestures we can make is to check in with our mates to see how they are doing, to see what, if anything, they need from us, and then get out of their way.

That may mean they will withdraw from us but it doesn't mean they don't love us anymore. It simply means they may need some time and space alone to make sense of what is going on in their lives. Nothing is constant. When we know that we can go away for a while and then come back to a loving partner, it makes our troubles pass more quickly. It also adds to the intimacy that exists between the partners.

When I take responsibility for how other people feel I rob them of the opportunity to learn and to grow.

Other thoughts

- ❐ Sex should never be used as a weapon to control someone. Rewarding someone for doing something they would not normally do or for being someone other than who they really are or want to be is a "spirit killer." It takes away from the person who uses sex this way, it lessens the esteem of the person who responds to the "reward," and it certainly damages the sense of intimacy the couple feels, and ultimately the relationship.

❒ Sex should never be painful, either physically, emotionally or spiritually, and should never happen against the other's wishes. When this happens the relationship is damaged, sometimes irreparably. There are no excuses to justify such behaviour.

❒ Sex should be fun and exciting. We engage in sex to explore each other's bodies and minds. It is a way of sharing pleasure with one another that says "You are very special to me." Some would say it is the ultimate way to share oneself. We all have the need to touch and be touched. It's basic. Being rejected sexually by your partner would rank right up there with the worst things that could happen to someone. We all have the right to change our minds but communicate why that is happening. We need to be very careful when we indicate we are interested in having sex with someone and then change our minds. Teasing someone in a sexual manner when both partners are enjoying the "game" is fun. Otherwise it can be dangerous.

❒ Men, generally, want to have sex first and then relax or talk (if they can stay awake). Women want to relax and talk first. They want to feel as though they are more than just a toy or a sex object. There have to be some feelings expressed, some emotions shared. They need to warm to the idea and the sexual experience. This is where intimacy plays an important role. We get to know what is important to our partners and try to make that happen for them. What do they like? What does making love mean to them? This is ALWAYS a two-way street.

For flavour, instant sex will never supersede the stuff you have to peel and cook.--Quentin Crisp

❒ When sex stops being fun or expressive of intimacy, people in relationships will wonder what they did or did not do that may have contributed to the decline. They will begin to wonder about the durability of the relationship and finally whether they could see themselves in a sexless relationship for any length of time.

This is the time when many people will try to re-invent the relationship. They go back to doing some of the things they did before with hopes of enlivening the relationship, often with success. But there are those who just toss in the towel and seek their validation outside the relationship. They have affairs. A man will often have sex outside of his relationship because he does not feel masculine enough: that is, admired, important, valued, intelligent or respected for being good at something. He goes looking for his validation elsewhere. A woman will have an affair so that she can be made to feel more feminine: that is, honoured, attractive, cared for, understood and treated with specialness, respected.

❐ Men like to have sex to feel good emotionally. They want to know that everything in the relationship is OK. Men will often want to have sex to help patch things up after an argument or disagreement. It's a way to make up and move on. There is some security in sex for men. It suggests that they are still loved or that their partner is not going to leave. Men have very fragile egos. Because men know how special making love is to a woman they assume that she wouldn't make love unless she still cared. He wants to feel secure.

Women have sex to feel good too. They want the same emotional security that men are looking for. But they feel differently about sex. It is more a way of feeling connected to someone, of being part of a relationship with meaning. To a woman the important selectivity process indicates a giving of herself to someone who occupies a special place in her heart. It also affords her a sense of personal control both of herself and for herself.

The best of reasons

We are all very different people with regard to what and how we attempt to get our needs met but are very much the same when it comes to the reasons. We all want to belong somewhere to someone. We all want to have a sense of place. Too often sex is used to attract and to hold on to a partner instead of being a way of saying or showing how two people feel about each other. For a woman it can be used as a way of overcoming a negative self-image, especially when age and gravity take over. For a man it can be used as a way of punishing or conquering someone in a physical, emotional or spiritual sense.

Premature sexual activity gets in the way of the conversations that are so vital to the survival of any satisfying and fulfilling relationship. Our objectivity can become clouded if we have sex with someone before we have had the opportunity to ask the questions we need to ask. The conversations that produce knowledge about the other person aren't as likely to take place. When it comes to seeing our prospective partners for who they are we will often deny the obvious if we don't like what we see. We will forsake close friendships with others when we hear what we don't want to hear. There is an emotional connection that is made before we take the time to find out just how compatible we are. We put the cart before the horse. Making love should fulfil the needs for communicating how we feel about that person in a way that is enjoyable to both. But when sex takes place before intimacy has developed it is often used for manipulative purposes. This will not create the solid foundation that is needed to build what it is we seek. I often hear people say of a new partner that "We'll learn to love each other." I seldom see that happen.

Of course, if the relationship is strictly based on mutual physical attraction and longevity isn't an issue, then asking about wants and needs, trust and compatibility are issues of less importance. Once the physical attraction wanes the relationship will end. The only concern in those situations should be safety and mutual consent.

Don't let romance die

Sex and intimacy provide the interior decorations for our lives. Romantic emotional experiences are a necessary part of those decorations. Weekends away or a picnic for two. Sunset walks along the beach--hand in hand. Sitting on the front porch together with your arms around each other but not saying anything. Just sitting enjoying each other's company. Those are the special times that money cannot buy. These are the experiences that keep intimacy and love alive in the relationship. They are as necessary as any other part when we are building or maintaining our relationships.

✎ Have your partner mark on the line where he or she feels you are, as a couple, when considering satisfaction with the level of sex and intimacy in your relationship. Then put your mark on the line. Don't be alarmed or disappointed at where your partner puts his or her mark. We seldom experience situations in the same way. If his or hers is lower than yours it does not mean that it is less important or satisfying to them. The important thing is to know what you need to do to make it better than it is now. Now go over the following questions together.

(Needs Work) 1___2___3___4___5___6___7___8___9___10 (Best)

1. Can you remember a time when you felt good about the sex and intimacy you experienced in the relationship? What was going on then? What was different?

2. What do we, as a couple, need to do to move each other's marks up a notch on the line scale?

3. If that happened how would you feel differently about the relationship? What difference would that make to each of you?

4. Each partner asks: "What do you need from me? How can I work to make this better for you? What do I need to do?"

5. How would I know--what would I notice that would indicate to me that you were feeling better about the level of intimacy in our relationship?

☞ Go back to the scale in a month's time and do it again. You can choose any length of time that suits you both. See if there has been any change. If there has been, keep doing what you are doing. If there hasn't been, sit down and discuss what happened and what else you could do.

The Golden Rule in relationships

I have been accused of being an idealist. I have said this before along our journey's path. It is a banner I wear with pride because I believe in the inherent good in most people. I believe that, should someone do a good deed for me, I am likely to do him or her one in return. If not him or her then someone else will benefit from it. It is the same in relationships. If one partner does something nice for the other, provided the goal is not to manipulate, the other is likely to respond in kind. The trick is to know what to give to our partners and when. If in doubt, ask. We often give to them what WE would need if we found ourselves in a similar situation. This seldom goes over well. People generally feel that they are not understood when this happens. Communication and trust must be a factor here. It is important for us to know and understand our partner's wants and needs. When we understand what they need from us and we give it to them in their time of crisis or stress we develop INTIMACY.

What goes around comes around. If we are there for them they will likely be there for us. For instance, being able to recognize when our partners want to be alone and when they need to have us near them will be invaluable. Understanding this will allow us to leave them be, if that's what they need, and not make us feel insecure or fearful regarding the strength of the relationship. Perhaps they just need someone to listen to them--not to make or help make any decisions about anything--just to listen. When we take the time to learn about our partners' needs we develop intimacy because we are saying that they are important to us and we want to be there for them. We TRUST they will return to us when they feel they can, when they have done the work they needed to do. People don't have to physically leave the relationship in order to withdraw from it.

We also have to be able to accept our DIFFERENCES. Lord knows we have them. We need to pay more attention to what our partners are saying and what that means to them instead of how they are saying it. Content over style. When we can do this we will find ourselves more in touch with our partners and arguing less often. If we could accept that we're different we would probably see that our partners have strengths in areas that may complement our weaknesses. We may be hard workers but poor money managers, for instance. Our partners may have good management skills. Let them take care of the money then. I'm not saying that we turn a blind eye here but rather learn that skill from them. We may have better organizational skills so perhaps we could look after scheduling events or appointments. We use each other's skills and strengths to our mutual benefit. When we try to change our partners' differences to suit our idea of how they should be, we will have nothing but grief to deal with. People resist change. Besides, those differences are often the things that attracted us to them in the first place. It doesn't make any sense for us to try to change them now. Celebrate the differences we have. We are who we are.

Let's remember the things that we used to do when we were trying to convince our partners that we were the best thing that was ever going to happen to them. Remember to do the little things every day so that they never forget how special we are. Holding hands, giving hugs in abundance--they don't hurt and they're free. A kind word and our undivided attention when they need it can be the difference between their having a good day and not. Dignity and respect should be the buzzwords of any relationship.

Relationships take work. Hard work. But when they are working there is nothing better because within them we get to make a difference in someone's life and get all of our needs met as well.

The Golden Rule is this: **"Don't wait--go first. That way you get to make up faster."**

Where are we now?

Put a mark on the line, either at one of the numbers or somewhere in between, that would gauge or record how you feel about your relationship--where you think it is with respect to what you hoped it would be. 1 would indicate that it needs some work and 10 would indicate that you feel it is the best it could be.

The focus is how WE move our marks up a notch at a time and not where they are initially marked. (Remember that we seldom see things the same way and usually process information quite differently.) What do WE need to do? Don't try to do it all at once. Steady growth and change is more fun and more realistic.

Going home

(Needs Work) 1___2___3___4___5___6___7___8___9___10___ (Best)

Understand that this is not an exercise to point fingers and judge. Anyone can be critical. Being critical does not take great skill. Rather see this as an opportunity to gain invaluable information that can help you and your partner work together on your relationship. The goal is to identify what is good about it now and decide what you can add to it or what has to happen to make it even better.

Here are some questions to ask each other to help discover what each can do to build a stronger relationship.

1. What are some of the positive things that we have done in the past that we could begin to do again that would enhance our relationship?

2. How can we improve on our ability to communicate? What has to happen? What can I do to make that happen?

3. How can I help you become all you want to be as a person? What do you need from me so that can happen for you?

4. What parts of our relationship mean the most to you?

5. What do you need from me that you are not getting enough of?

6. How will I know when you have moved up a notch? What would I see? What would I hear from you that is different?

7. If you woke up tomorrow and our relationship was all you wanted it to be, what would you say? How would you describe it to me? What would have changed?

8. If there were one thing that you needed more than anything else right now what would that be?

9. If you could be or do anything that you wanted to what would that be?

10. How can I help you move closer to that?

11. What skills could we learn that would help us grow in our relationship?

The perfect goal is not to be "perfect"

There are no perfect relationships. There are many great ones but no perfect ones. They are great because the people in them feel relaxed, fulfilled, safe, nurtured and free to be all they can be without conditions placed upon them. They feel contented to the point that there are no other options to be considered: "This is all I want. This is all I need." No relationship can sustain minute-by-minute intimacy, and joy, and peace, and harmony, and constant nurturing. We all need time to ourselves to continue our individual journeys. But if we want a good relationship we need to MAKE the time as often as we can to help it grow without losing sight of who we are and what we need ourselves. It's a fine balance that takes mutual understanding.

If we are looking for a relationship to ease our pain or to divert us from what troubles us, we are grossly mistaken and will be sorely disappointed. We can not take our "old baggage" into a new relationship and expect that it will magically disappear in the passion and excitement that comes with new beginnings.

At the very best you may forget about that baggage for a short time but those issues will surface again. It is not fair for us to expect that our new partners will somehow find a way to take away our pain or our anger. That is not their job. It is not a role we should expect them to assume. It is not their responsibility. It is ours. But if this is our goal we not only hurt ourselves but also the other innocent people we profess to love and who had wished for more.

The only way to start fresh is to take care of our business BEFORE we get involved with someone else. The only way to get through pain, anger, disappointment, grief or loneliness is to go through it. You can't run around it and you can't hide for long from it. Eventually our old issues will surface in our new relationship. Unfortunately those we are with now get the worst of it. We end up taking out our unfinished business on those who simply love us. Relationships are only as strong as the foundation upon which they are built. Good relationships are the result of managing all of the other parts of our lives. They occur when we are able to manage ourselves and the situations that we are asked to deal with. Only then can we really expect that we are ready to contribute to a healthy and fulfilling relationship.

Relationships are the rewards for managing our lives effectively.

Heaven and Hell

An old man knew that he was going to die very soon. Before he died, he wanted to know what heaven and hell were like, so he visited the wise man in his village. "Can you please tell me what heaven and hell are like?" he asked the wise man. "Come with me and I will show you," the wise man replied.

The two men walked down a long path until they came to a large house. The wise man took the old man inside, and there they found a large dining room with an enormous table covered with every kind of food imaginable. Around the table were many people, all thin and hungry, who were holding twelve-foot chopsticks. Every time they tried to feed themselves, the food fell off the chopsticks. The old man said to the wise man, "Surely this must be hell. Will you show me heaven?" The wise man said, "Yes, come with me."

The two men left the house and walked farther down the path until they reached another large house. Again they found a large dining room and in it a table filled with all kinds of food. The people here were happy and appeared well-fed, but they also held twelve-foot chopsticks. "How can this be?" said the old man. "These people have twelve-foot chopsticks and yet they are happy and well-fed?" The wise man replied, "In heaven the people feed each other."

--Unknown

Wonderful things can happen to us if we are willing to work together. If we are willing to "feed each other" we all will grow and benefit. Such is the way to happiness, to learning about ourselves and others, to peace and serenity. When we "feed each other" we create a system that enables all who participate in it to benefit equally. And the circle of people we influence grows too.

8.

WHAT TREASURES DID YOU FIND?

WHEN I UNDERSTAND THAT HOW I SEE MYSELF IS MY CHOICE, THE WINDOW THROUGH WHICH I SEE MY WORLD BECOMES MORE CLEAR.

Life is a journey--not a destination. It is a journey like no other. It can be a terrible, disastrous trip or a wonderful, thrilling adventure that is full of opportunity and wisdom. Our life's journey will consist of many smaller journeys. We will travel different roads and follow different paths. We can all experience greater peace, prosperity and happiness however if we are willing to see there may be a need to change our approach to living our lives as we do. If we want something more from life, if we develop a desire for making some changes, if we could be open to the possibilities that different perspectives and self-evaluation can bring, and if we are ready and committed to persist in our attempts to grow and evolve as people, we are ready to journey into our hearts and minds, our spiritual being, to seek the answers and the direction that awaits us.

However, must understand that we are not the sum total of our injuries and that we are not defined by our wounds. That might have been what happened to us but it is not who we are.

More people are recognizing the spiritual void that exists in the world today. They see wealth and success as the gods of these times. Many more are becoming fearful that they won't survive the changes which are coming at a rate few can fathom. We are moving away from the belief that the common good will prevail and are seeing that the "good" is going to fewer people. Our systems have developed to the point where human life is seen and treated as less valuable than material things. Hope is becoming a fleeting experience.

We have to get back to the time when we believed that our individual strengths and resources could and would carry our day, that if we depended upon and utilized our given talents we would be able to master whatever came our way. It is more important than ever for us to understand that what goes on inside of us determines what and how we do outside of us. We each have a fountain of strength and spirit within us. All we need to do is tap into it and great things will happen. For as much as the world has changed, some basic truths remain. For example, when we connect our attitudes and perspectives with our strength of character and well-being we can perform deeds beyond our expectations.

Each of our smaller journeys can bring us home with a greater belief in ourselves, our strengths, our resources and our abilities to manage ourselves in a way that provides the hope we need to face new challenges. We must understand that the quality of our life experience is, and has always been, up to us. What awesome power we hold within.

Journeys have purpose.

Journeys are not always meant to have destinations. Our spiritual journeys are travels of faith. They are undertaken for the sole purpose of learning something about ourselves that we didn't know before. We embark on them not knowing what we will find but with a belief that we will benefit somehow and that we will be more knowledgeable when we return. If, for instance, we travel inside ourselves to the real source of our anger, which is often pain and fear, and we learn not only about them but how to manage them effectively, then anger can become our ally instead of our enemy. We have learned a great lesson that can only serve to strengthen us and bring us more joy. But we cannot find what we don't believe is there. If it is a better life we seek we have to believe--have faith--that it is possible, and with hard work and a desire to change we will find what we are looking for.

So much of what we do is built on our beliefs. Success without faith is impossible. We need to have faith in ourselves and our abilities in order for us to attain the quality of life we so richly deserve. We continue to try new ways and remain open to change and new ideas. We believe that, with perseverance, we will triumph. Having faith allows us to succeed.

Faith has much to do with a quality of the heart. It is a principle by which we live. It is not religious in nature. We have heard of "blind" faith, so-called because we ask ourselves to believe in something that we cannot touch, feel or see. Embarking on our journeys provides us with opportunities to develop faith in ourselves. Faith also develops courage, wisdom and truth within us.

Our journeys are meant to create even more questions so that we will continue to seek within ourselves the answers which, in turn, create more questions which create the need for more journeys. I used the word "journey" metaphorically because that's what I believe we do when we seek a better way. We journey into our minds, hearts, and to the core of who we are as human beings--our spiritual centre. We cannot hide from ourselves. The journeys are the commitments we make to ourselves to seek a better way of doing things, to learn how we can be more honest with ourselves, and to risk accepting that we have something to learn. We don't know it all. We may need to consider discarding the methods we used or the mechanisms we created in order to be "safe" from those around us. We set aside our protective outer shells when we challenge our own beliefs.

Our journeys can be mental or physical. We can begin a journey and never leave town or we can seek wisdom and experience through travel. Many years ago I went on a journey to Mexico and Central America. While I was gone I saw things and experienced things that altered the course of my life. I was able to appreciate a different culture. I lived in a society that had different values. I could see the benefit of simplicity. I felt the loneliness of just surviving from day to day. But I also saw the wonder and the beauty of a culture that will soon be gone. I came away with a new appreciation for living a life built on simple values. My purpose for going was business related but once there my idea of what life was about and how it should be lived was challenged. I hadn't expected that. I have tried to live my life differently ever since. I've not always been as successful as I might have liked but I have never lost sight of those simple lessons I learned from that journey.

We will embark on several journeys before our time on this planet comes to an end. The sum total of all those journeys will help us understand the meaning of why we were here in the first place. Along the way we can pass on to others what we know and why we think it is important so they can learn from us and, in turn, pass whatever they get from us on to those they meet on their journey.

Recently I read *The Most Important Thing I've Learned in Life,* a book whose author is a 16-year-old boy named Beau Bauman. It struck me as remarkable that at that age he would be curious enough and dedicated enough to devote three years of his life to finding responses to his question. This is, or was, his journey. My hope is he is more curious now than ever and that he will enjoy another journey soon. There is much we can learn from Beau.

Each time we seek to know ourselves better we embark on a journey of discovery. We decide to risk being exposed so that others can get to know ourselves more deeply. Perhaps we can learn from them. Every time we "leave the terminal" we hope that the benefits of the journey outweigh the risks, but there are never any guarantees.

Even if you're on the right track you'll get run over if you just sit there.--Will Rogers

When we feel that we have gone as far as we can--that we learned what we needed to learn, we return home so that we can evaluate the experience, knowing full well that the next journey, the next adventure, is not far off. What did we learn about ourselves? How can we use this information to better our lives and perhaps the lives of those around us? Journeys are about learning and taking risks. When we return, we have a sense that we are more closely connected to those around us, that we are accepted, respected, and that we have a place. The search for that sense of place--the journey--is the driving force for us all. What do we have to do to find it?

"Buried Treasure"

There is a sense of peace that comes when we are able to act or respond to adversity in a way that leaves us feeling we did the best we could or that we handled it in a way that was not meant to hurt someone else. We feel good inside.

I asked that you keep an open mind when you began this journey with me. I asked that you at least consider the possibility that there were alternatives to think about. I wanted to challenge your beliefs and to provoke you to learn something new about yourselves.

There are risks and costs to a program of action, but they are far less than the long-range risks and costs of comfortable inaction.
--John F. Kennedy

When we are able to see new insights we become amenable to learning new skills. The key to learning new skills is contained in the act of self-evaluation. We must be able to look at ourselves and the natural outcomes of what we did and ask:

- ❐ "What did I learn from that experience?"
- ❐ "How could I have done that differently?"
- ❐ "Is what I am doing getting me closer to where I want to be?"
- ❐ "How did that affect the other guy?"

Caring enough to look at **our** role in what happens around us is the step that most people overlook. When you have done something for other people else and you know that they genuinely appreciated your help, how do you feel inside? When they help you understand that what you did made a difference to them, how do you feel then? When you are able to reach out to others who are close and they look at you in a way that says they think you are more special than any other, what is that like? How do you feel inside? That feeling is what I am talking about here. It is the feeling that accompanies our realization that we are getting closer to being all that we can be. This is a part of why I am here: to learn what it takes to be all I can be and to pass it on to those close to me. This is part of the "buried treasure" we can find along our way.

These journeys will continue for as long as we are held wondrous of their lessons. These are the lessons that we pass on to our children with the hopes that they pass them on to their children. This is a process that speaks on a spiritual level to the evolution of humankind. If we are to pass anything on to our children we first have to be open to scrutiny. We first have to be open enough to challenge our own belief systems. Then we have to have the courage to change what doesn't work anymore.

Our journey and the search for what?

What is it you want? What would have to be present in your life so that you could feel that you "had it all?" What would you need in your life for you to feel that you had found your peace and your place?

Make a list of six words that would define what you would **need** to have in your life so that you could say: "This life is as good as it gets. I'm satisfied." Write them on a piece of paper. We'll get back to this list in a bit.

Are we what we think?

How we see ourselves plays a large role in what we do. If we see ourselves as stupid or useless, or bad or no good, we will likely play out that self-fulfilling prophecy. Our healing and our work begin in our central core--our spiritual ground zero--and not outside of us. It is not what goes on around us that determines what we do next. It is how we see ourselves and our **beliefs** about the values that we live by that determine how we respond or what we do next. Just because someone says we are . ? . doesn't mean we are . ? .

What are our beliefs? What do we believe in? Do those beliefs still hold true? Which of our beliefs and values are still relevant and which are not? When we construct our mission statement these questions will be relevant. This statement is a declaration of what we are about and what we stand for, for how we see ourselves and how we choose to live our lives.

The world is not the same place that it was even 50 years ago. Some values may need to be re-evaluated and some should never change.

Consider the following, for example:

- ❒ "The Golden Rule" that states we should treat all others with the dignity and respect they deserve and we would want accorded to us still works for me.
- ❒ The idea that children should be seen and not heard, for instance, isn't relevant anymore, if it ever was.
- ❒ The idea that a women should stay at home and tend to the kitchen certainly doesn't apply anymore.
- ❒ A woman's place is not only in the kitchen but also in the factory. A man's place is not only in the factory but also in the kitchen. Both are now true.
- ❒ Men are every bit as capable of parenting with kindness, compassion and understanding as women. Being able to nurture and comfort a child is not a gender-specific issue. Other values and beliefs regarding parenting also need to be reconsidered.

There are more. Which ones do you need to re-think? Perhaps this is an exercise that you could do with your partner.

Is it possible?

To develop a more positive sense of ourselves, is it possible that we'll have to do some work? Feeling better about ourselves is about recognizing the strengths that we have and building on them as opposed to feeling bad about the strengths that we don't have or the ones we wish we had. Being angry or violent or depressed about what we don't have is useless. Our energy needs to be put into doing something positive for ourselves every day. It means that as we develop our rules for living we develop our sense of integrity. It means that we stay with them. We grow stronger as human beings when we DO things that maintain our sense of integrity. At this point the work begins. It is an inside job. Feeling more positive about ourselves helps us to develop the attitude we will need to accept change. We will look forward to change as an opportunity to grow and not as something to fear.

Is it possible that change is a part of growing? Life does not remain static no matter how much we want it to. We cannot control nature. We cannot control how or why other people make the decisions they do. What happens will happen regardless of how we feel about it. Do we throw up our hands and say "I quit" or "I give up?" Or do we say "How can I work myself through this? What do I need to do in order to survive? How can I benefit from what is going on?"

Do we need to look at how we sort out the issues that face us? We can ask, "What has worked for us in the past? What has not?" Then we do more of what's worked and less of what hasn't. Change can be stressful. Change can create havoc in our lives so we need to be organized in our response to change. Being organized helps us stay focused and helps us feel less overwhelmed. We need to keep some order in our lives when everything around us is becoming unhinged. Think about what we can do to be successful instead of what will happen if we are not. Above all else, we need to be able to look at the changes we face as opportunities to learn something about ourselves instead of something to fear.

We have no greater power than the power to heal ourselves.

Is it possible that stress is something that, for the most part, we create for ourselves? It is created by our beliefs about whether or not we can handle what comes our way. When we develop confidence in our ability to handle the issues with which we are presented, we become more "esteemed." The more confident we become, the less stress we will experience. Learning how to organize our lives and to recognize that we have personal assets and strengths we can use to work through what we face will be very helpful. Stress can also be created by feeling overwhelmed by life and all of its worries and fears. Do we expect too much? Have we set our sights so high that there is no possible chance we will succeed? The best way to reduce our stress is by being proactive. Think about how useful a reactive approach has been for us. While we are waiting for things to happen for us, they are likely to happen TO us. When we are making an effort to take care of ourselves and the needs of our families, we are doing something positive. When we do things that are positive for ourselves we maintain or increase our positive self-image.

☞ Remember that list of six words you put on a piece of paper a while back? Consider the list now and eliminate two of the six needs that you put down. Which two out of the six could you do without if you had to? Please put a line through the two you have chosen.

Is it possible that by being proactive we are merely taking control of ourselves and what we do? Taking control of ourselves is one thing we CAN control. It may mean that we assert our rights and define what we will and will not accept. When we do this we are engaging in an act of self-care and not self-centeredness. Taking care of our needs is vital to maintaining our positive sense of self--our self-image. It is OK for us to get our needs met as long as it is not at the expense of someone else's right to do the same. Being assertive is not being aggressive. We do not have to be aggressive to get what we want. We do have to be consistent in our expectations that our rights and needs be considered.

There may be times when we have to do things we don't want to do in order for us to get where we want to be. There will be times when we'll step back and ask ourselves whether or not we are acting in our own best interests if we pursue a particular tactic. If we are to continue growing as people we will need to assess and reassess our current methods of doing things. It will be necessary for us to develop ways and means of dealing with our automatic or learned responses to certain situations. Of course, some situations require an automatic response, for example when danger is imminent for us or others around us. When we have to go with our gut instincts our responses are more apt to be automatic. Often our instincts will be the only source of information upon which we can make a decision. However, reacting to anger, sadness, disappointment, loneliness, sarcasm or disrespect without thinking about the natural outcomes of our responses is not acting in our best interests.

This is where some people get stuck. They can't or won't see that it may be necessary to learn a new skill or try a new method of coping with things. Developing new ways of doing things always takes time and trust: time because we have to evaluate and re-evaluate our actions, and trust because we will have to depend on the feedback of others who are close to us. Our responses to these urges will vary. We might be passive and internalize everything; we may use food, alcohol, sex, drugs or gambling to respond to what goes on in our lives; or we may use violence as a way of dealing with things. All of these may work in the short run but will never end positively for us in the long run.

It is difficult to resist not responding right away. We want to get even--instantly. We want the "urge feeling" to go away because it is uncomfortable and provokes our anxiety. We sometimes believe that if we don't respond or react right away there is something wrong with us, or that we will be seen as weak somehow. But when we **THINK BEFORE WE ACT** we generally feel better about the outcomes.

Is it possible that anger is the most destructive of all our emotions, or is it possible our anger could become our most useful and powerful ally? Feeling angry can keep us safe when we are faced with danger. It can provide us with the energy we need to go beyond our ordinary limits. When we accept that our anger is about "us" and not about "them" we take a giant step toward becoming more productive and peaceful human beings. We also become more able to use our anger as a tool to use to our benefit and not our detriment. Our emotions belong to us so our anger belongs to us. Once we accept ownership of it we can do anything we want with it. There is an old saying which points out that "we would never give a bank robber our life savings to watch over." Neither should we give someone else the opportunity to control or be responsible for our emotions. To do that is to relinquish control over our happiness and our joy as well.

Identify the feeling for what it **really** is and then go to the source and deal with it there. It's OK to be angry. It is not OK to hurt ourselves or someone else with it.

☞ Go back to your list of words or phrases. You are now down to four words. Take a good look at your list and eliminate another two words. You are now down to two.

Is it possible that our relationships would be more fulfilled and enriched if we looked at what keeps US from putting forth the effort needed to make them all we want them to be? How much more enjoyable would they be if we felt more positive about ourselves and more trusting of our partners?

How would feeling less stressed add quality to the time we spend alone or time with our families or friends? Would we feel more positive? Would we argue less if we were able to be clear about what we needed from the important people in our lives and if we were able to hear what they needed from us?

When we are able to think before we act (either verbally or physically) and consider alternate responses, how would that add more quality to our lives? Would we fight less? When we are able to accept responsibility for our actions and own our emotions can we see that our lives and relationships with others would become more trusting and loving? How would our relationships be different if we had done some of this work before we became involved with our current partner?

Should any of this deter us from challenging our past beliefs? Do we choose to seek new information? Do we choose to continue on our journey? Our relationships can only get better when we begin to consider other possibilities by challenging our old ways of thinking and responding. They continue to get better when we remember that they need daily care. It will not be enough to say, "I love you" every 10 years or to engineer a special event once a year. **Daily care provides daily returns.**

☞ So now you're down to two words. Now eliminate one of the remaining two words. What's the word that represents the one want or need that, at this time, is more important to you than any other? If you fill that one need or satisfy that one want, how many of the other wants and needs that you crossed off would you have regardless? For instance, if you had crossed off emotional security as a need you felt was not as important to you as other needs and your last word was freedom would you not have a large measure of emotional security if you had freedom? In other words, by working toward what you believe is freedom (what you have indicated as your most important want/need) it is likely that, as a result, you would attain a level of emotional security anyway? In this example, all things flow from freedom or conversely if we don't have freedom nothing else matters.

We can get bogged down and overwhelmed with what we believe we want or need to be happy, secure, free, or whatever else we desire in this life. Often, if we can just move toward one basic goal, the others will come along as a result. Or we may understand that what we believed was important, isn't.

10 questions that could change your life

1. How much of what you want would be enough?
2. How will you know when you have enough? What would others see that would be different about you?
3. What are the different ways you could get to where you want to be?
4. What do you need to do to move closer to your goal?
5. What is doable for you right now?
6. What is realistic for you right now?
7. Is what you are now doing getting you closer to your goal?
8. How much time and effort are you willing to put into achieving your goal? (This might be the key question.)
   Imagine yourself in a wide open space with an unlimited number of doors facing you. You are told that behind one of the doors there is $1,000,000 in cash and it's yours for the finding. How many doors would you open? How much time would you spend trying to find it? Would you spend as much time and effort developing a positive self-image? Having a positive sense of ourselves and a faith in our abilities is a treasure like no other. Money can't buy it. You are wealthy when you have it.
9. If you were able to fill that "need" or get that "want," what would that mean to you?
10. How would your life be different?

To go where no man has gone before!

Question: What do you know about yourself now that you didn't know when you started this journey?

Question: How can you use that information and insight to get you closer to that which you want?

It is not enough to make this journey just once. Our journeys continue so that we gain knowledge and insight into ourselves as human beings. With new insights and information come new questions. With more questions come new journeys. It is in our nature to strive and struggle. History will bear that out. So it is with our need to be all we can be, however we define that for ourselves. Each time we embark upon another journey we do so as different people with different needs. We have new information so our insights have new meaning for us. Our perspective changes. Each time we embark on our journey of personal discovery we find new "treasures" that were always there. When the student is ready, the teacher will appear. So it goes with personal insights. When the person is ready to see them, they will present themselves.

Beyond all else, we all want to belong somewhere, to something. We want to be part of someone else's space. We want to know that there are those who cherish us and find our standards and rules for living vital, honourable and enriching. It is pleasing to know that we can fill a particular void as no other can. We want to feel that we are needed and wanted by others around us and that we have importance. We want to be able to share our spiritual part with someone who will not abuse the privilege. To accept the knowledge that we are connected with the universe we live in--that we are an equal and valued part of things and that there is a power that exists greater than ourselves--is a humbling experience. To feel that in some way we are part of it is a source of strength to draw on.
Can we have all of this? Yes, we can if we are willing to do the work. But we have to start at the beginning and that begins with a decision to manage ourselves in a way that benefits us and those around us.

The only person who can stop me from succeeding is me.

Growing does not have to be painful. Some believe that there can be no gain without some pain. Personal growth does not require pain. What it does require is honesty, effort and awareness. If you live by the truth that exists in your heart, your experiences will be learning opportunities. They don't have to hurt.

My goal is to encourage you to consider other ways of dealing with the roadblocks that stand in your way of having peace and happiness. I want to challenge you. I want to encourage you to create options for thinking and behaving. Having one alternative does not constitute choice. Our growth occurs when we evaluate the options we create, think them through, and then make our choice based on what we consider to be in our own best interests. The strength and wisdom to manage our lives has always been inside of us. All we have to do is have the faith that it is there and seek it out. That, to me, constitutes the true, continuing development of humankind. When we can manage ourselves we can manage how we respond to what goes on around us. And when we do that we don't have to depend on others to do that for us. We do not have to depend on other means.

All that we need--all the strengths, all the assets, all the resources we need to have the kind of life we want--are inside us. Other people cannot give us what we need. They can only provide the encouragement and the support that can move us to find it. The solutions to our issues lie within. There are many who suggest that the skills needed to succeed are called the Secrets of Life. I agree with Og Mandino who says, "They are not secrets. We have not discovered them yet is all."

Managing me truly is an inside job.

Afterword

Writing this book has been a journey for me. We should never pass on an opportunity to learn something about ourselves, regardless of how apprehensive we are. When I thought about how I would end this book I was filled with many feelings. Did I say what I wanted to say? Was I clear enough in my purpose for writing this book? Will anybody read it? Will anybody care? How will I end it? I wanted to end it with something that said it all in a page.

I chose this piece by a woman whose name is Nadine Stair. She was 85 years old when she wrote this. God bless her for her wisdom and her insight. She is a woman who has been on many journeys in her life. My hope is that she will have many more.

The regrets we feel are not for the things that we have done but rather for the things that we haven't done. Wishing it were other than how it is won't make it so. Journeys are about uncovering our strengths and initiating our personal power. The treasures that we seek are within us all. It is our journeys that aid us in discovering them. They are like a great diamonds which exist within the earth's crust--waiting. All we have to do is chip away the extraneous matter to uncover them.

A fellow traveller, Jim.

If I Had My Life To Live Over

I'd dare to make more mistakes next time.
I'd relax. I would limber up.
I would be sillier than I have been this trip.
I would take fewer things seriously.
I would take more chances.
I would take more trips.
I would climb more mountains and swim more rivers.
I would eat more ice cream and less beans.
I would, perhaps, have more actual troubles but I'd have fewer imaginary ones.
You see, I am one of those people who live sensibly and sanely hour after hour, day after day.
Oh, I've had my moments and if I had to do it over again, I'd have more of them. In fact I'd try to have nothing else. Just moments.
One after another, instead of living so many years ahead of each day.
I've been one of those people who never go anywhere without a thermometer, a hot water bottle, a rain coat and a parachute.
If I had to do it again, I would travel lighter next time.
If I had my life to live over, I would start barefoot earlier in the spring and stay that way later in the fall.
I would go to more dances.
I would ride more merry-go-rounds.
I would pick more daisies.

Nadine Stair

Research and Resource Materials:

Anger Management Group
Arleigh Porte
The Pastoral Institute, Calgary, Alberta

Believing In Myself
Earnie Larsen, Carol Hegarty
Prentice Hall Press, New York, New York, 1991

Characteristics of Healthy Parenting, Article
Janet G. Woititz. Ed.D

Chicken Soup for the Soul
Jack Canfield, Victor Mark Hansen
Health Communications Inc., Deerfield Beach, Florida 1993

Comprehensive Stress Management
Jerrold S. Greenberg
Brown & Benchmark, Madison, Wisconsin, 1995

Complete Stress Management Workbook, The
Dr. Thomas Whiteman, Dr. Sam Verghese, Randy Petersen
Zondervan Publishing House, Grand Rapids, Michigan, 1996

Couple's Comfort Book, The
Jennifer Louden
Harper San Francisco, Publishers, San Francisco, California, 1994

Discovering Life Skills
Shirley Allen, Shelley Altman et al
YWCA, Metropolitan Toronto, 1991

Hidden Keys to Loving Relationships
Gary Smalley
Gary Smalley Seminars Inc., Paoli, Pennsylvania, 1993

Light Her Fire: How to Ignite Passion and Excitement in the Woman You Love
Ellen Kreidman
Dell Publishing Co., Inc., New York, New York, 1992

Light His Fire: How to Keep Your Man Passionately and Hopelessly in Love With You
Ellen Kreidman
Dell Publishing Co., Inc., New York, New York, 1992

Make Anger Your Ally
Neil Clark Warren, Ph.D
Focus on the Family, Publishers, Colorado Springs, Colorado, 1990

Men are from Mars, Women are from Venus
Dr. John Gray
Beyond Words Publishing, Inc., Hillsboro, Oregon, 1993

On Death and Dying
Elisabeth Kubler-Ross
Macmillan Publishing Company, New York, New York, 1969

The Portable DO IT
John-Roger, Peter McWilliams
Prelude Press Inc., Los Angeles, California, 1993

The Relaxation and Stress Workbook
Davis, Eshelman, and McKay
New Harbinger Publications, Inc., Oakland, California, 1988

The 7 Habits of Highly Effective People
Steven R. Covey
Simon & Shuster Inc., New York, New York, 1990

The Solution Group
Bruce C. Dawson
New View Publications, Chapel Hill, North Carolina, 1993

Stage 2 Relationships-Love Beyond Addiction
Earnie Larsen
Harper and Row, Publishers, San Francisco, California, 1987

Think Again
Dr. Robert Anthony
Berkley Publishing Group, New York, New york, 1986

True Colors
Don Lowry
True Colors, Publishers, Corona, California, 1989